EDUCATING FOR SUSTAINABILITY

Educating for Sustainability presents fundamental principles, theoretical foundations, and practical suggestions for integrating education for sustainability into existing schoolwide systems and programs, organized in three sections:

- Principles of Education for Sustainability
- Fostering a Sustainability Worldview
- Learning and Thinking for Sustainability

Designed for teachers and teachers-to-be at all grade levels and across the content areas, the focus is on professional practices and pedagogical approaches rather than specific topics often associated with sustainability. Each chapter includes a number of supports to help readers monitor and improve their own professional practice and to deepen their own sustainability worldview, including textboxes in most chapters that provide more detailed or specialized information and a range of application exercises. All chapters include several "Consider This" activities and an "Extend Your Professional Knowledge" feature.

Future generations, including children in school today, will be confronted with a set of environmental, societal, and economic challenges unlike any ever before encountered. The goal of sustainability in this difficult environment is achievable, but it is a long-term process that requires people around the world to learn how to think and behave differently. Directly grounded in K–12 classroom practice, this book presents useful and realistic information for teachers looking to reorient their work toward sustainability and help their students develop new thinking and problem-solving abilities.

Victor Nolet is Professor of Secondary Education at Western Washington University, USA.

EDUCATING FOR SUSTAINABILITY

Principles and Practices for Teachers

Victor Nolet

Routledge
Taylor & Francis Group

NEW YORK AND LONDON

First published 2016
by Routledge
711 Third Avenue, New York, NY 10017

and by Routledge
2 Park Square, Milton Park, Abingdon, Oxon OX14 4RN

Routledge is an imprint of the Taylor & Francis Group, an informa business

First edition published by Routledge

Library of Congress Cataloging-in-Publication Data
Nolet, Victor.
    Educating for sustainability : principals and practices for teachers /
by Victor Nolet.
        pages cm
    Includes bibliographical references and index.
    1. Environmental education.   2. Sustainable development.   3. Teaching.
I. Title.
    GE70.N65 2015
    338.9'27071—dc23
    2015008675

ISBN: 978-0-415-72033-5 (hbk)
ISBN: 978-0-415-72034-2 (pbk)
ISBN: 978-1-315-86705-2 (ebk)

Typeset in Bembo
by Apex CoVantage, LLC

BRIEF CONTENTS

CONTENTS

ACKNOWLEDGEMENTS

This book exists because of the encouragement and kind support of a number of people. Rosalyn McKeown has been my colleague, friend, and mentor for many years and has contributed greatly to my own understanding of education for sustainability and to my thinking as I was writing this book. Similarly, Kim Corrigan has been unflagging in her encouragement and enthusiasm for over a decade as one of my earliest collaborators in educating for sustainability. Her keen insights have been invaluable over the years. I also am grateful to Faye Snodgress for her insights into the broader contexts in which education for sustainability exists today and to Ann Foster for helping me envision the more just and sustainable world that is possible through education. I am extremely grateful to Naomi Silverman, who has believed in this book from day one—in fact, years before it ever took form. I also am indebted to my colleagues Lauren McClanahan, Don Burgess, Bruce Larson, and Rosalie Romano for their encouragement and intellectual companionship along the way.

Finally, for her love and enduring support, I am grateful to Geneva Blake, without whose enthusiastic encouragement this book would not have been possible.

PREFACE

This book is for preservice and practicing teachers, particularly those who work or will work in formal education settings. It is relevant for teachers at any grade level and in any content area, but those working at the upper elementary through high school levels will find it particularly applicable to their context. The emphasis is on helping students develop tools that will help them engage with the complexities and tensions associated with creating a safe and just space for humans and other species now and in the future. The perspective of this book is that all teachers can teach for sustainability and that all learners can develop a way of seeing and interacting with the world through the lens of sustainability. The focus is on professional practices and pedagogical approaches, rather than specific topics often associated with sustainability. The goal is to help teachers and teachers-to-be become better thinkers, problem solvers, and decision makers.

Intended to be read as a coherent body of information, not a compilation of strategies and topics, the chapters build on one another, and earlier chapters provide background and contextual information that is employed in later chapters. The whole is intended to be greater than the sum of its many parts.

The book is organized in three sections. Section I, **Principles of Education for Sustainability**, presents the principles that underlie education for sustainability. Chapter 2, **The Future, Ready or Not**, creates a rationale for a focus on sustainability and particularly education for sustainability. This chapter describes the emergence of the Anthropocene, a geologic epoch marked by significant human impacts on planetary systems. During the Anthropocene, as a result of accelerating human impacts, a number of planetary systems upon which we depend for life support have become dangerously unstable. The reason we find ourselves in this situation is that our brains evolved when humans were primarily hunters and gatherers. We are not well adapted to engage in long-term thinking and planning or to consider consequences beyond our immediate environment. In many respects, we need to "speed up evolution" by learning to think and behave in ways that are evolutionarily atypical. We need to learn how to live within the limits imposed by planetary boundaries and at the same time ensure a minimal level of social foundations. This is why education and learning are so vitally important to the survival and future thriving of humans and other species.

Chapter 3, **Education for Sustainability**, explores the meaning of sustainability and the history and attributes of education for sustainability. This discussion attends particularly to the broad process of sustainable development and the various policy processes that have advocated for education for sustainable development over the past 30 years. Particular attention is paid to the Earth Charter, which provides a moral and conceptual basis for this book. The Earth Charter articulates a set of ethical principles that knit together the three interconnected spheres of environment, economy, and society that are of central concern in sustainability. Because of its importance, the Earth Charter is a leitmotif that recurs throughout the book.

Chapter 4, **Developing a Sustainability Worldview**, presents a discussion of the attributes of a sustainability worldview and the big ideas that inform it. This is a pivotal chapter in the book because it creates a conceptual basis for an emphasis on professional practices. A sustainability worldview involves seeing and interacting with the world through the lens of sustainability. It involves values, dispositions and knowledge, and a sense of agency and efficacy, and it is something that anyone can develop and refine through practice. A sustainability worldview is an inherently positive and optimistic outlook, but it is not necessarily instinctive or automatic. One way that teachers can help learners develop a sustainability worldview is through exploration of a constellation of sustainability big ideas. Chapter 4 includes an exploration of eight "bright stars" in that constellation.

Section II, **Fostering a Sustainability Worldview**, focuses on professional teaching practices. Chapter 5, **Teaching for Sustainability**, explores the philosophical orientations that are often associated with education for sustainability and leads the reader through an exploration of her or his own perspectives on the purposes of education for sustainability. This chapter also explores the relationship of a teacher's pedagogical content knowledge and domain knowledge as the basis for each teacher's own development of a sustainability worldview. It includes an extensive discussion of the United Nations Economic Commission for Europe framework of Competencies for Education for Sustainable Development. This framework describes what educators should know, what they should be able to do, how they should live and work with others, and how they should be to effectively teach for sustainability. In this respect, the framework supports a specialized teacher's version of a sustainability worldview.

Chapter 6, **Learning That Supports a Sustainability Worldview**, focuses on learning that underlies development of a sustainability worldview. It explores the attributes of learning for understanding and development of adaptive expertise as the basis for development of a sustainability worldview and also discusses the characteristics of seriously troubling problems and some instructional strategies for helping learners engage with them. Values play an important role in the development of a sustainability worldview, so Chapter 6 also discusses instructional implications and strategies for helping learners explore their own values systems and investigate the values of others and other cultures. Finally, because a sustainability worldview is focused on a positive future, the chapter explores strategies for helping learners develop a positive future orientation.

Chapter 7, **Powerful Pedagogies**, presents five families of instructional approaches that are used often in education for sustainability: collaborative small-group learning, inquiry-based learning, experiential learning, service learning, and place-based learning. While a number of variations and specialized applications can be found within each family, each shares a set of defining attributes. All of these pedagogies are considered powerful because they support high-leverage instructional practices and are learner centered. High-leverage practices are strategies that teachers use frequently and, when implemented effectively, can help teachers manage differences among students and advance the learning of all students. Learner-centered approaches are strategies in which the role of the teacher shifts from deliverer of content to facilitator of learning; the learners assume greater responsibility for and control over their own learning.

Section III, **Learning and Thinking for Sustainability**, focuses on thinking skills that can support a sustainability worldview. Chapter 8, **Critical Thinking and Decision Making**, explores strategies for helping learners become effective critical thinkers and decision makers. The section on critical thinking presents a number of research-validated strategies for helping learners to become better critical reasoners and more effective at using critical thinking to investigate and evaluate sustainability issues. The discussion of decision making focuses on the various errors of inference to which humans are prone and the instructional strategies that teachers can employ to help learners become better decision makers.

Chapter 9, **Systems Thinking**, presents an overview of systems dynamics and applications of systems thinking in the context of sustainability. The chapter includes numerous activities to support readers' learning about systems thinking and to support development of systems-thinking skills. This chapter discusses the use of indicators to monitor complex systems and presents a number of indicators systems focused on sustainability, including global footprint indicators and indicators related to happiness and well-being.

Finally, Chapter 10, **Happiness and Well-Being**, explores subjective well-being and happiness as elements of a sustainability worldview. The research on subjective well-being and positive education is discussed along with strategies for helping learners assess and monitor their own well-being and happiness.

Professional Practices

Focused on professional practices for teachers, with a particular emphasis on pedagogical approaches, this book is not a how-to guide on all things related to sustainability. Therefore, there are a number of things you will not find, for example, specific lesson plans for teaching about topics such as climate change or biodiversity, step-by-step instructions for setting up a specific project such as a school garden, or specific strategies such as how to launch a crowdsourcing campaign to fund new energy-saving inventions. Rather, the goal is to help teachers at all grade levels and across the content areas improve their professional practice. Each chapter includes a number of supports to help preservice and practicing teachers to monitor and improve their own professional practice and to deepen their own sustainability worldview. Most chapters include textboxes that provide more detailed or specialized information. Many of the boxes also include application exercises to help you better integrate the information into your professional practice. All chapters include several "**Consider This**" activities to encourage you to interact more directly with the text. These activities sometimes include reflection or discussion questions or prompt you to investigate your own beliefs, attitudes, or changing perceptions. At the end of each chapter, you will find an **Extend Your Professional Knowledge** box. These are extended application activities that encourage you to explore additional resources found on the Internet, including curriculum materials; resource guides; or, in some cases, web portals into a broader array of curriculum and professional development resources.

1

INTRODUCTION

O, wonder!
How many goodly creatures are there here!
How beauteous mankind is! O brave new world
That has such people in't

—William Shakespeare, *The Tempest V.i.184–187*

For many people, the phrase "brave new world" evokes images of Aldous Huxley's (1932) novel that portrays a future world where a powerful government protects individuals from the perils of overpopulation and excessive violence through a highly regulated caste system and state-mandated use of birth control and sedative drugs. Of course, Huxley borrowed the term "brave new world" from Shakespeare's *The Tempest*. Shakespeare used the word "brave" to refer to something splendid, bold, and exciting. For Shakespeare's Miranda, a 15-year-old girl in love, the "brave new world" is full of promise, optimism, and beauty. Indeed, this is also the way the character John in Huxley's novel views the world, at least until he realizes his own values are in direct conflict with the reality of the world in which he finds himself. For John, the notion of a bright and shining brave new world becomes a bitter irony.

Today, life on our planet often seems like something out of science fiction where multiple realities exist in the same time and space. On one hand, billions of people around the world experience an existence that would be immediately recognizable to the characters of the most pessimistic of dystopian fiction. These are the people who live under the repression of fundamentalist theocracies, dysfunctional kleptocracies, or military police states. These are the people for whom even the most rudimentary health care is nonexistent and survival involves a daily struggle for food, water, and safety. The people who live in this reality have limited opportunities to realize their full potential and diminished hopes for a positive future. Of course the most vulnerable, the most at risk in this version of reality are children. Consider that every 40 seconds, someplace on the planet, a child under the age of five dies from a diarrheal disease simply because she or he lacks access to clean water and the most basic health care (UNICEF, 2015).

At the same time, billions of other people around the world live an existence that just a few generations ago would have been imagined only as a futuristic utopian fantasy. These are the people who live in the developed areas of the world, where ready access to clean water is taken for granted, famine is largely unknown, education is nearly universal, and state-of-the-art health care is widely available (albeit for a price). Many of these well-fed, clothed, and sheltered people are in nearly constant contact with sophisticated and powerful technology devices, including smart mobile phones; miniature entertainment devices; televisions that can access hundreds of channels; and, of course, sophisticated portable computers connected to an ever-expanding Internet. Again, though, those most directly affected by life in this reality are children. For example, a recent study funded by the Kaiser Family Foundation (Rideout, Foehr, & Roberts, 2010) found that children in the United States spend as much as 6.5 hours each day interacting with some form of media; during that time they consume the equivalent of over eight hours of content. The word "content" here does not necessarily mean that they are being exposed to healthy or useful information. Often the content of the media with which these children interact perpetuates damaging stereotypes and is violent, racist, sexually charged, or highly commercialized. Meanwhile, the diseases of excess, including childhood obesity, heart disease, Type II diabetes, and addiction, are endemic in many areas in the developed world.

O brave new world that has such people in it! How can one planet sustain these parallel realities—these very different versions of a brave new world?

The answer to this question is "It cannot!"

Planet Earth simply does not have the capacity to provide enough breathable air, potable water, food, energy, and shelter for everyone on the planet to experience the standard of living enjoyed by those in the developed areas of the world (Global Footprint Network, 2015). Consider that since the beginning of the 20th century, there has been a nearly fivefold increase in the human population of the planet; as our population has grown, so has our impact on the planetary systems upon which we and all future generations must depend for our existence. Human behaviors have altered the physical, chemical, and biological properties of the entire planet, and most of that impact has been the result of overconsumption in the wealthy, developed regions of the world. Yet today, one sixth of the world populations still lives in extreme poverty. The unimaginable deprivations experienced by billions of people around the world creates a drag on the overall human prospect that is economically, ecologically, and morally untenable. Neither the dystopian nor utopian reality can be sustained. Unless we change our behaviors, the future of our own species and the future of many other species with whom we share this planet are in very real jeopardy.

The good news is that, unlike the characters in a play, we have the ability to write a different plot for our story. It *is* within our ability to stop perpetuating the dystopian existence that so many people around the world experience today and to ensure that future generations are able to take care of their needs. However, we also should not expect to create a utopia. For now, we should set our sights on creating a more positive future—one that includes more of what's better and less of what's worse. Quite simply, our collective goal today must be to create the conditions that foster the health and well-being of all . . . forever. Accomplishing this goal is the focus of a worldwide movement that has coalesced around **sustainability**.

Today, the noun **sustainability**, and its adjectival form **sustainable**, along with their close cousin, the sometimes verb–sometimes adjective **green**, can be found attached to hundreds of products, processes, policies, organizations, programs, and businesses. Even a cursory search of the Internet reveals dozens of putatively authoritative definitions of sustainability; if you enter the word in a library search engine, you will find thousands of articles, books, and reports focusing on a broad range of topics and ideas associated with sustainability in the popular and scholarly press. Indeed, the popularity of sustainability in recent years led John Engelman to write in the introduction to the Worldwatch Institute's *2013 State of the World Report*, "We live today in an age of *sustainababble*, a cacophonous profusion of uses of the word sustainable to mean anything from environmentally better to cool" (p. 3). There is no question that sustainability is a popular idea that has been commercialized and often co-opted. However, sustainability is far more than just another popular buzzword. Sustainability is popular because the goal of *achieving* sustainability is the defining idea of our era, while the consequences of *not achieving* sustainability are unthinkable.

A Popular but Complex Idea

The goal of this book is to help you understand what sustainability means so that you can begin to incorporate the values and ideas associated with sustainability into your professional practice as a teacher as well as your own day-to-day life. In the chapters that follow, you will have many opportunities to explore the ideas, values, and processes associated with sustainability. As you will discover, sustainability is a complex and multifaceted idea that defies simple definition. For example, descriptions of sustainability in the scholarly literature often characterize sustainability as an emergent paradigm that:

1. Considers environmental, economic, social, and political systems as interconnected systems rather than discrete entities;
2. Involves transformation of values and belief systems as well as technological, market, or policy approaches to problem solving;

3.   Views social and economic justice and intergenerational equity as inextricable from environmental stewardship; and
4.   Emphasizes personal and collective practices consistent with responsible global citizenship (Nolet, 2007, pp. 415–416).

The most common definition of sustainability was developed in 1987 by the World Commission on Environment and Development (WCED): Sustainability means "meeting the needs of the present without compromising the ability of future generations to meet their own needs" (WCED, 1987, p. 42). We will explore the origins and implications of this definition in Chapter 3. This conception of sustainability is based on an ecological perspective. Ecologists often refer to the capacity of an ecosystem to sustain interdependent forms of life by balancing the rate of resource removal with the rate of resource regeneration. In the broader context in which the term is used today, sustainability often refers to a balance among various human systems that influence and are influenced by the natural environment. In this context, sustainability represents an ideal that will be achieved when human-caused environmental degradation has been reversed and overconsumption and gross economic injustices that deprive future generations of the ability to meet their needs are eliminated.

While it is easy to embrace what sustainability stands for, it can be more difficult to understand all that it implies. This is because sustainability is a multidimensional construct—an abstract idea that cannot be observed directly or easily defined. Constructs allow us to refer to complicated phenomena such as "intelligence," "freedom," or "beauty" in everyday conversation without having to explicitly explain all of the underlying processes involved. Imagine how much less romantic the world would be if song writers and poets had to include detailed explanations of various physiological, psychological, and emotional phenomena every time they wanted express the sentiments embodied in the word "love"!

A construct label serves as a stand-in for a set of underlying processes or ideas called **dimensions** (Messick, 1989). We infer the presence of a construct by looking for evidence of its underlying dimensions. No single dimension is sufficient, but neither do all of the underlying dimensions need to be observed at any given time. Also, it is not unusual for some of the underlying dimensions to also act as constructs that require further description. So when we use the construct label "sustainability," we actually are referring to a broad range of ideas, values, beliefs, processes, principles, and outcomes. We make inferences about the presence of the construct "sustainability" by looking for evidence of its underlying dimensions.

For example, if we are interested in evaluating the extent to which a community development project would be considered "sustainable," we might look for indicators related to a variety of dimensions, such as the energy efficiency of the various buildings; the extent to which historically marginalized members of the community are involved in the planning process; the likely needs of future residents of the community, availability of green spaces for use by children, and strategies for ensuring economic equality within the community; availability of affordable, healthy food; preservation of various cultures and languages present in the community; health and safety issues; and so on. No single dimension alone would likely be enough to validate the "sustainability" of the community, but we might not need to see evidence of all the dimensions to make the claim of sustainability.

One of essential elements of the WCED definition of sustainability is the idea of "needs."

In the second half of the 20th century, our ideas about human needs were influenced greatly by Abraham Maslow's hierarchy (1943; 1970) that eventually included eight needs:

1. Physiological
2. Safety
3. Belonging and love
4. Self-esteem
5. Cognitive
6. Aesthetic
7. Self-actualization
8. Transcendence

In Maslow's hierarchy, basic or physiological and psychological needs must be met before an individual is able to move on to higher-level needs. This hierarchical view of needs often led to the assumption that some needs (e.g., physiological and safety) are far more important than others (e.g., self-actualization and transcendence) and that it might be acceptable if some people never have needs at the top of the pyramid met, particularly if resources are scarce. For example, Maslow's hierarchy has often been portrayed as a pyramid with physiological and basic needs at the bottom and self-actualization and transcendence at the top, occupying the smallest area. A hierarchical interpretation of "making sure that the current generation can meet its needs" might be interpreted as simply making sure that most people have sufficient food, water, and shelter while some people have opportunities for a more satisfying and fulfilling life. Similarly, the idea of "making sure future generations can meet their needs" might be interpreted as simply making sure *some* people in the future have sufficient food, shelter, and water, although it might be acceptable if the upper reaches of the needs hierarchy remain out of reach for vast numbers of people. Thus, when needs are viewed hierarchically, the two versions of a brave new world can exist simultaneously.

We understand that meeting the needs of people alive on the planet today and who will inhabit the planet in the future involves a more complex process that requires us to consider the interconnectedness of economic, environmental, and social justice issues. For example, economist Max-Neef (1991) investigated needs across cultures and found widespread agreement that humans have nine

fundamental needs that can be satisfied in a variety of ways that are often culturally dependent. In Max-Neef's matrix, illustrated in Table 1.1, needs are not hierarchical and can be satisfied in four existential categories (Being, Having, Doing,
and Interacting).

When we view needs in this more realistic and nuanced framework, the idea of
"meeting the needs of the current generation without compromising the needs of
future generations to meet their needs" clearly involves more than simply ensuring
that future generations have sufficient food, water, and shelter. Certainly people

TABLE 1.1 Fundamental Human Needs Manifested in Four Realms

Fundamental human needs	Being (qualities)	Having (things)	Doing (actions)	Interacting (settings)
Subsistence	Physical and mental health	Food, shelter, work	Feed, clothe, rest, work	Living environment, social setting
Protection	Care, adaptability, autonomy	Social security, health systems, work	Cooperate, plan, take care of, help	Social environment, dwelling
Affection	Respect, sense of humor, generosity, sensuality	Friendships, family, relationships with nature	Share, take care of, make love, express emotions	Privacy, intimate spaces of togetherness
Understanding	Critical capacity, curiosity, intuition	Literature, teachers, policies, educational	Analyze, study, meditate, investigate,	Schools, family, communities,
Participation	Receptiveness, dedication, sense of humor	Responsibilities, duties, work, rights	Cooperate, dissent, express opinions	Associations, parties, churches, communities
Leisure	Imagination, tranquility, spontaneity	Games, parties, peace of mind	Daydream, remember, relax, have fun	Landscapes, intimate spaces, places to be alone
Creation	Imagination, inventiveness, curiosity	Abilities, skills, work, techniques	Invent, build, design, work, compose, interpret	Spaces for expression, workshops
Identity	Sense of belonging, self-esteem, consistency	Language, religions, work, customs, values, norms	Get to know oneself, grow, commit oneself	Places one belongs to, everyday settings
Freedom	Autonomy, passion, self-esteem, open-mindedness	Equal rights	Dissent, choose, run risks, develop awareness	Anywhere

Source: Max-Neef, 1991.

need to be safe and have sufficient food, potable water, clean air, and adequate shelter, but they also need opportunities to fall in love, make music, collaborate, spend time in nature, engage in fulfilling work, take part in community life, create, speak out, read, play, learn, and grow. When we think about sustainability, then, we are not simply seeking to sustain a minimal existence for many and the good life for a few. Our goal is to be to create a safe and just planet on which humans and all other species can meet all of their needs, now and for generations to come in the future.

This is a monumental task, but it is achievable. We will not achieve sustainability through grand policy schemes or as a result of breakthrough technologies or unfettered market-based approaches, although policy, technology, and economics will play a role. Instead, the fundamental change that must occur is in our own thinking and behaviors. This is why the most viable pathway, perhaps the only pathway to sustainability is education—education for sustainability.

Education for Sustainability

In many respects, education is both the cause of unsustainability and the strategy for achieving sustainability. This dialectic was described cogently by Orr (2004):

> The crisis we face is first and foremost one of mind, perception, and values: hence, it is a challenge to those institutions presuming to shape minds, perceptions and values. It is an educational challenge. More of the same kind of education can only make things worse. This is not an argument against education but rather an argument for the kind of education that prepares people for lives and livelihoods suited to a planet with a biosphere that operates by the laws of ecology and thermodynamics. (p. 27)

Education for sustainability is decidedly not "more of the same kind of education" that helped create the problems we face today. Instead, education for sustainability seeks to equip learners to deal with the kinds of challenges that arise from the interconnectedness of environment, culture, society, and economy and that seem to typify life in the 21st century. These challenges often involve:

- Complexity caused by multiple causal and co-occurring relationships;
- Large scales associated with planetary and multinational processes;
- Long timeframes, often generational in scope;
- Unintended and unanticipated consequences;
- Invisibility and long-distance drivers (i.e., not all elements of the issue are apparent);
- Multiple and often competing perspectives;
- Interconnectedness among separate systems (particularly, environment, social, and economic);

- Globalized and highly monetized processes that privilege profits and corporations;
- Inequities and inequalities in benefits and impacts; and
- Problems that cannot be easily defined and for which solutions are not readily apparent.

Education for sustainability aims to help learners develop new ways of thinking, collaborating, and solving problems so that they can effectively engage with these kinds of challenges. To accomplish this aim, education for sustainability typically includes a number of key attributes. First, it is interdisciplinary and holistic. Ideally, learning for sustainability should be embedded in the whole curriculum, not as a stand-alone or drop-in subject. Second, education for sustainability is values based. The values and principles associated with sustainability are made explicit, examined, debated, tested, and applied in a variety of real-world contexts. Third, education for sustainability emphasizes open-ended, generative-thinking processes, including critical thinking, problem solving, participatory decision making and systems thinking. Fourth, education for sustainability is based in local contexts but connected to global issues. Learners are encouraged to engage directly with local, real-world issues and concerns, but then they are also encouraged to interpret these issues through a global or planetary perspective. Finally, being locally relevant means that education for sustainability also is culturally responsive. Multiple ways of knowing, engaging, and understanding are recognized and encouraged. At the same time, education for sustainability employs methods and pedagogies from a variety of disciplines and perspectives, with particular emphasis on learner-centered strategies. Transmissive strategies geared simply to passing on knowledge are discarded in favor of approaches in which teachers and learners work together to acquire knowledge and engage with real-world challenges.

The emphasis in this book is on professional teaching practices. Some of the practices and pedagogical approaches discussed in the book can be more readily applied in some disciplines or at some grade levels; however, the intent is that *all* teachers can teach for sustainability. This approach has been characterized as the **strengths model** (McKeown, 2006). This model assumes that:

1. No one discipline can claim ownership over education for sustainability. The ideas and issues associated with sustainability require a transdisciplinary perspective. Teachers from all disciplines share responsibility for weaving education for sustainability into their professional practice.
2. All members of the education community can contribute to education for sustainability, including teachers, administrators, para-educators, nonformal educators, community members, and the students themselves.
3. Education for sustainability includes content from a variety of disciplines. For example, it might involve quantitative reasoning from mathematics, inquiry processes from the natural sciences, creativity from the arts, critical thinking

and policy analysis from the social studies, communication and media literacy from Language Arts, and spatial reasoning from geography.

Based on the strengths model, education for sustainability can involve a variety of strategies and take place in a variety of settings, including nonformal education, community settings, formal education that takes place in elementary and secondary schools, and in technical and higher education.

While education can occur in a variety contexts, this book is primarily focused on education that occurs under the auspices of formal education institutions, such as elementary and high schools, and in colleges and universities. However, we should not confuse institutional formality with place. Education can occur in a wide range of settings beside classrooms, and this is particularly true of education for sustainability. Learners need opportunities to engage with sustainability-related issues in messy, real-world contexts. Therefore, education for sustainability occurs in gardens, neighborhoods, parks, laboratories, museums, under a tree, in a field, and, of course, in classrooms. Similarly, education for sustainability can occur at any grade level and in any discipline. It is not restricted to high school science or social studies, it is not environmental education, it is not civics education, and it is not based on a distinct set of curriculum standards or a particular body of content. It *is* education that helps learners develop thinking, collaboration, problem-solving, and critical-thinking skills. It *is* education that helps learners clarify and interrogate their own values and the values that underlie many of the challenges with which they will be forced to deal in their lifetime. It *is* education that can help learners develop compassion, empathy, cultural competence, and deeper understanding of the complex interconnectedness of the world.

Although, there are few techniques that are unique to education for sustainability, it does involves a set of perspectives that can inform professional teaching practices. These four perspectives help distinguish education for sustainability from other approaches (Wals, 2012):

- *An integrative perspective* that allows for integrating multiple aspects of sustainability such as environmental, economic, and social justice; local, regional, and global; past, present, and future; human and nonhuman, etc.;
- *A critical perspective* that involves investigating and challenging predominant patterns and policies that are unsustainable, such as hyperconsumerism, assumptions of unlimited growth, inequitable distribution of resources and impacts, and racist and sexist belief systems;
- *A transformative perspective* that involves moving beyond simple awareness to incorporate lasting change through empowerment and capacity building and through development of more sustainable lifestyles, values, communities, and businesses.

- *A contextual perspective* recognizes that that there are multiple ways of knowing, living, and valuing and that there is no single "correct" approach that will work for everyone; our approaches may need to be recalibrated as realities and times change.

Through these four perspectives, education for sustainability can help learners develop values, skills, and knowledge that will enable them to engage directly with the challenge of creating a safe and just space for all, now and in the future.

A Sustainability Worldview

The overarching perspective of this book is that the goal of education for sustainability is to help learners develop a **sustainability worldview**. This is a way of seeing and engaging with the world through the lens of sustainability. Our worldview influences our attitudes, decisions, choices, and behaviors. A sustainability worldview includes the belief that each of us can develop a sense of agency, efficacy, and hopefulness by becoming personally engaged with the work of creating the conditions that foster well-being for all forever. When we develop a sustainability worldview, we are prompted to go beyond mere criticism and analysis and to seek out ways to become personally involved with individual and collective actions that promote fairness and equity and that enhance the health and resilience of individuals and the systems upon which all life depends, now and in the future. A sustainability worldview prompts us to consider the impacts of our decisions and behaviors on others now and in the future. When we develop a sustainability worldview, we consider our own needs and wants in a larger, more interconnected context that transcends space and time. This process is facilitated by a number of sustainability big ideas that serve as portals into the broader sustainability discourse and to development of a sustainability worldview. We will explore this constellation of big ideas as well as the dimensions of a sustainability worldview in Chapter 4 and then return to those ideas frequently throughout the rest of the book.

Teaching for Sustainability

Teaching for sustainability is the process by which teachers turn the broad conceptual and often philosophical ideals of education for sustainability into specific elements of effective teaching practice. Teaching involves the day-to-day, hour-to-hour, and minute-to-minute work of creating learning environments that enable learning. The goal of this book is to help you become a better teacher of all students, regardless of grade level or discipline area. Obviously, it would make no sense for something called education for sustainability to interfere with helping all learners develop a strong foundation in basic academic skills and knowledge. Therefore, a central assumption of this book is that teaching for sustainability should enhance and augment teachers' day-to-day professional practices. Thus, many of the practices and strategies described in this book are not necessarily unique to education for sustainability. They are based on the empirical research about how people learn and the conditions that enable learners to become better thinkers, problem solvers, and decision makers. That research has shown that good teaching for sustainability is the same as good teaching for mathematics, good teaching for reading and language arts, good teaching for science, and good teaching for social studies. Regardless of discipline or topic, effective teachers are critical thinkers, have well-refined collaboration skills, reflect on their own impacts on student learning, and are skilled at balancing innovation with established practices (Cochran-Smith & Zeichner, 2005; Bransford, Darling-Hammond, & LePage, 2005; Darling-Hammond, 2011; Fraser, 2010).

Learning for Sustainability

One of the basic premises of this book is that universal access to high-quality education is an absolutely essential component of a sustainable future. Inequitable access to educational opportunity is, by definition, unsustainable. All learners, regardless of background, gender, economic status, race, culture, language, or ability must have opportunities to learn about the nature of various sustainability challenges and to develop knowledge and skills that will enable them to work individually and collectively to promote the well-being of all forever. Therefore, a sustainability worldview must be built on the bedrock of strong literacy, numeracy, communication, and problem-solving skills commensurate with one's age and developmental level. Anyone who aspires to teach for sustainability must be committed to the success of all students, and, similarly, any educational procedure that purports to be for sustainability must be first and foremost focused on improving the learning outcomes of all students.

As you will see in Chapter 6, one of the ways that education for sustainability supports the learning of all students is through a focus on active knowledge construction that leads to meaningful and authentic use of information. This process, often referred to as learning with understanding, helps students see meaningful patterns of information, transfer knowledge and abilities to novel situations, and successfully engage in a variety of thinking processes, including those associated with a sustainability worldview. As you will learn in Chapter 6, teachers who are most effective at supporting the process of learning for understanding consistently:

- Promote active learning that engages learners in meaningful activities and prompts them to think about, apply, and test out what they are learning,
- Make explicit connections to students' prior knowledge and provide opportunities for students to surface and test their preconceptions,
- Provide opportunities for students to interact with ambitious and meaningful tasks based on how knowledge is used in real-world contexts,

- Support students' use of metacognitive thinking and strategies to evaluate and guide their own learning, and
- Use ongoing formative assessments to diagnose student understandings and to provide step-by-step scaffolding to guide student learning.

Education for sustainability also supports the learning of all students through use of learner-centered approaches. These are active learning strategies in which the role of the teacher shifts from deliverer of content to facilitator of learning and the learners assume greater responsibility for and control over their own learning. In Chapter 7, we will explore a number of families of learner-centered approaches that promote improved learning outcomes for all students and are often employed in education for sustainability. Those approaches are:

- Collaborative small group learning;
- Inquiry-based learning;
- Experiential learning;
- Service learning; and
- Place-based learning.

While values are an essential element of a sustainability worldview, it is equally important for learners to develop skills in critical thinking, decision making, and systems thinking. These are not processes that can be learned by observing. Learners need scaffolded opportunities to try out their ideas, test their assumptions, and investigate their preconceptions and biases. At the same time, teachers need strategies for supporting learners in development in these skills. That is the focus of Chapters 8 and 9.

A sustainability worldview is positive and solutions focused. Values and thinking skills can help learners investigate and engage directly with sustainability challenges. However, learners also need to be disposed to engage with difficult, sometimes discouraging problems. Teachers need strategies to help learners develop a positive future orientation and character strengths associated with happiness and well-being. As you will see in Chapter 10, helping learners develop habits of mind that support happiness and well-being can have positive impacts that go far beyond day-to-day functioning and school success.

Finally, while this book is intended to help you become better at the job of teaching, it is also intended to help you get better at the job of living. As you read the chapters in this book and work through the various activities, you will find that your own perspectives, beliefs, and dispositions change as you develop and refine your own sustainability worldview. This, too, is part of the design of this book. After all, if our goal is to transform the way humans think, behave, and interact with the world, shouldn't we begin with our own worldview?

EXTEND YOUR PROFESSIONAL KNOWLEDGE 1.1

1. Download the Education for Sustainable Development Sourcebook at
    http://unesdoc.unesco.org/images/0021/002163/216383e.pdf.
    a. After reading the descriptions of education for sustainable develop-
        ment, complete the Project Y activity.
2. Go to Facing the Future at www.facingthefuture.org.
    a. Explore the resources at the site and download a lesson plan on a
        topic that interests you.
3. As you explore these resources, notice how your understanding of sus-
    tainability changes.
4. As you think about these resources and the ideas that were introduced
    in this chapter . . . .
    a. What questions arise?
    b. What ideas are you looking forward to exploring in the chapters that
        follow?
    c. What ideas did you encounter that you found troubling or problematic?

References

Bransford, J., Darling-Hammond, L., & LePage, P. (2005). Introduction. In L. Darling-Hammond & J. Bransford (Eds.), *Preparing Teachers for a Changing World: What Teachers Should Learn and Be Able to Do* (pp. 1–40). Washington, DC: Jossey-Bass.

Cochran-Smith, M., & Zeichner, K. (Eds.). (2005). *Studying Teacher Education: The Report of the AERA Panel on Research and Teacher Education.* Mahwah, NJ: Lawrence Erlbaum.

Darling-Hammond, L. (2011). Teacher education and the American future. *Journal of Teacher Education, 61* (1–2), 35–47.

Fraser, J.W. (2010). A tale of two futures: A fable of teacher education in the United States in 2015. *Kappan, 92* (2), 29–31.

Global Footprint Network. (2015). Footprint Basics: World Footprint: Do We Fit on the Planet? Retrieved from: www.footprintnetwork.org/en/index.php/GFN/

Huxley, A. (1932). *Brave New World.* London: Chatto & Windus.

Maslow, A.H. (1943). A theory of human motivation. *Psychological Review, 50*, 370–396.

Maslow, A.H. (1970). *Motivation and Personality* (2nd ed.). New York: Harper and Row.

Max-Neef, M. (1991). *Human Scale Development.* New York: Apex Press.

McKeown, R. (2006). *Education for Sustainable Development Toolkit.* Paris: UNESCO.

Messick, S. (1989). Validity. In R.L. Linn (Ed.), *Educational Measurement* (3rd ed.). New York: Macmillan.

Nolet, V.W. (2007). Preparing sustainability literate teachers. *Teachers College Record, 111*, 409–442.

Orr, D.W. (2004). *Earth in Mind: On Education, Environment, and the Human Prospect.* Washington, DC: Earth Island Press.

Rideout, V.J., Foehr, U.G., & Roberts, D.F. (2010). *Generation M2: Media in the Lives of 8- to 18-Year-Olds.* Menlo Park, CA: Henry J. Kaiser Foundation.

Shakespeare, W. (1983). The tempest. In Staunton, H. (Ed.) *The Globe Illustrated Shakespeare: Complete Works Annotated* (p. 1570). New York: Greenwich House.

United Nations Children's Fund (UNICEF). (2015). *The State of the World's Children 2015*. New York: Author.

Wals, A. (2012). *Shaping the Education of Tomorrow: Full-length Report on the UN Decade of Education for Sustainable Development*. Paris: UNESCO.

World Commission on Environment and Development (WCED). (1987). *Our Common Future*. Oxford: Oxford University Press.

SECTION I
Principles of Education for Sustainability

2

THE FUTURE, READY OR NOT

People like us, who believe in physics, know that the distinction between past, present and future is only a stubbornly persistent illusion.

—Albert Einstein, March 21, 1955

We are now faced with the fact that tomorrow is today. We are confronted with the fierce urgency of now. In this unfolding conundrum of life and history there is such a thing as being too late.

—Martin Luther King, April 4, 1967

Humans have existed in their present form on this planet for such a short time, it is impossible to say yet whether we are a successful species. Certainly other organisms have lasted longer. The great dinosaurs appeared during the Triassic Period and lasted to the end of the Cretaceous Period, a span of about 100 million years. Ants probably began to appear on the planet about 150 million years ago, and fungi have been around for more than 300 million years. By comparison, *Homo erectus* appeared a mere two million years ago, and *H. sapiens sapiens* (that's us) have been around for only about 200,000 years. By planetary standards, we are a brand new species.

Despite our short time here, humans like to believe that we have accomplished much as a species. After all, just look at all the things we can do—we can use tools, read, make music, solve quadratic equations, Salsa dance, love, and search the Internet. As far as we know, no fungus or ant has figured out how to do any of those things yet. Compared to other species, we have some pretty handy upgrades. We have relatively large and plastic brains, we are omnivorous, we walk upright and have opposable thumbs, we have adequate (although not spectacular) sensory organs, and we have developed quite a few useful communication and problem-solving strategies.

Yet, have we really accomplished all that much? Other than being a little bigger, the basic structures and functions of our bodies and brains today are probably not too different from those of our first *Homo sapiens* ancestors. After all, 200,000 years is just an eye blink on an evolutionary time scale. We still experience a flight or fight response when confronted with new situations, our mating rituals often entail more hormones and raw emotions than cognition or compassion, and we regularly do things we know are unhealthy (such as eating too much) or just plain stupid (such as texting while driving). We also have not managed to put our supposedly superior cognitive and communication abilities to particularly effective use at a societal level. We routinely wage wars; we have not eliminated deaths from even very preventable illnesses, and we seem to be unable to refrain from destroying the natural systems that provide us with air, water, and food.

In many respects, humans have remained relatively unchanged since first appearing on the planet. Perhaps one of the reasons for this is that for most time we've been around, the conditions of our existence have changed very little. Throughout most of our history, human life has revolved around the rhythms of the planet—migrations and harvests synchronized with the passing seasons. Humans rarely moved faster than they could slide down a snowy hill or than a horse could gallop (about 25 miles an hour). For the most part, our impact on the world around us was minimal and rarely permanent. Our hunting and gathering practices may have temporarily changed a local species population or habitat, but the effect was usually not beyond the capacity of the local ecosystem to restore itself after humans moved on. As tertiary consumers at the top of the food chain, few other species relied on our existence for their survival. If humans had never appeared, or had gone extinct after a few dozen millennia, the planet would still be humming along today just fine without us, thank you very much.

BOX 2.1 VARIABILITY SELECTION HYPOTHESIS

One hypothesis that is gaining acceptance among scientists is that human evolution accelerated during periods of climate variability that began about three million years ago. According to the *variability selection hypothesis* (Grove, 2011; Potts, 1998), the challenges of finding food and keeping warm during periods of climate variability eventually led to development of larger, more complex brains. By the time *Homo sapiens* evolved about 200,000 years ago, humans had figured out how to manage fire, build shelters, make tools, use language to communicate and form social groups, interact and trade with strangers, and find their way around over large areas.

Other hominid species that existed at that time also could do these things but have since gone extinct. Our species survived because we had evolved a large, highly adaptable brain that was energy efficient, good at making quick decisions, and adept at spatial and symbolic reasoning. Throughout most of human history, individual decisions and behaviors focused on outcomes in the immediate environment with short-term consequences, and those evolutionary adaptations served us quite well under those conditions. However, those same brains are less well adapted to decision making under uncertainty or to managing complexity. We can learn how to do those things, but it takes more effort, and we are prone to making mistakes.

Dawn of the Anthropocene

Everything began to change about 10,000 years ago when we learned how to domesticate animals and plants. The cultivation of crops, particularly grain crops such as rice, and the maintenance of fowl and ruminant mammals, such as goats, sheep, and cattle, allowed humans to settle in one place rather than to migrate seasonally. As a result, we developed more stable and nutritious food sources and more durable shelters organized into villages and communities. In time, as humans settled, we developed increasingly more sophisticated written communication systems that allowed us to store, share, and pass on to successive generations the knowledge gained from experience. We also began to develop more complex epistemologies and systems of philosophy and religion. These new ways of thinking and sharing knowledge helped humans make sense of the world, get along with one another in ever larger communities, and begin to better understand the systems upon which our survival depended.

CONSIDER THIS 2.1 FROM HUNTER TO FARMER

Think about the transition from a nomadic way of life to a settled, agrarian way of life.

How do you think this change came about? What thinking and problem-solving process would those early humans have used to make this transition? Imagine and describe some scenarios in which humans first begin keeping seeds and domesticating animals.

As this knowledge accumulated and was passed along from generation to generation, humans became more adept at exploiting and modifying their environment to meet their needs. Over time, agricultural and herding practices became more systematic, efficient, and widespread. Animal domestication practices soon began to resemble what today would be recognized as selective breeding as farmers systematically kept animals that thrived on local food sources and that produced more eggs, milk, meat, or fiber for textiles.

After a few more thousand years, humans learned how to use animals to do work and as a means of transportation. In time, we also got better at using minerals and metals to create tools that increased our power and efficiency. We found ways to capture, store, and use energy sources other than human or animal labor, particularly water power, thus enabling us to maintain larger farms and herds and to clear larger areas of forested land for agricultural use. These innovations allowed more humans to survive and reproduce, to live longer, and to enjoy a more comfortable existence; the human population has increased inexorably worldwide ever since.

However, when humans began to employ more systematic agricultural and herding practices, we also began to exert a more permanent, wide-ranging, and ultimately destructive impact on the planet. A variety of forms of evidence, including paleontological, climatic, geologic, archeological, cultural, and historical data indicate that, as early as 8,000 years ago, agricultural and forest clearing practices in Eurasia had already begun to result in atmospheric increases in methane (CH_4) and carbon dioxide (CO_2) inconsistent with a previous long-term downward trend in concentrations of these gases (Fuller et al., 2011; Ruddiman, 2003).

These **anthropogenic** (i.e., human-caused) increases in CH_4 and CO_2 represented a major turning point in the history of the planet and marked the early beginning of what is becoming increasingly recognized as a distinct geologic epoch called the **Anthropocene**. The Anthropocene (Crutzen & Stoermer, 2000) is an informal but increasingly popular term that refers to our current era. The distinguishing feature of the Anthropocene is the extent to which various planetary conditions and processes have been profoundly altered by human activities. The geologic record shows no evidence that humans had a lasting impact on any earth system prior to the emergence of agriculture, but from that point forward, human impacts on other species and ultimately on the entire planet have increased in scope and number and at an ever-accelerating rate.

BOX 2.2 WHAT'S IN A NAME?

The International Union of Geological Sciences (IUGS, 2014) is the professional organization charged with naming the various intervals or "epochs" on the Earth's geologic time scale. According to the IUGS, we are officially in the Holocene epoch, which began at the end of the last major ice age, about

12,000 years ago. The IUGS is currently considering whether the Anthropocene should be considered a geological epoch at the same hierarchical level as the Pleistocene and Holocene epochs. The implication of this decision would be that the current epoch, the Holocene, has ended. Alternatively, the IUGS might decide that the Anthropocene is a subdivision of the Holocene, a lower hierarchical level called an "age." A number of geologists feel that there is not enough evidence in rock strata to justify naming our current epoch the Anthropocene. Other scientists agree that we are in the Anthropocene but argue that we should mark its start about 250 years ago when increases in carbon dioxide and methane first appear in ice cores and lake sediments. In any event, while scientists disagree about whether the Anthropocene began with the advent of agriculture about 8,000 years ago or with the dawn of the Industrial Revolution, there is virtual unanimity among credible scientists in all disciplines that humans have irreparably altered planetary climate systems, caused the extinction of plant and animal species, and have caused lasting damage to major hydrologic and ocean systems.

The Great Acceleration

Today, it is widely acknowledged among credible scientists and scientific organizations that human activity has increased so dramatically over the past 250 years that our impact on the planet is no longer in doubt or insignificant. What is most alarming, though, is that the scale and speed of change has been accelerating rapidly in the last 60 years. As a result, the years since World War II are often referred to as the **Great Acceleration**.

These processes can be seen in Figures 2.1 and 2.2. Figure 2.1 shows the increasing rates of change in various types of human activity since the beginning of the Industrial Revolution on a variety of indicators. These varied indicators all show a sharp change in the slope of the curves occurring in the 1950s, illustrating how the past 60 years have been a period of rapid and unprecedented change in human history. Figure 2.2 shows similar changes in a variety of earth systems during this same time period.

To fully appreciate what the graphs in Figures 2.1 and 2.2 are showing, it might be helpful to review two terms you probably learned in your high school general science class. Velocity refers to the rate at which something is moving in a particular direction. Something moving at a constant velocity is not accelerating. Acceleration does not refer to the speed at which something is happening but rather refers to a *change* in the rate at which something occurs. For example, in Figure 2.1a we can see that the population of humans on the planet grew at a fairly constant rate between 1750 and 1900 to about 1.6 billion. In 1900, the rate of growth began to increase; it had grown about 60% to 2.5 billion people by 1950. Then, during the

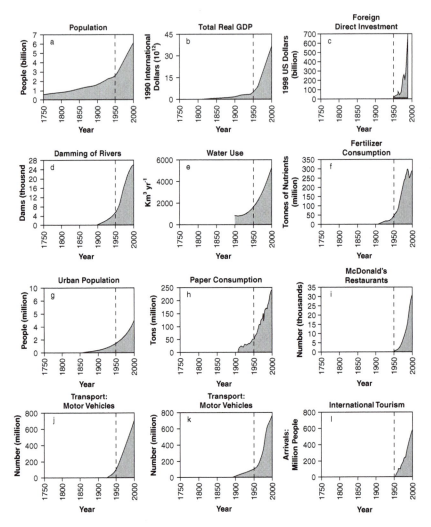

Figure 2.1 The increasing rates of change in human activity since the beginning of the industrial revolution

Data sources for graphs in Figure 2.1: a. United States Bureau of the Census (2000); b. Nordhaus (1997); c. World Bank (2002); d. World Commission on Dams (2000); e. Shiklomanov (1990); f. International Fertilizer Industry Association (2002); g. United Nations Centre for Human Settlements (2001); h. Pulp and Paper International (1993); i. McDonald's (2002); j. UNEP (2000); k. Canning (2001); l. World Tourism Organization (2001).

Source: Adapted from Steffen et al. (2005), p. 132, Fig. 3.66. Used with permission.

Great Acceleration, the rate of growth in world population increased each year, resulting in a 295% overall increase to about 7.3 billion people in 2015.

This drastic acceleration in human population growth is remarkable enough on its own, but the distinguishing characteristic of the Great Acceleration is the sheer number of processes that show this pattern of rapid acceleration beginning in the 1950s.

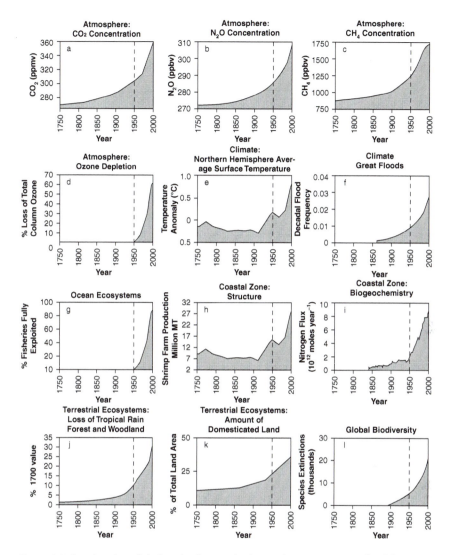

Figure 2.2 Accelerating global-scale changes in the earth system as a result of dramatic increases in human activity

Sources of information for Figure 2.2: a. atmospheric CO$_2$ concentration (Etheridge et al., 1996); b. atmospheric N$_2$O concentration (Machida et al., 1995); c. atmospheric CH$_4$ concentration (Blunier et al., 1993); d. percentage total column ozone loss, using the average annual total column ozone, 330, as a base (Shanklin & Gardine, 1989); e. northern hemisphere average surface temperature anomalies (Mann et al., 1999); f. decadal frequency of great floods (one-in-100-year events) after 1860 for basins larger than 200,000 km^2 with observations that span at least 30 years (Milly et al., 2002); g. percentage of global fisheries either fully exploited, overfished or collapsed (FAOSTAT, 2002); h. annual shrimp production as a proxy for coastal zone alteration (WRI, 2003; FAOSTAT, 2002); i. model-calculated partitioning of the human-induced nitrogen perturbation fluxes in the global coastal margin for the period since 1850 (Mackenzie et al., 2002); j. loss of tropical rainforest and woodland, as estimated for tropical Africa, Latin America and South and Southeast Asia (Richards, 1990; WRI, 1990); k. amount of land converted to pasture and cropland (Klein Goldewijk, & Battjes, 1997); l. mathematically calculated rate of extinction (based on Wilson, 1992).

Source: Adapted from Steffen et al. (2005), p. 133, Fig. 3.67. Used with permission.

The issue here is not just that the human population growth is accelerating but also that the number of harmful human activities is also accelerating. A *general* conclusion we can draw is that a rapid acceleration in human activities in the last half century, such as those shown in the examples in Figure 2.1, has resulted in a rapid acceleration in the deterioration of systems upon which we depend for our survival, such as those shown in Figure 2.2. However, the causal relationship between specific human activities and specific planetary impacts is complex, so we cannot say that specific activities shown in Figure 2.1 *caused* specific impacts shown in Figure 2.2. This complexity can operate in a variety of ways.

Sometimes, a single type of human activity can result in multiple responses in planetary systems, and those responses can then trigger additional responses. For example, the combustion of fossil fuels such as coal, petroleum, and natural gas results in atmospheric deposition of **greenhouse gases** (GHG) such as carbon dioxide (CO_2), methane (CH_4), nitrous oxide (N_2O), nitric oxide (NO), and sulfur dioxide (SO_2). Greenhouse gases trap heat energy in the atmosphere, leading to an overall rise in terrestrial surface temperatures and associated disruptions of numerous climate systems.

Increased levels of atmospheric CO_2, NO, and SO_2 due to fossil fuel combustion also affect vegetation growth and contribute to changes in ocean chemistry, causing oceans to become more acidic. This increasing acidity in turn is a factor in the death of coral reefs and the decline of other marine species that depend on coral reefs for food and shelter, resulting in an overall loss of biodiversity.

Sometimes multiple types of human activities contribute to specific planetary responses. For example, a wide range of human activities other than fossil fuel combustion can contribute to loss of biodiversity, including various forms of pollution; destruction of habitats; or overharvesting, such as in the case of commercial fisheries and forests. Similarly, fossil fuel combustion is not the only source of greenhouse gas emission. A variety of industrial processes such as aluminum and semiconductor manufacturing and the transmission of electrical energy can result in release of **fluorinated gases** such as hydrofluorocarbons, perfluorocarbons, and sulfur hexafluoride. Fluorinated gases have no natural sources and only come from human-related activities. They are the most potent and longest lasting type of greenhouse gases emitted by human activities so that even small atmospheric concentrations can have large effects on global temperatures.

BOX 2.3 ECOLOGICAL THRESHOLDS

A threshold is the critical tipping point at which a small change can bring about an abrupt qualitative change in a larger system (Groffman et al., 2006; Lenton et al., 2008). Often the changes that occur when a threshold is crossed are nonlinear. This means that the change in the overall system may be much more drastic than the effect of the small change that triggers it. When referring to ecosystems, these tipping points are often referred to as **ecological thresholds**. Crossing an ecological threshold implies that the ecosystem has moved from a stable, sustainable state to less stable and usually less sustainable state. Often, an ecosystem reaches this state of instability as a result of multiple small changes, bringing about a large response in the ecosystem. Here are some common examples of ecological threshold crossings:

- Overfishing of one species in an area eventually leads to a complete collapse of multiple fish populations over a much broader region (Hamilton, Haedrich, & Duncan, 2004).
- Runoff of phosphorus and nitrogen from sewage effluent or agricultural practices leads to decreased oxygen levels in the water of a lake. Increased rates of algae growth lead to higher levels of turbidity and drastic changes in species populations (Larsen, Schultz, & Malueg, 1981; Jeppesen et al., 1999).
- After the population of Easter Island grew to an estimated high of around 10,000 people around 800 CE, the rate of tree cutting exceeded the ability of forests to regenerate. Without trees, soil erosion occurred and canoes, used for fishing and hunting, could no longer be built. The society resorted to cannibalism, and the population eventually collapsed to an estimated 2,000 people (Rainbird, 2002).

What is particularly alarming about the Great Acceleration is that human-driven impacts are operating at such simultaneity, magnitude, and rapidity that they often exceed the range of natural variability observed over at least the last 800,000 years (Steffen et al., 2005). These impacts are causing a number of Earth systems to become unstable in ways that have no precedent in the geologic record. In other words, we simply do not know what happens when these systems grow unstable because there is no previous example from which to learn. The growing concern among many scientists is that as these various systems become less stable, they will cross the planetary equivalent of an ecological threshold; the possibility of abrupt, irreversible changes on a planetary scale can no longer be ruled out. What is fairly certain, though, is that if changes of that scale occur, they will ultimately make the planet less able to sustain life—or at least less able to sustain human life.

Planetary Boundaries

Of course, the planet is not just a single unitary system but actually involves many complexly interconnected subsystems and, therefore, many separate threshold tipping points. Because many of those thresholds are not fully understood, Rock-ström et al. (2009a, 2009b) have proposed establishing "planetary boundaries" for nine variables that pertain to the planetary systems most essential for sustaining life on Earth. Whereas thresholds are intrinsic features of a system and represent a dangerous point of no return, a boundary is a human-determined variable that is set at a safe distance from the threshold. Think of a guardrail and sign erected several meters back from the precipice of a cliff to warn people about the dangers of going too close to the edge. The nine variables that form the basis for planetary boundaries are described briefly here:

Climate Change

The United Nations Framework Convention on Climate Change (1992/2015) defines this as a "change of climate which is attributed directly or indirectly to human activity that alters the composition of the global atmosphere and which is in addition to natural climate variability observed over comparable time periods" (p. 2). Climate change primarily is responsible for an overall warming trend in surface temperatures, and this warming process triggers a cascade of other impacts, including loss of polar ice sheets, sea level rise, planetary changes in ocean and weather circulation patterns, extreme weather events, changes in seasonal rainfall and snowpack, changes in species migration patterns, ocean acidification, and loss of species habitats. As noted above, while a number of human activities contribute to climate change, the primary driver is emission of greenhouse gases, including CO_2. Atmospheric concentration of CO_2, measured in parts per million (ppm) is widely accepted to be a reliable indicator of overall climate change, with 350 ppm considered a safe planetary boundary. At the time this book was published in 2015, atmospheric concentrations of CO_2 hovered around 400 ppm.

Loss of Biodiversity

The term **biodiversity** is a portmanteau that combines the words biological and diversity. Generally, the term refers to the overall variety of species found in a particular area or ecosystem. Increasingly, the term is also used to refer to the diversity of species at the planetary level. In this broader context, loss of biodiversity refers to species extinction. As can be seen in Figure 2.2.1, rates of species extinctions have increased drastically during the Great Acceleration, at more than 100 times the normal background rate. The impacts of loss of biodiversity are varied but can affect the overall health of local ecosystems, changes in migration patterns, loss of livelihood, and threats to food security.

Nitrogen and Phosphorous Cycling

Nitrogen is a major ingredient of chlorophyll, amino acids, and proteins and thus is an essential element for all life forms. Humans have impacted the nitrogen cycle by converting atmospheric N_2 into accessible forms at a faster than natural rate. This occurs primarily through the manufacture and excessive use of fertilizers as well as through combustion of fossil fuels. As a result, freshwater and coastal marine ecosystems often undergo rapid **eutrophication**, a process in which they receive excess nutrients that result in excessive plant growth and species imbalances such as algae blooms. Eutrophication can cause a severe drop in biodiversity and an eventual collapse of a freshwater or marine ecosystem.

Phosphorous is also an essential nutrient for plants and animals and, like nitrogen, is not readily available in an accessible form to plants and other organisms. Phosphorus occurs primarily as part of a phosphate ion $(PO_4)^{3-}$ in rocks and minerals and becomes accessible to plants as a result of various weathering processes. The plants are then consumed by other species; the phosphorus is then excreted or incorporated into tissue and transmitted further up the food chain. During the Great Acceleration, humans have greatly increased the availability of phosphorus by mining it and then including it in fertilizers. As with nitrogen, this increased availability of phosphorus can disrupt species balances by contributing to overgrowth of aquatic plants and algae and loss of biodiversity in lakes and coastal waterways.

Ozone Depletion

The ozone layer is a region in the stratosphere, 10–50 km above the surface of the Earth. This layer is essential to the survival of life on Earth because it filters harmful ultraviolet (UV) radiation from sunlight. If the ozone layer thins, more UV radiation reaches the ground. This higher level of UV radiation can cause higher rates of skin cancer as well as damage to a variety of marine and terrestrial ecosystems. Human use of chlorofluorocarbons (CFCs) as refrigerants, solvents, foam blowing agents, and in other applications contributed to ozone-layer depletion and the formation of ozone holes in the second half of the last century. However, as a result of international agreements, the use of CFCs has been severely limited so that ozone depletion is currently within planetary boundaries.

Ocean Acidification

Anthropogenic addition of CO_2 to oceans has the effect of lowering the pH of surface seawater, reducing the availability of carbonate ions for use by various marine organisms. As a result, organisms that form protective calcium carbonate shells, such as coral, many mollusks, and numerous other species, find it increasingly difficult to survive. Surface ocean acidity has already increased by 30% compared to preindustrial times, and ocean acidification is resulting in massive coral reef die-offs and conversion of coral reefs to algal-dominated systems. Coral reefs are sometimes referred to as the rainforests of the ocean because they are the most diverse of all marine ecosystems. It is estimated that as much as one quarter of all ocean species depend on reefs for food and shelter. Therefore, crossing the ocean acidification boundary has ramifications for the whole planet because it will change the structure and dynamics of entire ocean ecosystems and could potentially lead to drastic reductions in fish stocks.

Global Freshwater Use

The amount of freshwater on the planet remains fairly constant over time, at about 2.5% of all water on the planet. Freshwater is continually recycled through the atmosphere and then back into various terrestrial aquifers and hydrologic systems. However, only 1% of the planet's freshwater is readily accessible for human use. The freshwater cycle is strongly affected by climate change and human activities. As human population has soared during the Great Acceleration, global demand for freshwater is overtaking its supply in many parts of the world. The United Nations Environment Program (UNEP) predicts that by 2025, more than half of the countries in the world will be experiencing water stress or outright water shortages (UNEP, 2010). In some cases, overuse has caused permanent changes in aquifer levels over wide geographic areas. At the same time, drastic changes in hydrologic systems through damming or other modifications to freshwater systems can cause abrupt and irreversible changes at a global scale.

Changes in Land Use

Land system changes are primarily driven by agriculture and industrial expansion. These changes can affect freshwater, carbon, and other cycles; reduce biodiversity; and reduce the effectiveness of naturally occurring carbon sinks. Agricultural processes including conversion of forests, wetlands, and other vegetation types to agricultural land as well as industrial processes such as mountaintop removal mining and hydrologic fracturing oil extraction can irreversibly affect land systems over large areas. While these land-system changes may occur on a local level, the aggregated impacts of these changes occur around the planet by reducing global resilience to climate change, ocean acidification, freshwater flow, and loss of biodiversity.

Atmospheric Aerosol Loading

Aerosols are formed when fine solid particles or liquid droplets become suspended in the atmosphere. Naturally occurring aerosols can form after a volcanic eruption or from desert dust. Human activities that contribute to atmospheric aerosol loading include emission of pollutant gases that condense into droplets and particles and land-use changes that increases the release of dust and smoke into the air. Human-made aerosols generally are the result of burning coal or oil. Aerosols can directly affect climate by changing how clouds absorb and reflect sunlight or by changing the amount of sunlight that is radiated back into space, in some cases creating localized cooling by reflecting more sunlight. However, it is not known how this localized cooling will interact with the more generalized warming process created by greenhouse gases and large-scale changes to climate and monsoon systems already seen in highly polluted environments. In addition to climate impacts, human-made aerosols directly affect air quality. They can contribute to higher rates of pollution-caused illnesses such as asthma and contribute to an increase in the number of premature, pollution-related deaths each year. While many relationships between aerosols, climate, and ecosystems are well established, many causal links are yet to be determined, so it has not yet been possible to set a safe boundary for atmospheric aerosol loading.

Chemical Pollution

Concerns about chemical pollution have a long-standing history, dating back to the work of Rachel Carson (1962) early in the environmental movement. Chemical pollution can involve a wide range of toxic substances, including heavy metals, radioactive compounds and a variety of human-made organic compounds. Many of these compounds can persist in the environment for very long times, and their effects on humans and other species are irreversible. Many of these substances can bioaccumulate to create increased risk for organisms with longer-term exposure or biomagnify to create increased risks for organisms at higher trophic levels. Chemical pollution has no natural occurring source and is only caused by human activity. It has not yet been possible to identify a chemical pollution planetary boundary on the basis of empirical science; however, there is a well-established body of research that documents the very considerable health and environmental risks associated with chemical pollution.

The nine planetary boundaries proposed by Rockström and his colleagues, along with a brief description of the parameters used to measure them, are shown in Table 2.1.

These nine variables are not an exhaustive list of all possible threats to the various environmental systems upon which humans and other species depend for their survival. For example, we might add to chemical pollution the threats created by the tons of plastic and other garbage that has found its way into the oceans. However, the nine planetary boundaries serve as indicators of the overall health of the planet. If we manage to stay on the safe side of these boundaries, we can at least have some assurance that we will be able to preserve the integrity of planetary systems for future generations. Rockström et al. (2009a, 2009b) described this area as the **safe operating space for humanity**. The relative status of the nine variables with respect to this safe operating space can be observed directly in Figure 2.3. In the figure, the two inner circles with dotted shading represent the area on the safe side of the planetary boundaries.

As Figure 2.3 shows, three of the nine systems (loss of biodiversity, climate change, and nitrogen) are already in a state of **overshoot**. This means the

TABLE 2.1 Nine Planetary Boundaries That Establish a Safe Operating Space for Humanity.

Planetary boundary	Description of boundary parameters	Proposed boundary	Current status	Preindustrial value
Climate change	Atmospheric CO_2 concentration parts per million (ppm)	350 ppm	387 ppm	280 ppm
	Ratio of sunlight absorbed by Earth to energy radiated back into space (also known as **radiative forcing**) watts/meter squared (Wm^{-2})	$+1.0\,Wm^{-2}$	$+1.5\,Wm^{-2}$	0
Rate of biodiversity loss	Extinction rate per million species per year (E/MSY)	10	> 100	0.1–1
Nitrogen cycle (part of a boundary with the phosphorus cycle)	Amount of N_2 removed from the atmosphere for human use measured as millions of tonnes per year (Mt N yr-1) 1 tonne = 1,000 kg = 2,204.6 lbs.	35 (about 25% of the total amount of N_2 fixed per annum by natural processes	121	0
Phosphorus cycle (part of a boundary with the nitrogen cycle)	Quantity of P flowing into the oceans (Mt N yr-1)	< 10 times natural rate due to weathering	8.5–9.5	~1
Stratospheric ozone depletion	Concentration of ozone (Dobson unit or DU)	276 DU 5% reduction from pre-industrial level	283 DU	290 DU
Ocean acidification	Global mean saturation state of aragonite in surface sea water (Ω arag)	2.75 Ω arag > 80% of pre-industrial level	2.90 Ω arag	3.44 Ω arag
Global freshwater use	Consumption of freshwater by humans (km^3 per $year^{-1}$)	4,000 km^3 per $year^{-1}$	2,600	415
Change in land use	Percentage of global land cover converted to cropland	> 15% of global ice free land surface converted to cropland	11.7	Low
Atmospheric aerosol loading	Overall particulate concentration in the atmosphere on a regional basis	To be determined		
Chemical pollution	Not yet determined. One example would be concentration of persistent organic pollutants, plastics, endocrine disrupters, heavy metals, and nuclear waste in the global environment.	To be determined		

Source: Rockström et al., 2009a, p. 472; Rockström et al. 2009b, pp. 31–32. Used with permission.

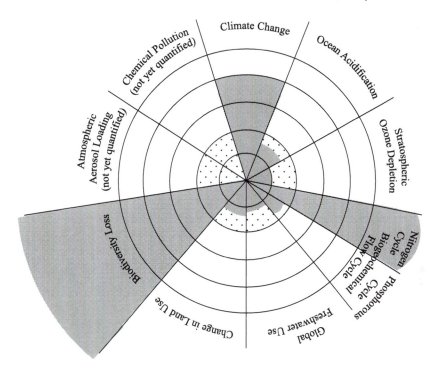

Figure 2.3 Beyond the planetary boundary

Source: Rockstrom et al, 2009/Azote Images/Stockholm Resilience Centre. Used with permission.

recommended boundaries for these variables already been crossed, and the systems are in the danger zone on the wrong side of the guardrail, approaching the precipice. The figure also shows that several other systems are also nearing their boundaries but have not yet crossed into the danger zone. Also, it is entirely possible that we have already crossed into a danger zone for chemical pollution and atmospheric aerosol loading, but the scientific knowledge has not yet been fully developed for these systems to allow verification of this possibility.

When a system goes into overshoot, one of two things can happen. The system itself might undergo a drastic change to adjust to a new, higher limit or threshold. For example, it is possible that the planet might move permanently to much warmer climate regime as a result of global climate change. Those species that can rapidly adapt would survive, and those that cannot would go extinct. Alternatively, a system in overshoot could simply collapse, which, of course, has catastrophic consequences. At this point, we simply do not know what will happen as the planet moves further and further into the unknown territory beyond the barriers. However, it is almost certain that life will become increasingly more difficult if not impossible for billions of humans and other species, not in some distant future but during the lifetime of the children who are in school today and who will enter school this year.

Whether we are ready or not, this is the future that our distant ancestors set in motion more than 8,000 years ago when they first started domesticating animals and plants and that our more recent ancestors locked us into during the Industrial Revolution.

The question for us today is this: What future are we creating for future generations?

CONSIDER THIS 2.2 INVESTIGATE THE BOUNDARIES

Look at the variables illustrated in Figure 2.3 and described in Table 2.1. How often do you interact with each of these systems? Are there things that you do on a regular basis that might contribute to the instability of these various systems?

Choose one of the planetary boundary variables and investigate ways that you could reduce your impact.

A Safe and Just Space for Humanity

The Rockström et al.'s (2009a) planetary boundaries framework is helpful because it identifies a set of parameters for monitoring the status of key Earth systems vital for the survival of humans and other species. However, the planetary boundaries do not reflect the various social systems that also must be in place to prevent deprivations that limit the potential of individuals to live healthy, productive, and empowered lives.

The relationship between environmental boundaries and social foundations is complex. Often, sustainability is conceived as a concern for environmental systems and, particularly, the preservation of those systems for future generations. Concerns for human development, human rights, and social justice often focus on improving outcomes, capabilities, and opportunities for people alive today. In this respect, sustainability and social justice are similar in that both are about distributive justice—a socially just allocation of goods, services, and consequences in a society. The underlying value is that inequitable processes are unjust, whether across groups or generations. The injustice created when the current generation destroys the environment for future generations is no different than the injustices created when a present-day group acts in ways that diminish the aspirations of another present-day group for equal opportunities to jobs, health, or education (UNDP, 2011, p. 11).

To address this expanded notion of sustainability, Raworth (2012) has extended the Rockström et al. (2009a) concept of planetary boundaries to include a set of social foundations that establish the floor of **a safe and just space for**

humanity. As Rockström et al. (2009a) have done with the planetary boundaries, Raworth (2012) has proposed a set of essential variables that form the social foundations floor of the safe and just space for humanity. These are described briefly in Table 2.2.

As Raworth (2012) emphasizes,

> Ensuring all people's lives are built upon a social foundation is essential for sustainable development, but so is staying below the environmental ceiling: crossing over either of these boundaries can trigger both social and ecological crises. Sustainable development can only succeed if poverty eradication and environmental sustainability are pursued together. (p. 8)

TABLE 2.2 Examples of Indicators of the Social Foundations of Safe and Just Space for Humanity.

Social foundation	Extent of global deprivation (illustrative indicators)	Current percentage	Year data collected
Food security	Population undernourished	13%	2006–8
Income	Population living below $1.25 (PPP) per day	21%	2005
Water and sanitation	Population without access to an improved drinking water source	13%	2008
	Population without access to improved sanitation	39%	2008
Health care	Population estimated to be without regular access to essential medicines	30%	2004
Education	Children not enrolled in primary school	10%	2009 2009
	Illiteracy among 15–24 year olds	11%	
Energy	Population lacking access to electricity	19%	2009
	Population lacking access to clean cooking facilities	39%	2009
Gender equality	Employment gap between women and men in waged work (excluding agriculture)	34%	2009
	Representation gap between women and men in national government	77%	2011
Social equity	Population living on less than the median income in countries with a Gini* coefficient exceeding 0.35	33%	1995– 2009
Voice	Example: Population living in countries that do not permit political participation or freedom of expression.	To be determined	
Jobs	Example: Labor force not employed in decent work	To be determined	
Resilience	Example: Population facing multiple dimensions of poverty	To be determined	

Source: Raworth, 2012/Oxfam. Used with permission.

*The Gini index is a measure of income inequality in a society. A Gini index of 1.00 represents maximum inequality—one person has all the resources and everyone else has none. A Gini index of 0.00 represents perfect equality—everyone has the same income.

The safe and just space for humanity, then, is the area above the floor of critical social foundations and below the ceiling of planetary boundaries. This is the space "in the doughnut" illustrated in Figure 2.4.

Unlike the planetary boundaries, there is no earlier preindustrial baseline that can be used to interpret the social foundations. In fact, there has never been a time in the history of the planet when there has been a commitment to ensuring universal access to social foundations. The tipping points for the various social foundations will vary from context to context, but just as overshoot can result in a disruptive and long-term if not permanent transformation of a system, "undershoot" of any of the social foundations is likely to have similar impacts. Examples of the kind of disruptions that can occur when one of the social foundations goes into "undershoot" include examples such as these:

• Poor sanitary conditions and a lack of an adequate medical infrastructure in very poor nations leaves them unprepared to deal with outbreaks of deadly viruses. In the case of HIV/AIDS, this situation can be exacerbated by low levels of education, persistence of misinformation, and superstitions about how the disease is transmitted. In the case of Ebola, poor West African nations

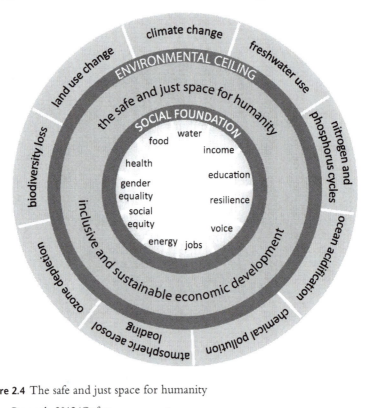

Figure 2.4 The safe and just space for humanity

Source: Raworth, 2012/Oxfam

were unprepared to deal with a fast-moving epidemic in 2014. In contrast, people living in wealthy countries often have access to state-of-the-art treatments and technologically advanced treatment facilities.

- Long histories of discriminatory policies and practices have created gross inequalities in many American cities that include high numbers of poor and minority youth. Public outcry and demonstrations occurred across the United States in 2014 when large numbers of people felt that many urban police departments exercise racist practices, resulting in the higher rates of incarceration and death of black and Hispanic men.
- Political upheaval and ethnic conflicts resulted in widespread famine in 2011–2012 after years of drought at the Horn of Africa.
- A pattern of extremist and corrupt governments led to a broad wave of revolutionary protests and demonstrations that occurred during Arab Spring in 2010–2012.
- Deep-rooted inequalities in a society can result in gender-based discrimination in education. Millions of girls around the world are excluded from the benefits of education due to practices such as gender-based violence, discriminatory education laws, early marriage and pregnancy, and traditional attitudes about the status and role of females.

Learning to Live Within the Doughnut

The problems of unsustainability are not caused by a sinister cabal of evil-doers intent on destroying the world. Rather, they are the cumulative result of hundreds of years of people all over the world going about the everyday business of trying to live their lives the best way they know how. For example, as Figure 2.5 shows, most greenhouse gases are generated by processes that serve the desires and needs of "just plain folks" to heat their homes and the other buildings, use public or private transport, use electricity, or consume goods and services provided by agriculture and forestry. Broad categories of threats such as disruption of nitrogen and phosphorus cycles, threats to global freshwater, or loss of biodiversity are the result of each of us engaging in such prosaic activities as disposing of our bodily waste, washing our clothes, turning the tap to fill a water glass, or eating takeout from a fast food restaurant. Think about how often you do any of these things in a day!

Similarly, it can be tempting to think of practices and policies that lead to undershoot of social foundations as things that "other people" do. It is easy to take for granted privileges such as access to an adequate education, health care, housing, and employment without considering that those privileges are not universally available.

But take heart! Living within the doughnut does not necessarily mean you need to totally transform your life so that you can stop doing all those things that get you through the day but that contribute to unsustainability. Rather, it means making better, smarter decisions on a day-to-day and minute-to-minute basis about

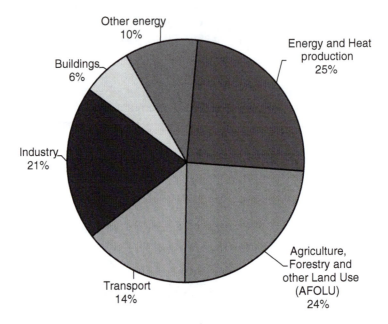

Figure 2.5 Anthropogenic GHG emissions by sector

Data Source: International Panel on Climate Change (2014).

how you do those things. Many small steps and small decisions can lead to large changes. The goal of education for sustainability is to help people learn how to "live within the doughnut" (Raworth, 2012) by working to create the conditions that enable everyone alive today equal access to the necessary freedoms and opportunities associated meaningful human development and at the same time working to avoid seriously compromising the freedoms and opportunities of future generations. The chapters in this book will help you learn how to begin incorporating that decision process into your personal and professional practice as a teacher.

EXTEND YOUR PROFESSIONAL KNOWLEDGE 2.1

Visit one of these websites and investigate the various curriculum programs and resources listed. Think about how the information presented in this chapter can help you implement some of these lesson plans.

National Wildlife Fund: www.nwf.org/Eco-Schools-USA/Become-an-Eco-School/Pathways/Climate-Change/Curriculum.aspx

Facing the Future: www.facingthefuture.org/ (click on Issues and Solutions)

References

Blunier, T., Chappellaz, J., Schwander, J., Barnola, J.-M., Desperts, T., Stauffer, B., & Raynaud, D. (1993). Atmospheric methane record from a Greenland ice core over the last 1,000 years. *Journal of Geophysical Research, 20,* 2219–2222.

Canning, D. (2001). *World Bank: A Database of World Infrastructure Stocks, 1950–95.* Washington, DC: World Bank.

Carson, R. (1962). *Silent Spring.* Boston: Houghton Mifflin.

Crutzen, P.I., & Stoermer, E.F. (2000). The Anthropocene. *IGBP Newsletter, 41,* 12.

Einstein, A. (1955, March 21). *Letter to Family of Michel Angelo Besso.* Einstein Archives Online call number 75–839. Retrieved from: http://alberteinstein.info/.

Etheridge, D.M., Steele, L. P., Langenfelds, R. L., Francey, R. J., Barnola, J.-M., & Morgan, V. I. (1996). Natural and anthropogenic changes in atmospheric CO_2 over the last 1,000 years from air in Antarctic ice and firn. *Journal of Geophysical Research, 101,* 4115–4128.

FAOSTAT. (2002). Statistical Databases. Food and Agriculture Organization of the United Nations, Rome. Retrieved from: www.apps.fao.org.

Fuller, D.Q., van Etten, J., Manning, K., Castillo, C., Kingwell-Banham, E., Weisskopf, A., . . . Hijmans, R.J. (2011). The contribution of rice agriculture and livestock pastoralism to prehistoric methane levels: An archaeological assessment. *Holocene, 21*(5), 743–759.

Groffman, P. M., Baron, J.S., Blett, T.J., Gold, A.J., Goodman, I., Gunderson, L.H., . . . Wiens, J. (2006). Ecological thresholds: The key to successful environmental management or an important concept with no practical application? *Ecosystems, 9,* 1–13.

Grove, M. (2011). Speciation, diversity, and Mode 1 technologies: The impact of variability selection. *Journal of Human Evolution, 61,* 306–319.

Hamilton, L. C., Haedrich, R. L., & Duncan, C. M. (2004). Above and below the water: Social/ecological transformation in northwest Newfoundland. *Population and Environment, 25*(3), 195–215.

International Fertilizer Industry Association. (2002). Fertilizer Indicators. Retrieved from: www.fertilizer.org/ifa/statistics/indicators/ind_cn_world.asp

International Panel on Climate Change (IPCC). (2014). Summary for policymakers. In Edenhofer, O., Pichs-Madruga, R., Sokona, Y., Farahani, E., Kadner, S., Seyboth, K., . . . Minx, J. C. (Eds.), *Climate Change 2014, Mitigation of Climate Change. Contribution of Working Group III to the Fifth Assessment Report of the Intergovernmental Panel on Climate Change.* Cambridge: Cambridge University Press.

International Union of Geological Sciences (IUGS). (2014). What Is the "Anthropocene"?—Current Definition and Status. Retrieved from: http://quaternary.stratigraphy.org/workinggroups/anthropocene/

Jeppesen, E., Sondergaard, M., Kronvang, B., Jensen, J. P., Svendsen, L. M., & Lauridsen, T. L. (1999). Lake and catchment management in Denmark. *Hydrobiologia, 396,* 419–32.

King, M.L. (1967, April 4). *Beyond Vietnam: A Time to Break the Silence.* Speech delivered at the Riverside Church, New York.

Klein Goldewijk K, Battjes R (1997) One Hundred year database for integrated environmental assessments. Reprinted with permission from National Institute for Public Health and the Environment (RIVM), Bilthoven, Netherlands.

Larsen, D.P., Schultz, D.W., & Malueg, K.W. (1981). Summer internal phosphorus supplies in Shagawa Lake, Minnesota. *Limnology and Oceanography, 26*(4), 740–753.

Lenton, T.M., Held, H., Kriegler, E., Hall, J.W., Lucht, W., Rahmstorf, S., & Schellnhuber, H.J. (2008). Tipping elements in the Earth's climate system. *Proceedings of the National Academy of Sciences, 105*, 1786–1793.

Machida, T., Nakazawa, T., Fujii, Y., Aoki, S., & Watanabe, O. (1995). Increase in the atmospheric nitrous oxide concentration during the last 250 years. *Geophysical Research Letters, 22*, 2921–2924.

Mackenzie, F.T., Ver, L. M., & Lerman, A. (2002). Century-scale nitrogen and phosphorus controls of the carbon cycle. *Chemical Geology, 190*, 13–32.

Mann, M. E., Bradley, R. S., & Hughes, M. K. (1999). Northern hemisphere temperatures during the past millennium: Inferences, uncertainties, and limitations. *Geophysical Research Letters, 26*, 759–762.

McDonald's. (2002). Our Company: Getting to Know Us. Retrieved from: www.mcdonalds.com.

Milly, P.C.D., Wetherald, R.T., Dunne, K. A., & Delworth, T. L. (2002). Increasing risk of great floods in a changing climate. *Nature, 415*, 514–517.

Nordhaus, W. (1997). Do real wage and output series capture reality? The history of lighting suggests not. In: Bresnahan T., & Gordon, R. (Eds.), *The Economics of New Goods*. Chicago, IL: University of Chicago Press.

Potts, R. (1998). Variability selection in hominid evolution. *Evolutionary Anthropology, 7*, 81–96.

Pulp and Paper International. (1993). PPI's International Fact and Price Book. In: *FAO Forest Product Yearbook 1960–1991*. Rome: Food and Agriculture Organization of the United Nations.

Rainbird, P. (2002). A message for our future? The Rapa Nui (Easter Island) ecodisaster and Pacific Island environments. *World Archaeology, 33*(3), 436–451.

Raworth, K. (2012, February). A safe and just space for humanity: Can we live within the doughnut? *Oxfam Discussion Papers*. Oxford: Oxfam.

Richards, J. (1990). Land transformation. In: Turner, B.L., Clark, W. C., Kates, R. W., Richards, J. F., Mathews, J. T., & Meyer, W.B. (Eds.), *The Earth as Transformed by Human Action: Global and Regional Changes in the Biosphere Over the Past 300 Years* (pp. 163–201). Cambridge: Cambridge University Press.

Rockström, J., Steffen, W., Noone, K., Persson, A., Chapin, S., Lambin, E.F., . . . Foley, J.A. (2009a). Planetary boundaries: Exploring the safe operating space for humanity. *Ecology and Society, 14*(2), 32.

Rockström, J., Steffen, W., Noone, K., Persson, A., Chapin, S., Lambin, E.F., . . . Foley, J.A. (2009b). A safe operating space for humanity. *Nature, 461*, 472–475.

Ruddiman, W. F. (2003). The Anthropogenic greenhouse era began thousands of years ago. *Climatic Change, 61*, 261–293.

Shanklin, J. D., & Gardine, B.G. (1989). The Antarctic ozone hole. *British Antarctic Survey*. London: Natural Environment Research Council.

Shiklomanov, I. A. (1990). Global Water Resources. *Nature Resource, 26*(3).

Steffen, W., Sanderson, A., Tyson, P. D., Jäger, J., Matson, P. A., Moore, B., . . . Wasson R.J. (2005). *Global Change and the Earth System: A Planet Under Pressure*. Heidelberg: Springer Verlag.

United Nations Centre for Human Settlements. (2001). *The State of the World's Cities, 2001*. Nairobi: Author.

United Nations Development Programme (UNDP). (2011). Sustainability and Equity: A Better Future for All. *Human Development Report 2011*. New York: United Nations Development Programme, Human Development Report Office (UNDP/HDRO).

United Nations Environment Programme (UNEP). (2000). *Global Environmental Outlook 2000*. Nairobi: Author.

United Nations Environment Programme (UNEP). (2010). *Clearing the Waters: A Focus on Water Quality Solutions*. Nairobi: UNEP.

United Nations Framework Convention on Climate Change (UNFCCC). (1992/2015). Article 1. Definitions. *United Nations Framework Convention on Climate Change* (p. 7). Bonn: Author.

United States Bureau of the Census. (2000). International Database. Retrieved from: www.census.gov/ipc/www/worldpop.htm

Wilson, E.O. (1992). *The Diversity of Life*. Boston, MA: Harvard University Press.

WRI. (1990). Forest and rangelands. In: A guide to the global environment. World Resources Institute, Washington DC, pp. 101–120.

WRI. (2003). A guide to world resources 2002–2004: Decisions for the Earth. A joint publication with UN Development Program, UN Environmental Program, World Bank and World Resources Institute, Washington DC.

World Bank. (2002). Foreign Direct Investment. *Data/Indicators*. Retrieved from: http://data.worldbank.org/indicator

World Commission on Dams. (2000). Dams and development: A new framework for decision-making. *The Report of the World Commission on Dams*. London: Earthscan.

World Tourism Organization. (2001). Tourism Industry Trends. *Industry Science Resources*. Retrieved from: http://www.world-tourism.org

3

EDUCATION FOR SUSTAINABILITY

What is rooted is easy to nourish.
What is recent is easy to correct.
What is fragile is easy to break.
What is small is easy to scatter.
Prevent trouble before it arises.
Put things in order before they become chaotic.
The giant tree grows from a tiny sprout.
A great tower rises from a basket of dirt.
Even the longest journey starts from beneath your feet.
                    —Lao Tzu (c. 605 BCE—c. 535 BCE), *Tao Te Ching*, ch. 64

Creating a safe and just space for humans and other species means making sure the various systems upon which our survival depends stay on the safe side of planetary boundaries. As was discussed in Chapter 2, we are already in dangerous territory with respect to climate, biodiversity, and nitrogen cycling; not only do we need to bring those systems back into the safety zone, we also have to prevent other systems from crossing their respective boundaries. At the same time, we need to create conditions that ensure everyone has access to minimal social foundations. This is something that has never yet been achieved in human history, and as you saw in Table 2.2, we are a long way from achieving this goal today.

The challenge of creating a safe and just space for humanity and other species is a very ambitious goal indeed! It will require the same kind of revolution in thinking and values that occurred during the Age of Enlightenment when we moved from a geocentric to heliocentric understanding of the universe—a fundamental transformation of the way we see, think about, and interact with the world and with one another. Clearly this is not something that can be accomplished through decree or policy agreements, it is not something that will occur quickly or effortlessly, and, of course, education will be a critical process in the transformation to a more just and sustainable planet.

Education for sustainability is a vibrant, evolving, and sometimes contested domain that often poses more questions than solutions. There is broad agreement among educators around the world that education for sustainability is a desirable pursuit, but there is not wide agreement about what exactly it is or how we should do it. A wide variety of curriculum frameworks, pedagogical approaches, program configurations, and intended outcomes can be found around the world today, and education for sustainability is redefined continuously as it responds to local values, cultures, priorities, and interpretations in widely diverse contexts.

The task of trying to decide what is and what is not effective education for sustainability can be confusing and frustrating. Sometimes it can seem that we are left with nothing more robust than the "I know it when I see it" standard.[1] Unfortunately, much of what gets labeled "education for sustainability" is poorly planned, superficial, of too-short duration, incomplete, or just plain wrong—the educational equivalent of greenwashing. Not only do many educators *not* "know it when they see it," they may not even know what they are looking for. Therefore, one of the most important challenges teachers face when implementing education for sustainability is to develop a deep and integrated understanding of the body of information that makes up the sustainability knowledge domain. In this chapter, we will explore the origins of education for sustainability, and in the next chapter we will examine the core principles and concepts that make up the sustainability knowledge domain.

Origins of Sustainability

Sustainability is an ancient concept that involves a concern for the long-term availability of those things most important for the preservation of life. The ideas that underlie sustainability are nearly universal in the human experience and can be found in Chinese philosophy as early as 400 BCE, ancient Roman and Greek teachings about the natural world, and in the belief systems of indigenous people from around the world (Manuel-Navarrete, Kay, & Dolderman, 2004).

The English word *sustain* derives from the 9th-century Old French verb *sustenir* meaning to withstand or endure; to support or hold up; to remain standing; or to provide sustenance for. These words derive from the Latin roots *sub* (from below) and *tenere* (to hold). The closely related term **sustenance**, which refers to a means of earning a living or livelihood or of sustaining life through food, is derived from the same Latin roots. These early senses of the words evoke images of sturdiness, dependability, perseverance, and timelessness. Think of a magnificent tree, hundreds of years old.

Later usages of sustain added the idea of defending or supporting an opinion (for example in legal proceedings); in the 19th century, journalists began using the word to mean suffer, as in "she sustained an injury." Arguably, these more recent uses were really just nuanced interpretations of the original meaning of sustainability rather than completely different definitions. Indeed, sustain is something of an etymological marvel in that its earliest meaning—"to endure"—has in fact endured as its primary definition for over a millennium.

In the second half of the 20th century, common usage of the term **sustainability** typically referred to the process of keeping something such as an initiative, program, or effort going. This usage became popular among business and school administrators about 10 years ago when concern was often expressed about the difficulty of keeping reform and innovation efforts moving. For example, Fullan (2005) referred to "leadership sustainability" in this context. However, this usage has lost popularity in the last decade as the more contemporary context for sustainability has gained ascendancy.

In recent years, the term sustainability has typically referred to the idea of development that "meets the needs of the present without compromising the ability of future generations to meet their own needs." This conception of sustainability was first expressed in 1987 by the World Commission on Environment and Development in a report entitled *Our Common Future* (WCED, 1987, p. 42). The commission was chaired by Gro Harlem Brundtland, the prime minister of Norway at the time, so the report often is referred to as the *Brundtland Report*. This definition of sustainability has come to be known as the **Brundtland definition of sustainability**. Embedded within the Brundtland definition are the concept **needs**, particularly the essential needs of poorest people in the world, and the concept **limits**, especially the limits imposed by the finitude of planetary systems.

CONSIDER THIS 3.1 WHOSE DEVELOPMENT MATTERS?

When we unpack the Brundtland Definition, a number of questions arise. Think about how you'd answer these questions. What other questions arise as you contemplate these?

Whose development matters?

- Do those who have benefited from development have a right to tell those who have not "too bad, you're out of luck"?
- Do future generations have a right to the same opportunities we've experienced?

What does it mean to meet ones needs?

- How do we distinguish needs from wants?
- How do we distinguish basic needs versus needs associated with an improved quality of life?
- What processes interfere with one's ability to meet needs?

Who are future generations?

- How far into the future should we look?
- Is it our responsibility to be concerned for future generations?

The *Brundtland Report* made two important assertions that have since formed the core of contemporary notions of sustainability: economic, social, and environmental concerns must be viewed as interconnected and equal in importance, and the rights and needs of future generations are equal to those of people alive today. The first assertion, that human survival requires the support of economic, social, and environmental systems and that these systems are intricately interconnected, originates in the field of ecology. From an ecological perspective, sustainability refers to the capacity of an ecosystem to perpetuate interdependent forms of life by balancing the rate of resource removal with the rate of resource regeneration. Ecologists view a sustainable ecosystem as one in which resource use is in balance with resource regeneration and in which growth slows or at some point. Meeting the needs of humans now and in the future entails finding the right balance among economic, environmental, and societal processes so that planetary boundaries are not crossed but social foundations are ensured.

BOX 3.1 ATTEMPTS TO REPRESENT SUSTAINABILITY GRAPHICALLY

In the 30 years since the *Brundtland Report* was published, a number of metaphors and diagrams have been employed to illustrate the interconnectedness of economic, social, and environmental systems the definition of sustainability. Often these three systems are referred to as the "three pillars" of sustainability or the "three legs" of a sustainability stool. Sometimes the term **triple bottom line** is used to call attention to the need to focus on environmental and social systems as well as financial costs and benefits.

(Continued)

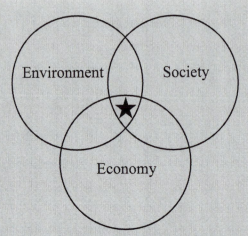

Intersecting Systems

The Intersecting Systems diagram shows that the "sweet spot" for considering whether a process is sustainable is in the area where the three systems overlap. A process that considers only one or two of these systems would not be considered sustainable.

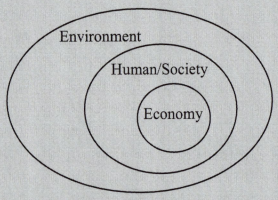

Nested Systems

The Nested Systems diagram illustrates that the economy is subset of human society and that a healthy economy depends on healthy social and human systems such as good governance, equitable distribution systems, and conditions that support human development. At the same time, humans are part of and depend on various environmental systems and earth systems.

The second assertion of the Brundtland definition, that that the rights and needs of future generations are of equal importance to those of people alive today, often is referred to as *intergenerational equity*. This assertion is follows directly from earliest definitions of sustainability (withstand, endure, remain standing, etc.). However, intergenerational equity is a difficult idea to implement because it requires us to rethink most of the assumptions that underlie life in the developed areas of the world in the 21st century. Challenges such as overreliance on nonrenewable fossil fuels, gender and economic inequities, human-caused climate change, loss of biodiversity, and the demise of indigenous cultures and languages are all examples of processes that threaten the ability of future generations to meet their various needs.

By linking these four ideas (i.e., essential needs; planetary limits; interconnected economic, social, and environmental systems; and intergenerational equity) in a single goal, the World Commission proposed **sustainable development** as an alternative to the exploitative international development practices that occurred in much of the world during the postcolonial era following World War II. Although the intent of the *Brundtland Report* clearly was very different from previous decolonization and international development processes, the notion of coupling an ecological conception of sustainability with a dubious economic process was, for many people, problematic.

Recall that the Brundtland Commission issued its report in 1987, at the end of the Cold War and at the height of an international movement toward widespread adoption of neoliberal economic policies. This movement, led by British Prime Minister Margaret Thatcher and U.S. President Ronald Reagan, was based on assumptions of unlimited economic growth and unregulated markets. Many people believed that the kind of unlimited economic growth advocated by the neoliberals was impossible from an ecological perspective because continual growth makes demands on resources that eventually outstrip rates of renewal. Thus, the idea of sustainable development under a neoliberal regime was considered to be an oxymoron.

BOX 3.2 UNSUSTAINABLE DEVELOPMENT

To understand the significance of the *Brundtland Report*, it is helpful to review what unsustainable development looked like. In the second half of the 20th century, economic development was seen as a strategy for helping poor countries move toward standards of living enjoyed in wealthier countries in Europe and North America. Right after World War II, this process generally involved wealthy countries providing aid directly to poor countries,

(Continued)

generally in the form of food, medical supplies, or other material goods. During the 1960s, aid took the form of loans and often resulted in saddling less-developed countries with crushing debts that further limited their ability to raise standards of living. In the Thatcher/Reagan era, international economic development was driven by market-based strategies that favored private sector initiatives rather than government-to-government processes. This internationalized privatization process later became known as globalization. Globalization was often viewed as both inevitable and beneficial, and it was widely thought that a benign 21st-century global marketplace would create a rising tide of economic prosperity that would raise all boats. However, we know today that this was an unrealistic vision. Not only has globalization created greater inequity, but the entire project of economic development in the industrial age has resulted in the Great Acceleration described in Chapter 1.

Discomfort with the idea of sustainable development led to a preference in many areas for the term **sustainability** instead of **sustainable development**. Today, the term sustainability often is used in developed countries, particularly in North America and Europe, and the term sustainable development often is used in less-developed areas and in international contexts such as the United Nations Educational, Scientific, and Cultural Organization (UNESCO), and the Organization for Economic and Cultural Development (OECD). However, from a practical standpoint, these two terms are virtually interchangeable and refer to the same set of ideas and values. The term sustainability is used in this book, largely for the sake of parsimony, grammatical simplicity, and clarity.

Sustainable Development Goals

Five years after the WCED issued its report, the United Nations convened the first Conference on Environment and Development (UNCED), also known as the Earth Summit in Rio de Janeiro. The *Rio Declaration on Development and the Environment* (UNCED, 1992a) that was developed at the Earth Summit included 27 principles intended to guide sustainable development practices around the world. Most of the principles focused directly or indirectly on processes for preventing or reducing the impacts of environmental damage in the development process, although the accompanying implementation plan, known as *Agenda 21*, focused more directly on social foundations, particularly strengthening the roles of women, indigenous people, youth, and nongovernmental organizations (NGOs); promotion of peace; eradication of extreme poverty; and processes for ensuring governance.

These 27 principles were further refined over the next eight years; in 2000, all 189 member states of the United Nations ratified the *Millennium Declaration* (United Nations, 2000), which was in many respects a direct outgrowth of the *Rio Declaration* principles. The resultant *Millennium Development Goals* (MDGs) were adopted as a worldwide agenda for sustainable development. The eight MDGs were:

GOAL 1.   Eradicate extreme poverty and hunger
GOAL 2.   Achieve universal primary education
GOAL 3.   Promote gender equality and empower women
GOAL 4.   Reduce child mortality
GOAL 5.   Improve maternal health
GOAL 6.   Combat HIV/AIDS, malaria, and other diseases
GOAL 7.   Ensure environmental sustainability
GOAL 8.   Develop a global partnership for development.

Implementation targets, measureable indicators, and timelines were developed for each goal, with the expectation that all would be accomplished by 2015. For example, one of the targets for MDG Goal 1 (eradicate extreme poverty) was to halve the proportion of people whose income is less than $1.25 a day between 1990 and 2015. This goal was met in 2010, when the number of people living on less than $1.25/day was half of what it was in 1990.

Overall, the MDG program has been successful. Real progress was made in most areas, although none of the MDGs were met completely (United Nations, 2014). Areas of success included:

- Reduction of rates of malaria and tuberculosis infections;
- Improved access to an drinking water and sanitation;
- Reduction of disparities in primary school enrolment between boys and girls; and
- Improved political participation of women.

At the same time, progress has been disappointing in other areas. For example,

- Global emissions of greenhouse gasses continued to rise;
- Undernourishment and hunger among children is still a problem in many areas;
- Maternal and child health has not improved sufficiently, and deaths due to preventable conditions continues to be a problem in many areas;

- Enrollment of children in primary education is still not universal, and high school graduation rates are unacceptably low in many areas of the world.

CONSIDER THIS 3.2 MILLENNIUM DEVELOPMENT GOALS PROGRESS

Go to the website shown below and find the most recent Millennium Development Goals Progress Chart. Think about how your community would do on each of the target areas shown on the Progress Chart. Are there areas where you think your community could do better?

Examine some of the other documents at the website. Do any of the reports include findings that surprise you? Why?

Get the MDG progress reports here: www.un.org/millenniumgoals/reports.shtml.

Because they are seen as an overall success, the world community has committed to the continuation of the MDGs after their 2015 expiration. Thus, the **Sustainable Development Goals** (SDGs) pick up where the Millennium Development Goals leave off. The development of the SDGs was one of the major outcomes of the 2012 Rio+20 summit, the 20-year follow up to the original Earth Summit. In the final report for Rio+20, the United Nations (2012) acknowledged the need to achieve sustainable development by:

> promoting sustained, inclusive and equitable economic growth, creating greater opportunities for all, reducing inequalities, raising basic standards of living; fostering equitable social development and inclusion; and promoting integrated and sustainable management of natural resources and ecosystems that supports inter alia economic, social and human development while facilitating ecosystem conservation, regeneration and restoration and resilience in the face of new and emerging challenges. (p. 1)

The final report called for "an inclusive and transparent intergovernmental process on sustainable development goals that is open to all stakeholders, with a view to developing global sustainable development goals to be agreed by the General Assembly" (p. 46). This process involved a multistakeholder "open working group" that solicited a diverse range of opinions and voices to develop a preliminary set of 17 sustainable development goals shown in Box 3.3. The UN General Assembly was set to approve a final, consolidated set of Sustainable Development Goals in September 2015.

BOX 3.3 PROPOSED SUSTAINABLE DEVELOPMENT GOALS

GOAL 1.   End poverty in all its forms everywhere

GOAL 2.   End hunger, achieve food security and improved nutrition, and promote sustainable agriculture

GOAL 3.   Ensure healthy lives and promote well-being for all at all ages

GOAL 4.   Ensure inclusive and equitable quality education and promote lifelong learning opportunities for all

GOAL 5.   Achieve gender equality and empower all women and girls

GOAL 6.   Ensure availability and sustainable management of water and sanitation for all

GOAL 7.   Ensure access to affordable, reliable, sustainable, and modern energy for all

GOAL 8.   Promote sustained, inclusive, and sustainable economic growth; full and productive employment; and decent work for all

GOAL 9.   Build resilient infrastructure, promote inclusive and sustainable industrialization, and foster innovation

GOAL 10. Reduce inequality within and among countries

GOAL 11. Make cities and human settlements inclusive, safe, resilient, and sustainable

GOAL 12. Ensure sustainable consumption and production patterns

GOAL 13. Take urgent action to combat climate change and its impacts

GOAL 14. Conserve and sustainably use the oceans, seas, and marine resources for sustainable development

GOAL 15. Protect, restore, and promote sustainable use of terrestrial ecosystems; sustainably manage forests; combat desertification; halt and reverse land degradation; and halt biodiversity loss

GOAL 16. Promote peaceful and inclusive societies for sustainable development; provide access to justice for all; and build elective, accountable, and inclusive institutions at all levels

GOAL 17. Strengthen the means of implementation and revitalize global partnerships for sustainable development

Source: United Nations, 2014.

Contemporary Notions of Sustainability

The *Brundtland Report* and subsequent *Rio Declaration* and MDGs led to broad acceptance of sustainable development as the dominant paradigm for international development programs. However, an entire generation has come of age since the *Brundtland Report* as published, and, as was discussed in Chapter 2, we are still failing at both aspects of the WCED definition of sustainable development. We are not adequately making sure that people who live in the present are able to meet their needs, and we are rapidly destroying the systems upon which future generations must rely to meet their needs.

The ideals expressed in the *Brundtland Report* are more relevant than ever, but our understanding of the difficulty and complexity of the challenges associated with accomplishing sustainability has grown immeasurably in the last three decades. There is much greater appreciation now than there was in 1987, that to bring about the kind of broad-ranging transformation in thinking that will be necessary to accomplish sustainability, our conceptual models must match the complexity of the challenges we hope to address.

Thus contemporary discussions of sustainability have moved away from earlier top-down, policy-driven approaches that focused primarily on the intersection of economic and environmental systems toward more locally relevant and multidimensional strategies for bringing about changes in behaviors and practices.

Today, sustainable development is seen as a "bottom-up plus top-down" approach that relies on multistakeholder networks and participatory knowledge-sharing processes to address **glocal issues**. These are issues that are simultaneously locally and globally relevant. As a result, contemporary notions of sustainability embrace a complex set of interconnected outcomes and strategies.

For example, Raworth's (2012) safe and just space for humanity framework, introduced in Chapter 2, reflects the complexity of the various interconnections among social foundations and planetary boundaries and is explicit in creating the expectation that we need to be as concerned with *intra*generational equity as we are with *inter*generational equity (Anad & Sen, 1994). Similarly, Agyeman (2013) argues that the goal of achieving sustainability cannot focus solely on processes that privilege "green" or "environmental" outcomes. He urges a **just sustainabilities** approach that "ensures a better quality of life for all, now and into the future, in a just and equitable manner, whilst living within the limits of supporting ecosystems" (Agyeman, 2013, p. 5). Agyeman's (2013) definition of just sustainabilities focuses on four conditions for creating just and sustainable communities on any scale, from very local to global:

- Improving our quality of life and well-being;
- Meeting the needs of both present and future generations;
- Justice and equity in recognition, process, procedure, and outcome; and
- Living within ecosystem limits (Agyeman, 2013, p. 7).

It is somehow fitting, though, that one of the clearest expressions a contemporary view of sustainability that addresses both social foundations and planetary boundaries be found in the **Earth Charter**, a document that grew directly out of the *Brundtland Report*.

The Earth Charter

The Earth Charter (Earth Charter International, 2015) is a visionary call to action that sets forth a set of fundamental ethical principles for building a just, sustainable, and peaceful global society. Development of the Earth Charter was initiated in response to a recommendation in the Brundtland Report for a "universal declaration on environmental protection and sustainable development" (WCED, 1987, p. 21) that would eventually serve as the basis for a United Nations convention. Work began on this new charter prior to the 1992 Earth Summit in Rio de Janeiro, but international politics prevented agreement on language for the document in time for the Rio meeting.

The drafting process continued over the next eight years, co-led by Maurice Strong, a Canadian businessman and secretary general of the Earth Summit, and Mikhail Gorbachev, former head of the Soviet Union. During that time, hundreds of international documents were consulted, and many thousands of people from all over the world participated in the process. Particular efforts were made to include the voices of historically marginalized people, including indigenous people, youth, women, poor people, and individuals representing a broad spectrum of cultures, languages, races, and belief systems. As a result, the development of the Earth Charter is considered one of the most open and participatory processes ever conducted in the framing of an international document. This open and inclusive process for drafting the Earth Charter is the primary source of its legitimacy as an ethical framework. The Earth Charter was formally launched in 2000 at the Peace Palace in The Hague. Since then, it has been endorsed by over 6,000 governmental agencies, local governments, NGOs, schools, universities, businesses, faith/religious groups, and youth organizations. Today, the Earth Charter is widely recognized as a global consensus statement on the core principles of sustainability.

The Earth Charter conceptualizes environmental protection, human rights, equitable human development, and peace as interdependent and indivisible processes. The Preamble to the Earth Charter summarizes the global context for sustainability by addressing both the challenges we face, such as those discussed in Chapter 1, and the universal responsibility we all share for finding solutions to those challenges. The main body of the Earth Charter is organized in four major parts with 16 principles and 61 supporting principles. The full collection of Earth Charter principles is shown in Figure 3.1.

The four principles in Part I, *Respect and Care for the Community of Life*, establish a foundation for other three parts, focusing on the relationship between human beings and the greater community of life, the relationship between human beings and society, and the relationship between present and future generations. The twelve principles in the other three parts (*Ecological Integrity*, *Social and Economic Justice*, and *Democracy, Nonviolence, and Peace*) provide further explanation of the first four principles. The 61 supporting principles add additional detail, elaboration, and clarity.

Part I.   Respect and care for the community of life

1.   *Respect Earth and life in all its diversity.*

a.   Recognize that all beings are interdependent and every form of life has value, regardless of its worth to human beings.

b.   Affirm faith in the inherent dignity of all human beings and in the intellectual, artistic, ethical, and spiritual potential of humanity.

2.   *Care for the community of life with understanding, compassion, and love.*

a.   Accept that with the right to own, manage, and use natural resources comes the duty to prevent environmental harm and to protect the rights of people.

b.   Affirm that with increased freedom, knowledge, and power comes increased responsibility to promote the common good.

3.   *Build democratic societies that are just, participatory, sustainable, and peaceful.*

a.   Ensure that communities at all levels guarantee human rights and fundamental freedoms and provide everyone an opportunity to realize his or her full potential.

b.   Promote social and economic justice, enabling all to achieve a secure and meaningful livelihood that is ecologically responsible.

4.   *Secure Earth's bounty and beauty for present and future generations.*

a.   Recognize that the freedom of action of each generation is qualified by the needs of future generations.

b.   Transmit to future generations values, traditions, and institutions that support the long-term flourishing of Earth's human and ecological communities.

In order to fulfill these four broad commitments, it is necessary to:

Part II.   Ecological integrity

5.   *Protect and restore the integrity of Earth's ecological systems, with special concern for biological diversity and the natural processes that sustain life.*

a.   Adopt at all levels sustainable development plans and regulations that make environmental conservation and rehabilitation integral to all development initiatives.

b.   Establish and safeguard viable nature and biosphere reserves, including wild lands and marine areas, to protect Earth's life support systems, maintain biodiversity, and preserve our natural heritage.

c.   Promote the recovery of endangered species and ecosystems.

d.   Control and eradicate non-native or genetically modified organisms harmful to native species and the environment, and prevent introduction of such harmful organisms.

e.   Manage the use of renewable resources such as water, soil, forest products, and marine life in ways that do not exceed rates of regeneration and that protect the health of ecosystems.

f.   Manage the extraction and use of nonrenewable resources such as minerals and fossil fuels in ways that minimize depletion and cause no serious environmental damage.

6.   *Prevent harm as the best method of environmental protection and, when knowledge is limited, apply a precautionary approach.*

a.   Take action to avoid the possibility of serious or irreversible environmental harm even when scientific knowledge is incomplete or inconclusive.

(continued)

Figure 3.1 (continued)

b. Place the burden of proof on those who argue that a proposed activity will not cause significant harm, and make the responsible parties liable for environmental harm.

c. Ensure that decision making addresses the cumulative, long-term, indirect, long-distance, and global consequences of human activities.

d. Prevent pollution of any part of the environment, and allow no build-up of radioactive, toxic, or other hazardous substances.

e. Avoid military activities damaging to the environment.

7. *Adopt patterns of production, consumption, and reproduction that safeguard Earth's regenerative capacities, human rights, and community well-being.*

a. Reduce, reuse, and recycle the materials used in production and consumption systems, and ensure that residual waste can be assimilated by ecological systems.

b. Act with restraint and efficiency when using energy, and rely increasingly on renewable energy sources such as solar and wind.

c. Promote the development, adoption, and equitable transfer of environmentally sound technologies.

d. Internalize the full environmental and social costs of goods and services in the selling price, and enable consumers to identify products that meet the highest social and environmental standards.

e. Ensure universal access to health care that fosters reproductive health and responsible reproduction.

f. Adopt lifestyles that emphasize the quality of life and material sufficiency in a finite world.

8. *Advance the study of ecological sustainability, and promote the open exchange and wide application of the knowledge acquired.*

a. Support international scientific and technical cooperation on sustainability, with special attention to the needs of developing nations.

b. Recognize and preserve the traditional knowledge and spiritual wisdom in all cultures that contribute to environmental protection and human well-being.

c. Ensure that information of vital importance to human health and environmental protection, including genetic information, remains available in the public domain.

Part III.   Social and economic justice

9. *Eradicate poverty as an ethical, social, and environmental imperative.*

a. Guarantee the right to potable water, clean air, food security, uncontaminated soil, shelter, and safe sanitation, allocating the national and international resources required.

b. Empower every human being with the education and resources to secure a sustainable livelihood, and provide social security and safety nets for those who are unable to support themselves.

c. Recognize the ignored, protect the vulnerable, serve those who suffer, and enable them to develop their capacities and to pursue their aspirations.

10. *Ensure that economic activities and institutions at all levels promote human development in an equitable and sustainable manner.*

a. Promote the equitable distribution of wealth within nations and among nations.

b. Enhance the intellectual, financial, technical, and social resources of developing nations, and relieve them of onerous international debt.

(continued)

Figure 3.1 (continued)

c.	Ensure that all trade supports sustainable resource use, environmental protection, and progressive labor standards.
d.	Require multinational corporations and international financial organizations to act transparently in the public good, and hold them accountable for the consequences of their activities.

11. *Affirm gender equality and equity as prerequisites to sustainable development, and ensure universal access to education, health care, and economic opportunity.*

a.	Secure the human rights of women and girls, and end all violence against them.
b.	Promote the active participation of women in all aspects of economic, political, civil, social, and cultural life as full and equal partners, decision makers, leaders, and beneficiaries.
c.	Strengthen families and ensure the safety and loving nurture of all family members.

12. *Uphold the right of all, without discrimination, to a natural and social environment supportive of human dignity, bodily health, and spiritual well-being, with special attention to the rights of indigenous peoples and minorities.*

a.	Eliminate discrimination in all its forms, such as that based on race; color; sex; sexual orientation; religion; language; and national, ethnic, or social origin.
b.	Affirm the right of indigenous peoples to their spirituality, knowledge, lands, and resources and to their related practice of sustainable livelihoods.
c.	Honor and support the young people of our communities, enabling them to fulfill their essential role in creating sustainable societies.
d.	Protect and restore outstanding places of cultural and spiritual significance.

Part IV. Democracy, nonviolence, and peace

13. *Strengthen democratic institutions at all levels, and provide transparency and accountability in governance, inclusive participation in decision making, and access to justice.*

a.	Uphold the right of everyone to receive clear and timely information on environmental matters and all development plans and activities that are likely to affect them or in which they have an interest.
b.	Support local, regional, and global civil society, and promote the meaningful participation of all interested individuals and organizations in decision making.
c.	Protect the rights to freedom of opinion, expression, peaceful assembly, association, and dissent.
d.	Institute effective and efficient access to administrative and independent judicial procedures, including remedies and redress for environmental harm and the threat of such harm.
e.	Eliminate corruption in all public and private institutions.
f.	Strengthen local communities, enabling them to care for their environments, and assign environmental responsibilities to the levels of government where they can be carried out most effectively.

(continued)

Figure 3.1 (continued)

14. Integrate into formal education and life-long learning the knowledge, values, and skills needed for a sustainable way of life.
a. Provide all, especially children and youth, with educational opportunities that empower them to contribute actively to sustainable development.
b. Promote the contribution of the arts and humanities as well as the sciences in sustainability education.
c. Enhance the role of the mass media in raising awareness of ecological and social challenges.
d. Recognize the importance of moral and spiritual education for sustainable living.
15. Treat all living beings with respect and consideration.
a. Prevent cruelty to animals kept in human societies and protect them from suffering.
b. Protect wild animals from methods of hunting, trapping, and fishing that cause extreme, prolonged, or avoidable suffering.
c. Avoid or eliminate to the full extent possible the taking or destruction of nontargeted species.
16. Promote a culture of tolerance, nonviolence, and peace.
a. Encourage and support mutual understanding, solidarity, and cooperation among all peoples and within and among nations.
b. Implement comprehensive strategies to prevent violent conflict, and use collaborative problem solving to manage and resolve environmental conflicts and other disputes.
c. Demilitarize national security systems to the level of a nonprovocative defense posture, and convert military resources to peaceful purposes, including ecological restoration.
d. Eliminate nuclear, biological, and toxic weapons and other weapons of mass destruction.
e. Ensure that the use of orbital and outer space supports environmental protection and peace.
f. Recognize that peace is the wholeness created by right relationships with oneself, other persons, other cultures, other life, Earth, and the larger whole of which all are a part.

Figure 3.1 Earth charter principles

Source: The Earth Charter Initiative (2012). Used with Permission.

Education for Sustainability

The value of the Earth Charter is that it helps create a vision of what it would look like if we accomplished sustainability and provides very clear guidance about the things we can do to accomplish that goal. Certainly, if all of the Earth Charter principles were enacted and the SDGs were fully accomplished by 2030, we could feel that much progress had been made toward creating a safe and just space for humanity and other species. However, it is difficult to imagine enacting the Earth

Charter or accomplishing the SDGs unless the thinking and values that create unsustainability change. The only way to accomplish this kind of broad transformation in thinking is through education.

The importance of education for accomplishing sustainability was recognized early. The *Brundtland Report* called for a "vast campaign of education, debate, and public participation" (p. 27), and *Agenda 21*, the implementation document for the *Rio Declaration*, devoted an entire chapter to education. That chapter, Chapter 36, emphasized that:

> While basic education provides the underpinning for any environmental and development education, the latter needs to be incorporated as an essential part of learning. Both formal and non-formal education are indispensable to changing people's attitudes so that they have the capacity to assess and address their sustainable development concerns. It is also critical for achieving environmental and ethical awareness, values and attitudes, skills and behaviour consistent with sustainable development and for effective public participation in decision making. (United Nations, 1992b, § 36.3)

UNESCO was charged with overseeing Chapter 36, and in 2005, UNESCO launched the United Nations Decade of Education for Sustainable Development (UNDESD). The UNDESD was an explicit global movement focused on improving and reorienting education systems to address sustainable development. The four major thrusts of the UNDESD were to:

1. Improve quality and retention rates in basic education;
2. Reorient existing education programs to address sustainability;
3. Increase public understanding and awareness of sustainability; and
4. Provide training to advance sustainability in all sectors (UNESCO, 2005).

Implicit in these four thrusts is the expectation that education for sustainability should occur in all levels of education, in a wide range of settings. Those contexts include:

*   *Formal education* that occurs in elementary, middle, and secondary schools and is based on established curricula and approved teaching and assessment methods;
*   *Nonformal education* that occurs outside the formal system through various organized learning settings such as youth groups, zoos, and museums; community organizations; and adult literacy classes;
*   *Informal education* that occurs as a result of daily life activities related to work, family, or leisure. Informal education might involve families, religious organizations, community groups, and traditional culture as well as news organizations, social media, and various forms of entertainment.
*   *Training*, which could occur in community and technical education programs, work settings, or other contexts intended to improve an individual's

performance or to help him or her attain a required level of knowledge or skill (Fien & Guevara, 2012, p. 3).

Thus, the broad process of educating for sustainability can include three types of procedures. *Basic* education provides generic competences and subject-specific knowledge and skills necessary for all individuals to develop their capacities to live effective and fulfilling lives. This is the minimal education that should be afforded to every human being on the planet but that is denied to millions of people around the world. Ensuring that all children have access to high-quality basic education is the preliminary level of education for sustainability.

Education *about* sustainability provides foundational knowledge about various sustainability-related issues and challenges to support a minimal level of sustainability literacy. At more advanced education levels, education *about* sustainability also could include more in-depth or technical information associated with specific vocational or disciplinary preparation. For example, a high school earth and space science class might include information about the processes associated with climate change, or a technical education college might include a program focused on design and installation of solar panels. An individual could be sustainability literate or acquire specific knowledge about some aspect of sustainability but not necessary possess the values and dispositions necessary to engage fully with the work of helping to create a safe and just space for humanity.

Education *for* sustainability focuses on the values, thinking skills, and dispositions that enable an individual to live in a sustainable way and to participate fully in the work of helping to build a just and sustainable future (Buckler & Creech, 2014). In one of UNESCO's final evaluation reports for the UNDESD, Wals (2012) identified nine different pedagogical approaches in use in the thousands of education for sustainability projects represented in a 102-country sample. Traditional disciplinary and transmissive methods were used least frequently while constructivist, collaborative, transdisciplinary, and project-based approaches were found most often. Similarly, in a review of literature focusing on the teaching and learning processes associated with education for sustainability, Tilbury (2011) found that successful education for sustainability efforts have four key features in common.

First, they are highly collaborative and provide ample opportunities for intercultural dialogues and participation. Learning is viewed as a social process, in which stakeholders learn from one another and knowledge is cocreated. The focus of learning is not on acquisition of knowledge to be recapitulated on a test but rather on learning in communities for the purpose of finding just and equitable solutions to various sustainability-related challenges.

Second, successful projects engage the whole education system. Education for sustainability efforts often are not confined to the classroom of a single teacher or a specific subject area. Instead, education for sustainability efforts frequently involve multiple classes or entire schools, multiple disciplines, and all education levels from early childhood to university. Successful programs also create permeable boundaries among schools and various sectors in the community including nonprofit and nongovernmental organizations, business and industry, nonformal education, and various governmental agencies.

Third, successful education for sustainability efforts employ innovative curriculum and teaching approaches. These are approaches that move away from a focus on the teacher as the disseminator of knowledge toward more interactive approaches that encourage learners to question assumptions and to push back against dominant ways of thinking and behaving. These approaches are transformative in that they promote new ways of seeing, interpreting, understanding, and interacting with the world. Learners are encouraged to get to the root of issues, to clarify their own values, and to develop a positive orientation toward the future based on a belief in their own efficacy to help bring about meaningful societal changes.

Fourth, successful education for sustainability programs promote these three processes through use of pedagogical approaches that support active and participatory learning. These are instructional approaches that encourage learners to engage directly with the material to be learned rather than simply absorb information passively from a lecture or readings. In her review, Tilbury (2011) identified a wide variety of strategies that promote active learning, including those based in the performing and visual arts (e.g., storytelling, dance, drama, painting), field-based inquiry, case studies, simulations, outdoor learning, critical reading and writing, and collection of first-person narratives and oral histories. The common element in these approaches is that learners actively explore the various dimensions of sustainability issues and assume a direct role in charting the course of their own learning.

These four dimensions of successful education for sustainability combine to create a transformative model of education that focuses on helping learners develop a **sustainability worldview**—a way of seeing and interacting with the world through the lens of sustainability. We will explore the dimensions of a sustainability worldview in the next chapter.

EXTEND YOUR PROFESSIONAL KNOWLEDGE 3.1

Visit the Earth Charter International website at: www.earthcharterinaction.org/content/

1. Read the entire Earth Charter, including the Preamble.
2. Under the *Areas of Work* tab, click on Education under Network Activities.
3. Download the Earth Charter Guide for Education and investigate the resources it contains.
4. Under the *Get Involved* tab, click on the *What you Can Do* and *Action Guidelines* links.
5. Identify some strategies that will help you begin to incorporate the Earth Charter into your professional practice as a teacher.

Note

1 In 1963, the United States Supreme Court was asked to decide whether the film *Les Amants* was protected under the First Amendment right to free speech. The manager of a theater that had shown it was convicted under Ohio state law of possessing and exhibiting an allegedly obscene film. The U.S. Supreme Court decided that the film did not qualify as obscenity and therefore was constitutionally protected speech. However, the four justices who formed the majority in the opinion did not agree on the criteria that should be used to decide what qualifies as obscenity, so each wrote a separate opinion. One of those justices, Potter Stewart, famously wrote that while he was unable to define succinctly what might qualify as hard core pornography, "I know it when I see it, and the motion picture involved in this case is not that" (*Jacobellis v. Ohio*, 378 U.S. 184 (1964)).

References

Agyeman, J. (2013). *Introducing Just Sustainabilities: Policy, Planning, and Practice.* London: Zed Books.

Anand, S., & Sen, A. (1994). *Human Development Index: Methodology and Measurement. HDRO Occasional Papers.* New York: United Nations Development Programme, Human Development Report Office (UNDP/HDRO).

Buckler, C., & Creech, H. (2014). *Shaping the Future We Want: UN Decade of Education for Sustainable Development (2005–2014) Final Report.* Paris: UNESCO.

Fien, J., & Guevara, J.R. (2012). Skills for a green economy: Practice, possibilities and prospects. In R. Maclean, S. Jagannathan, & S. Jouko (Eds.), *Skills for Inclusive and Sustainable Growth in Developing Asia-Pacific* (pp. 255–263). Dordrecht: Springer.

Fullan, M. (2005). *Leadership and Sustainability: System Thinkers in Action.* Thousand Oaks, CA: Corwin Press.

Lao Tzu. (c. 605 BCE–c. 535 BCE). *Tao Te Ching*, ch. 64 (S. Mitchell, Trans.). (Reprinted 1988, New York: Harper Collins)

Manuel-Navarrete, D., Kay, J.J., & Dolderman, D. (2004). Ecological integrity: Linking biology with cultural transformation. *Human Ecology Review, 11*(3), 215–229.

Raworth, K. (2012, February). A safe and just space for humanity: Can we live within the doughnut? *Oxfam Discussion Papers.* Oxford: Oxfam.

The Earth Charter International. (2015). *Earth Charter: Values and Principles for a Sustainable Future.* Retrieved from: www.earthcharterinaction.org/

UNESCO. (2005). *United Nations Decade of Education for Sustainable Development (2005–2014): International Implementation Scheme.* Paris: Author.

United Nations. (1992a, June 3–14). *Rio Declaration on Environment and Development: United Nations Conference on Environment and Development (UNCED).* New York: Author.

United Nations. (1992b, June 3–14). *Agenda 21: Programme of Action for Sustainable Development Earth Summit. United Nations Conference on Environment and Development (UNCED).* New York: Author.

United Nations. (2000). *Millennium Declaration: Resolution Adopted by the General Assembly* [without reference to a Main Committee (A/55/L.2)]. New York: Author.

United Nations. (2012, June 20–22). *The Future We Want.* Rio+20: United Nations Conference on Sustainable Development. Rio de Janeiro: Author.

United Nations. (2014). *The Millennium Development Goals Report, 2014.* New York: Author.

Wals, A. (2012). *Shaping the Education of Tomorrow: Full-Length Report on the UN Decade of Education for Sustainable Development.* Paris: UNESCO.

World Commission on Environment and Development (WCED). (1987). *Our Common Future.* Oxford: Oxford University Press.

4

DEVELOPING A SUSTAINABILITY WORLDVIEW

When you plant a tree and you see it grow, something happens to you. You want to protect it, and you value it. I have seen people really change and look at trees very differently from the way they would in the past.

—Wangari Maathai, 2000

After the United States dropped atomic bombs on Hiroshima and Nagasaki at the end of World War II, many of the scientists who participated in the development of the bombs were deeply conflicted about their own contributions to the creation of these weapons of tremendous mass destruction and about the future proliferation of atomic weapons. In May 1946, Albert Einstein sent a telegram to several hundred prominent U.S. citizens asking them to support an education campaign aimed at helping people understand the risks and potential benefits associated with atomic energy. In the telegram,[1] which was published in the *New York Times* (*Atomic Education Urged by Einstein*, 1946), he asserted that:

> Our world faces a crisis as yet unperceived by those possessing power to make great decisions for good or evil. The unleashed power of the atom has changed everything save our modes of thinking and we thus drift toward unparalleled catastrophe.
>
> We scientists who released this immense power have an overwhelming responsibility in this world life-and-death struggle to harness the atom for the benefit of mankind and not for humanity's destruction....
>
> We need ... a nation-wide campaign to let the people know that a new type of thinking is essential if mankind is to survive and move toward higher levels. (p. 13)

In a follow-up interview published in the *New York Times Sunday Magazine* shortly after he sent the telegram (The Real Problem is in the Hearts of Men, 1946), Einstein elaborated on what he meant by "a new type of thinking." He called for "a great chain reaction of awareness and communication" and encouraged individuals to work actively on behalf of peaceful approaches to resolving international conflicts. This interview included his now-famous quote that "we cannot simultaneously plan for war and peace" and was, in general, a statement of Einstein's concern that unless individuals became personally engaged in working for peace, the atomic bomb would be used again and again, with the same horrific results seen in Hiroshima and Nagasaki.

Clearly Einstein was worried about the proliferation of atomic weapons, but what really concerned him was the proliferation of the thinking that led to the development of those weapons. It is apparent that what Einstein meant by a "new type of thinking" was not that he wanted people to engage in a newly discovered form of mental activity but rather that he wanted people to apply thinking abilities already in their repertoire to the challenge of finding peaceful alternatives to war and the use of atomic weapons. For Einstein, those abilities involved a spirit of cooperation, effective communication, critical thinking, courage, and trust in the "realities of faith, good will, and honesty in seeking a solution" (The Real Problem, 1946).

Today, 70 years after he sent his telegram, we still face the same dilemma that concerned Einstein: the continued proliferation of obsolete and ineffective thinking. The tremendous challenges we face today are unparalleled in human existence, but the thinking that informs our public policy, our educational institutions, and our financial systems has changed very little since the dawn of the Industrial Revolution. This is the thinking that created the challenges, but it is not helping us solve them. When we ponder the planetary boundaries that have already been crossed and when we consider the abysmal lack of social foundations for millions of people around the world, it can seem as though we are once again drifting toward "unparalleled catastrophe."

The new type of thinking we need today is a **sustainability worldview**—seeing and interacting with the world through the lens of sustainability. We recognize today, as Albert Einstein did 70 years ago, that the way to bring about new ways of thinking is through education that can move humanity toward "higher levels." Thus the ultimate goal of education for sustainability is to help learners develop a sustainability worldview. Supporting learners in development of a sustainability worldview prepares them to engage effectively with the complexities, tensions, and uncertainties associated with creating a safe and just space for humans and other species today and in the future.

A Sustainability Worldview

Your worldview is the unique combination of perspectives, values, knowledge, and beliefs that determine the way you see, interpret, and interact with the world. Philosophers sometimes refer to a worldview as *Weltanschauung*—the fundamental way a person views life as a whole. We each enact our worldview in the things we say, the choices we make, and the way we behave on a day-to-day and minute-to-minute basis.

A sustainability worldview is a thoughtful and skillful way of being in the world that is positive, life affirming, future oriented, and solutions focused. An individual who has developed a sustainability worldview holds values consistent with the goals of sustainability, has sufficient knowledge to understand the dimensions of various sustainability issues and challenges, is willing to act on behalf of the well-being of all forever, and has skills and abilities to act meaningfully and with effect. Development of a sustainability worldview can lead to that "great chain reaction of awareness" to which Einstein referred. Here's how:

A sustainability worldview prompts us to seek out ways to become personally engaged with individual and collective actions that help create a safe and just space for humans and other species now and in the future.

↓

Direct engagement with the tensions and challenges associated with promoting fairness, equity, and the health and resilience of the systems upon which all life depends, promotes a sense of agency, efficacy, and hopefulness.

↓

We begin to see our individual decisions and behaviors as elements in larger, interconnected systems of ideas and decisions.

↓

Understanding this interconnectedness helps us see the ways our personal choices and decisions can have direct impacts that extend into our individual futures as well as the futures of countless others humans and other species.

↓

Consideration of those current and future impacts prompts us to consider the fairness and equity dimensions of our own choices as well as the decisions to which we each contribute as members of communities.

↓

We begin to see that even small changes in our own thinking and behavior can matter profoundly for our own well-being as well as that of others now and in the future.

A sustainability worldview is something that almost anyone can acquire through learning and refine through practice. It does not require a qualitatively different kind of mental process or newly discovered type of intelligence located in a previously unmapped region of the brain, and a sustainability worldview is not something that a person either has or does not have—there is no "sustainability gene" that someone might be lucky enough to inherit. However, sustainability worldview is not simply a collection of facts, opinions, and beliefs about sustainability-related problems. For example, knowing facts about how the nitrogen cycle works would not necessarily lead someone to change behaviors that contribute to eutrophication of a local waterway. At the same time, a sustainability worldview entails more than just being disposed to become engaged with sustainability problems. Someone could care deeply about the impacts of gender inequality in education or the impacts of climate change on vulnerable populations but not know how to become directly involved with these problem in ways that would have a meaningful impact. Thus, a sustainability worldview is a holistic phenomenon that involves a combination of **values**, **knowledge, dispositions**, and **agency**.

Values

Values refer to an individual's beliefs about what is important or should be held dear. Values inform decisions of right versus wrong, good versus bad, and desirable versus undesirable. Often sets of values shared by members of a society or culture take the form of accepted moral standards or principles, articulated in documents such as the Universal Declaration of Human Rights and the Earth Charter. Because values typically are linked to highly contested domains such as religious or spiritual belief systems or political beliefs, teachers often are reluctant to address values directly in formal educational settings. Yet, as McKeown (2006) notes:

> [E]ven if values are not taught overtly, they are (often) modeled, explained, analyzed, or discussed . . . understanding values is an essential part of understanding your own worldview and other people's viewpoints. Understanding your own values, the values of the society you live in, and the values of others around the world is a central part of educating for a sustainable future. (p. 23)

Values are central to the broader sustainability discourse and are an essential element of a sustainability worldview. For example, the Earth Charter clearly expresses a value-based perspective in principles such as these:

- Respect the Earth and life in all its diversity.
- Care for the community of life with understanding, compassion, and love.
- Build democratic societies that are just, participatory, sustainable, and peaceful.
- Secure the Earth's bounty and beauty for present and future generations.

- Eradicate poverty as an ethical, social, and environmental imperative.
- Affirm gender equality and equity.
- Uphold the right of all, without discrimination.
- Treat all living beings with respect and consideration.
- Promote a culture of tolerance, nonviolence, and peace.

There is no single "correct" set of values, so the goal of education must not be to indoctrinate or to tell learners which values they should adopt. Instead, we need to provide learners with tools and information that will help them choose values systems that are consistent with creating a safe and just space for humanity and other species now and in the future. Learners must be provided opportunities to clarify their own values and to understand the values of others. It also is important for learners to investigate the values that underlie a sustainability worldview, such as those found in the Earth Charter, to find out how those values statements overlap with their own personal values system and the broadly accepted universal values that underlie most major religious and cultural traditions.

Knowledge

Knowledge refers to the broad array of types of information (e.g., facts, concepts, principles, and strategies) that an individual can bring to bear on a particular issue or problem. Knowledge also can include the mental procedures an individual employs while acting on various types of information (e.g., follow a plan, solve a problem, compose a letter, or read a map) as well as physical procedures that involve application of information (e.g., playing basketball, welding, dancing, or building a chicken coop) (Marzano & Kendall, 2007).

The formal body of information associated with a field of study or thought is the **knowledge domain.** The knowledge domain that underlies a sustainability worldview is contained within a number of **big ideas**. Big ideas are overarching constructs that reflect the core ideas in a discipline (Wiggins & McTighe, 2005). Big ideas can enable learners to develop a deeper understanding of complexities and subtleties associated with a sustainability worldview by helping them bind disparate facts and concepts into coherent and meaningful patterns of information. We will explore a number of sustainability big ideas that inform a sustainability worldview later in this chapter.

As you saw in the discussion in Chapter 2, sustainability-related issues often involve technical and discipline-based knowledge, but it would be a mistake to suppose that a sustainability worldview requires a deep understanding of the specialized knowledge domains found in fields such as ecology, physics, economics, sociology, or political science. Certainly, there are issues that can be understood and investigated through a disciplinary perspective, but sustainability belongs to and is the responsibility of everyone, not just people who call themselves scientists or economists or environmentalists.

A sustainability worldview involves a perspective on how humans relate to one another and to the planet. Thus anyone can develop a sustainability worldview, and a sustainability worldview can be applied in any discipline area. In fact, it is important for learners to have opportunities to apply sustainability perspectives across disciplinary classes and levels so that they can more readily connect ideas across disciplines and at the same time begin to apply disciplinary perspectives while engaging with sustainability challenge.

Dispositions

Dispositions refer to an individual's tendency or likelihood to behave or think in a particular way. Dispositions involve clusters of preferences, attitudes, and intentions, as well as a set of capabilities that allows these preferences to become realized in a particular way (Perkins & Salomon, 2012). These are closely related but not identical ideas. Our preferences are our likes and dislikes. Attitudes refer to a habitual stance or mode of responding to a type of situation or issue. An intention is a volition or purposeful aim to behave or think in a particular way, and capabilities refer to our capacity, ability, or power to act. Clearly, none of these is fixed, and all are generally thought to be under our direct control. We all experience changes in preferences, develop new attitudes, and establish new intentions regularly throughout our lives. These are all factors that affect our disposition to behave or think in a particular way. At the same time, our dispositions can be highly contextual. For example, an individual with the ability to think critically under certain conditions will actually do so only if she or he has formed the habit to think critically or chooses overtly to use critical-thinking abilities (Ennis, 1996). Similarly, an individual might be disposed to be outgoing and gregarious in one situation but reserved and quiet in another. Teachers can help learners develop dispositions associated with a sustainability worldview when they:

- Create experiences that allow learners to confront preconceptions and unsubstantiated preferences;
- Provide positive models and examples that support development of new preferences and attitudes (e.g., locally grown food; use of a refillable bottle; taking the bus, etc.);
- Help learners develop new capabilities that support dispositional changes;
- Provide guidance and support that encourages learners to follow through on intentions to make changes; and
- Link dispositional changes to positive outcomes in learners' own lives as well as the lives of others (e.g., well-being, school or job success, relationships, etc.).

Agency

Agency refers to an individual's ability to make choices and to act effectively so as to bring about a desired effect. To enact a sustainability worldview, an individual needs to know *what* needs to be done, know *how to do* it, and have the *ability* to act in a way that has meaningful impact. Assuming the individual has sufficient knowledge, she or he also needs to believe that acting will bring about a desired result. This belief in one's own capacity to organize and execute a course of action is often referred to as **self-efficacy** (Bandura, 1977). According to Bandura, people develop self-efficacy as a result of mastery experiences (i.e., having opportunities to learn how to perform a task successfully), social modeling (i.e., seeing other people successfully complete the task), social persuasion (i.e., receiving positive messages, encouragement, and pep talks), and psychological responses (i.e., learning how to minimize stress and elevate one's mood when facing a difficult or challenging task).

The notion of agency as it is used here aligns with Bandura's (1997, 2000) term **human agency**, which refer to one's capacity to coordinate learning, motivation, and emotions to reach a goal. Human agency can take three forms. **Personal agency** refers to management of events that affect one's own life. **Proxy agency** refers to efforts to get others who have direct control or power over conditions that affect one's life to take action that results in a desired outcome. Examples of proxy agency might include writing a letter to a legislator to try to get a law changed or donating to an advocacy group that is bringing a lawsuit against a polluter. **Collective agency** involves working with others to bring about a desired outcome. Collective agency involves not only pooled knowledge but also the interactive, synergistic, and coordinated efforts of the group as they act on a shared vision and belief in their collective efficacy.

Helping Learners Develop a Sustainability Worldview

Recapitulating the key points discussed above, education aimed at helping learners develop a sustainability worldview would provide opportunities for them to:

1. Clarify their own values, understand the values of others, and investigate the values that underlie a sustainability worldview, such as those contained in the Earth Charter. Investigate areas where their own values coincide with or conflict with broader societal values or the values associated with creating a safe and just space for all now and in the future. Understand that ultimately, we each choose our beliefs and values.
2. Develop a broad knowledge base that includes basic skills and disciplinary knowledge, as well as more specialized information pertaining to sustainability issues and challenges. Sustainability big ideas can form the basis for this broad knowledge domain.
3. Engage directly with real-world problems and challenges that enable them to apply theory in authentic contexts and to develop habits of thinking and dispositions to act on behalf of sustainability goals.
4. Gain direct experience and practice that supports development of self-efficacy and leads to personal, proxy, and collective agency.

5. Investigate and test their own assumptions, biases, beliefs, and preconceptions and continue to assess and adjust their own evolving worldview as they develop deeper understanding and experience with the world.

CONSIDER THIS 4.1 DO YOU HAVE A SUSTAINABILITY WORLDVIEW?

Do you think you have a sustainability worldview?

How do your values, knowledge, dispositions, and skills converge to form your worldview?

In what ways to the sustainability big ideas inform your daily activities and decisions?

What areas do you feel that you want to work on with respect to your worldview?

A Constellation of Big Ideas

There is no single "correct" version of a sustainability worldview. It can mean different things to different people and just as sustainability has many dimensions, so does a sustainability worldview. What binds the various dimensions of sustainability worldview into a coherent whole is a constellation of big ideas.

Constellations are perceived patterns in the night sky, formed by stars that appear to be close to one another. The perception of a constellation is a holistic process in which a few brighter stars appear to form a pattern. Many other stars are visible within the constellation, but it is those brighter stars that stand out to create the recognizable pattern. Most ancient societies assigned names to constellations, and sometimes constellations assumed mythical or spiritual significance. More often, though, constellations served the very practical purpose of helping people orient themselves, navigate unfathomably complex environments, and travel long distances.

The constellation of sustainability big ideas functions the same way. Big ideas can help learners see the interconnectedness among the values, knowledge, disposition, and agency components of a sustainability worldview; navigate unfamiliar terrain to learn new knowledge and skills; and apply knowledge and skills in new situations. The lived experience of a sustainability worldview involves integration of these big ideas into one's day-to-day thinking, decision making, and interactions. At the same time, when teachers understand the big ideas associated with sustainability, they are better able to prioritize content, identify learning progressions, develop coherent long-term plans, anticipate student preconceptions, and guide student learning.

As with any constellation, there is a small set of "bright star" big ideas that stand out and serve as key navigation aids. We will explore eight bright stars in the constellation of sustainability big ideas shortly. In addition, a much larger set of less vivid stars also are visible and can assume importance from time to time. These include a flexible and evolving set of topics and themes that might be important in a particular community or cultural context, and ideas that emerge in the various disciplines. So while the discussion here will focus on the bright stars in the constellation, you should not consider this to be an exhaustive list of sustainability big ideas.

As you review the descriptions of big ideas below, you might find it useful to bear in mind some essential characteristics of big ideas:

First, big ideas are not vocabulary words. Big ideas come in many shapes and sizes, including broad topics or themes difficult problems, or ongoing debates or issues (Wiggins & McTighe, 2005). The goal is not for learners to memorize definitions but to dig deeper into the meaning and implications of each big idea. In this respect, the big ideas are intended to be generative—investigation of the big ideas leads to a deeper inquiry into the meaning of sustainability and the dimensions of a sustainability worldview.

Second, sustainability big ideas usually are transdisciplinary and often involve information from multiple ways of knowing, multiple disciplines, and multiple cultures. Truly understanding a big idea may require perspectives from multiple disciplines and traditions. At the same time, each discipline has its own set of big ideas that can intersect with sustainability. They are not competing ideas but rather different perspectives on a single idea. For example, systems thinking can be applied in many disciplines to understand processes as distinct as the flow of energy through trophic levels, cultural diffusion, the economics of the industrial revolution, and the effect of climate change on deep ocean currents. At the same time, "thinking in systems" can have different connotations across cultures and contexts. Truly understanding interconnectedness can involve use of systems dynamics, such as will be discussed in Chapter 9, as well as ideas from non-Western cultures that view interconnections among humans and other species and across time nonlinearly and nonsequentially.

Third, while sustainability big ideas can involve a variety of types of information (e.g., facts, generalizations, values, skills, etc.), it can be particularly helpful for learners to focus on the overarching **principles** and core **concepts** embedded in big ideas.

Principles and Concepts

Principles are statements of the primary assumptions upon which all other knowledge in a discipline is based and from which other assumptions and theories follow. They typically are stated as general laws or rules, widely accepted within the discipline as guides to action. **Knowledge-based principles**, often found in the physical and life sciences and many social sciences, refer to primary self-evident propositions or to previously validated relationships among variables. Examples include the laws of thermodynamics (energy cannot be created or destroyed), the principle of exchange in economics (two parties will voluntarily make an exchange only if they each perceive that they get more than they give), and the Greenhouse Effect (some thermal radiation reflected from the surface of the Earth is absorbed by atmospheric gasses and reradiated back to the surface). **Ethical principles** are rules for determining whether an individual or group behavior is right or wrong, or good or bad, or better or worse. Where knowledge-based principles are based on a body of verifiable evidence, often obtained through scientific experimentation, ethical principles are based on an assessment of a body of law, values, or moral standards. For example, the principles in the Earth Charter very clearly articulate the ethical underpinnings of a sustainability worldview. Recall that the Earth Charter principles are listed in Figure 3.1.

Concepts are generalizations for which multiple examples can be provided (Marzano & Kendall, 2007). Concepts can vary greatly in the extent to which they lead to deeper understandings. Some concepts simply add to a learner's overall knowledge but have little impact on overall understanding of the discipline. However, others can lead to profound changes in learner perceptions and understandings. Recently Meyer and Land (2006) introduced the idea of **threshold concepts** to describe this latter form of the concept. These are concepts that, once learned, lead to a deeper and significantly different understanding of the discipline. According to Meyer and Land (2006), threshold concepts are:

- *Transformative.* After learning a threshold concept, a learner thinks about the subject in a fundamentally different way. Threshold concepts lead to significant new insights into the subject area and may be accompanied by changes in values or attitudes.
- *Irreversible.* Once learned, a threshold concept is not likely to be forgotten or unlearned. Because threshold concepts are transformative, it is impossible for a learner to go back to seeing the subject from the previous, untransformed perspective.
- *Integrative.* Threshold concepts reveal interrelatedness that was previously not recognized by the learner and lead to development of more elaborate and connected knowledge representations.

The notion of threshold concepts is relatively new and has yet to be fully validated empirically with precollege learners; however, it seems clear that a number of the big ideas that underlie a sustainability worldview would likely qualify as threshold concepts. They are potentially difficult for learners to grasp initially, but, once understood, they create a portal into a broader understanding of the world.

CONSIDER THIS 4.2 INVESTIGATE THE BIG IDEAS

1. As you investigate the sustainability big ideas discussed below, refer back to the Earth Charter Principles to see which of the principles includes each of the big ideas. Think about both knowledge and ethical components of the big idea.
2. For each big idea, decide whether you think it is a threshold concept. Review the characteristics of threshold concepts listed above and think about the conditions under which the big idea might meet those conditions.

There are eight bright stars in the constellation of sustainability big ideas:

1. Equity and justice
2. Peace and collaboration
3. Universal responsibility
4. Health and resiliency
5. Respect for limits
6. Connecting with Nature
7. Local to global
8. Interconnectedness.

As noted, this is not an exhaustive list of all of the topics and themes that can be associated with sustainability. Numerous other ideas and topics will arise in consideration of sustainability challenges. These eight big ideas might be best thought of as a minimal set that forms the basis for a sustainability worldview. Education aimed at helping learners develop a sustainability worldview should provide opportunities for them to explore these ideas in a variety of contexts and disciplines, to dig deeper in to the meaning and implications of these ideas, and to incorporate these ideas into their own thinking, problem solving, and decision making. We will explore each of the ideas in the sections that follow.

Equity and Justice

Clearly, a focus on creating a safe and just space for humans and other species, now and in the future, is at the very center of a sustainability worldview. This big idea attends to equitable access to opportunities and resources, as well as just distribution of the impacts of consequences of unsustainability. It comprises a number of related and overlapping ideas that arise in the context of sustainability, including social justice, economic justice, environmental justice, gender equity, food justice, climate equity, and so on. Attention to equity and justice leads to consideration of number of issues, including various dimensions of privilege, distinctions among needs and wants, and consideration of interspecies equity. Issues such as the ethical and humane treatment of other species, preservation of biodiversity, genetic engineering, invasive species, and habitat protection can all be explored through the lenses of justice and equity.

One of the core concepts embedded in this big idea is the notion of **intergenerational equity**. Intergenerational equity refers to the rights of future generations to have access to adequate resources and opportunities necessary meet their needs. This perspective encourages consideration of future generations whose ability to meet their needs might be jeopardized if resources such as water and arable land are used up by the current generation or if the impacts of current human activities results in a compromised climate system.

Consideration of intergenerational equity prompts consideration of the distinctions between equity and equality. Equity refers to a sense of fairness and evenhandedness, whereas equality usually refers to the idea of "leveling the playing field" so that everyone gets the same portion or has similar access. However, we recognize today that future generations will inherit a planet with a greatly diminished reserve of nonrenewable resources, decreased biodiversity, and a lessened capacity for renewal. Therefore, intergenerational equality is no longer an option. Thus the term **equity** is often preferred because it communicates a greater sense of urgency and a moral obligation that has a justice or rights basis. Our moral obligation to future generations involves a concern for equity—taking steps now to ensure that they are able to meet their needs.

The overarching principle at work here is often referred to as the **Precautionary Principle**. The Precautionary Principle states that "When an activity raises threats of harm to human health or the environment, precautionary measures should be taken even if some cause and effect relationships are not fully established scientifically" (Wingspread Statement on the Precautionary Principle, January 1998). Less formal expressions of the Precautionary Principle include Hippocrates' admonition to "first do no harm" and any number of cautionary aphorisms, such as "an ounce of prevention is worth a pound of cure." The Precautionary Principle applies equally to current and future generations. Threats could involve direct damage to natural systems upon which future generations will rely (e.g., climate change or ocean acidification) or to depletion of resources that will be needed by future generations (e.g., clean water, wilderness areas, or nonrenewable resources). The precautionary principle also could be applied to the preservation of human resources such as cultures and languages threatened by the hegemony of a globalized media that privileges the languages and cultures dominant in developed areas.

Intergenerational equity is most likely a threshold concept because it is a transformative and irreversible idea. Consideration of the needs of individuals who will live their lives many decades in the future fundamentally restructures one's notions of fairness to include an intertemporal component. Intergenerational equity also is a potentially troublesome concept. It calls for a level of altruism that is foreign to the belief systems of individuals immersed in a culture of short-term gratification and "present-ist" thinking. It also is conceptually difficult because it involves long time frame phenomena. Throughout most of human existence, there was no reason to plan further into the future than one's own lifespan or the lifespan of one's children. Our brains are adept at reactive and short-term thinking but less well-adapted to long-term planning or long-term analysis processes.

Peace and Collaboration

Along with our basic needs for food, water, and shelter, the most fundamental human need is for peace and security, and one of humanities most persistent challenges is to help people learn how to get along. Thus a sustainability worldview must include the knowledge, values, skills, and attitudes associated with living together peacefully. Ultimately, the goal is for each of us to learn to treat the needs of others around the world today and who will live in the future as equal in importance with our own wants and needs.

Current ideas of peace often are based on Johan Galtung's (1996) two-sided definition that pushes the definition of peace beyond merely the cessation or lack of violence. According to Galtung, **negative peace** is the absence of violence among individuals, groups, or governments while **positive peace** involves social justice, fair distribution of power and resources, equitable opportunity, equal protection, and impartial implementation of laws. In Galtung's framework, negative and positive peace represent separate dimensions that are each necessary but not sufficient for the state of peace to exist.

Today there is a growing awareness that positive peace involves not only human interactions with each other but also human interactions with the planet (Do & Iyer, 2010; Zohar, Schoenfeld, & Alleson, 2010). The notion that there are environmental dimensions to issues of peace is not new, and, of course, history includes many examples of conflicts that grew out of disputes over access to natural resources such as water, productive land, or minerals. However, as the human population of the planet continues to increase, conflicts over diminishing resources will become increasingly likely. At the same time, mounting scientific evidence of the extent to which human behaviors are directly impacting the health of natural systems has led to new concerns over inequitable distribution of environmental impacts and the violence that could result from those inequities (Homer-Dixon, 1991). As the complexity of human-planet interconnectedness becomes better understood, it is becoming evident that the factors that contribute to positive peace (e.g., social justice, fair distribution of power and resources, equitable economic opportunity, equal protection, and impartial implementation of laws) also contribute to the health and preservation of natural systems and that the variables associated with violence also have a deleterious effect on the environment.

Universal Responsibility

This big idea focuses on helping learners assume personal responsibility for the consequences of their own decisions and behaviors as well as develop an understanding of the broader responsibility each of us has to promote the creation of a safe and just space for all forever. The premise is that while each of us has universal human rights, we also have universal human responsibilities. Those responsibilities include the expectation we each treat other humans with respect and dignity, refrain from taking what was not freely given (including not taking from future generations), and a responsibility to avoid harming the natural systems upon which humans and other species depend for their survival. At the center of this big idea is the value of **reciprocity**, which means treating others the way you want to be treated. This is the "golden rule" found at the core of numerous religious and belief systems followed by billions of people around the world.

Universal responsibility is not simply a matter of refraining from doing harm. A sustainability worldview is focused on active and collaborative engagement to find positive solutions. So in many respects, the big idea of universal responsibility involves putting sustainability into practice. Direct engagement with sustainability-related issues can provide learners opportunities to develop a sense of agency, efficacy, and hopefulness by taking on issues that might otherwise seem distant in time and space. This is why inquiry-based pedagogies such as those discussed in Chapter 6 are an essential element of education for sustainability. These approaches can help learners clarify their own roles and responsibilities with respect to sustainability-related issues and then develop efficacy and agency to act on those responsibilities.

Health and Resiliency

Health can involve our individual habits and lifestyle choices, or it can involve issues that have broader, societal impacts, such as hunger; malnutrition; malaria; waterborne diseases; drug and alcohol abuse; HIV, AIDS, and other sexually transmitted diseases; and, of course, a wide range of environmentally related health conditions caused by poor air quality, climate change, and agricultural and industrial practices that damage the environment.

A sustainability worldview is centrally concerned with the health and well-being of individuals and the various systems upon which they depend. Education that supports development of a sustainability worldview aims to help people exercise control over and improve their health through personal and collective action.

Resiliency refers to the capacity of a system to deal with change but continue to function and develop. In the context of sustainability, resilience often refers to socioecological systems such as communities and ecosystems, but the term also has been used extensively to refer to the capacity of individuals, particularly children, to bounce back from hardship or trauma. Both of these applications of the idea resiliency are pertinent in the context of education for sustainability, although they have generally involved completely separate lines of research. The terms **resiliency** and **resilience** often are used interchangeably and have nearly the same meaning. However, to be precise, resiliency refers to a capacity, and resilience refers to the action itself.

Resiliency was not originally associated with sustainability, but it is now viewed as an essential element of sustainable systems. Earlier definitions of resiliency often referred to the amount of time it takes a system to return to an initial state after being disturbed. However, more recently, this notion of resilience as a process of "returning to normal" is being replaced with a definition of resiliency as the amount of disturbance a system can withstand before moving to another state. For example, in a resilient community, government and essential services would continue to function after a devastating flood, but a less resilient community might simply shut down. This conception of resiliency is based on the view that change is a normal process in any complex system, such as cities, companies, or ecosystems. These systems experience numerous cycles of growth, transition, and renewal and frequently assume new configurations. Resilient systems remain healthy and thrive throughout those cyclical changes. For example, a caterpillar that has not been compromised by pesticides metamorphoses into a butterfly, a community becomes an vibrant urban village when a nearby city expands to surround it, or a group of indigenous people form a farming cooperative when their ability to pursue a traditional livelihood is threatened by development.

The big idea of health and resiliency provides students a context for investigating characteristics of healthy, thriving systems. When the various themes and issues associates with sustainability are examined through the lens of resilience thinking, students are encouraged to adopt assets-based strategies and to see change as a natural process in complicated systems. At the same time, students can be encouraged to investigate the variables that contribute to their own resiliency and adaptability to life events.

A related idea that often arises in the context of health and resiliency is the constancy of change in all elements of the universe. Life, by definition, is impermanent and our entire existence is defined by change, yet we often behave as though "nothing ever changes." There are two ways that our reluctance to embrace change can impact our thinking and decision making. First, in the same way that people often find it difficult to understand complex, large-scale phenomena, they also often struggle with processes that occur over long time frames. Our brains are well adapted to think and solve problems in the here and now, but we are not as adept at thinking in terms of multiple years, much less generations. Second, contemplation of impermanence can be challenging when it reminds us of our own mortality.

Helping learners see change as an element of healthy, resilient systems can enable them to better understand and embrace change as a positive element in their own lives. Also, helping learners understand change as a universal phenomenon can facilitate a better understanding of long time frame phenomena associated with various planetary systems.

Respect for Limits

In the context of sustainability, the term **limits** refers to the finite capacity of the Earth to supply its inhabitants with the things they need for survival, such as clean air, fresh water, food, the ability to recycle waste, and preserve the health of the planet's biodiversity. This idea is foundational in the broad sustainability discourse and is referenced often in the sustainability literature (Nolet, 2007). The idea of limits maps directly onto the discussion of planetary boundaries and social foundations in Chapter 2.

The macro principles that overarch this big idea are the first and second the laws of thermodynamics that describe how energy changes and behaves anywhere in the universe. The first law of thermodynamics states that energy can neither be created nor destroyed, but it can be converted from one form to another. The second law states that energy tends to become more dispersed (disordered) until a state of equilibrium is reached. From a human point of view, energy that has been dispersed is usually less useful than energy that is well ordered or concentrated. For example, the energy stored in a lump of coal is highly organized and concentrated. After the coal is burned, the energy is dispersed in the form of heat, ash, and gasses such as CO and CO_2.

Our planet, including the atmosphere that surrounds it, behaves like a closed system. Energy is introduced into the system in the form of sunlight, but with the exception of the few meteors that strike the planet, very little new matter is added to the system. Similarly, some energy can leave the planet in the form of light or heat reflected or radiated into space, but very little matter gets out, largely due to the Earth's gravitational pull. Therefore, there are finite limits to matter-based energy contained within this system that are available for human use.

For the last several centuries, we have been converting and dispersing the energy stored in resources like coal and petroleum in ways that make it unavailable for use by future generations. However, we do not simply use this matter and energy up and it goes to some magical place called "Away." Because we live in a closed system that is governed by the laws of thermodynamics, some of that matter and energy returns to the Earth; some of it is dispersed in forms that we consider waste, such as excess heat; and some of it is released into the atmosphere. At the beginning of the 20th century, when there were one billion people on the planet, matter and energy were being converted and dispersed at a much slower rate than is occurring now that the world human population is nearly seven billion. As population growth accelerated in the last century, so did the rate of our dispersion of matter and energy.

The concept respect for limits is most likely a threshold concept. Recognition of and respect for the natural limits imposed by the laws of thermodynamics is central to many of the other ideas associated with a sustainability worldview. It is transformative and irreversible because it changes the way we think about ideas like consumption, fairness, and justice. When we move from the perception of the Earth as an unlimited store of resources to a perception of Earth as finite, we begin to think differently about our relation with other humans alive today, our responsibility to future generations, our relationship with other species, and our own needs and wants. At the same time, the concept of limits, and the broader idea of respect for limits, is potentially troublesome because it reflects a fundamentally different way of thinking about our own behaviors and beliefs. The idea of respect for limits also runs counter to the dominant economic model in most of the world today and the messages that many people around the world receive from popular media and politicians. Neoliberal economic models are based on the assumptions of unlimited capacity, unlimited growth, and consumption as social responsibility if not a patriotic duty.

Connecting With Nature

This big idea involves a variety of issues that have to do with the way humans interact with the natural world. One of the core elements of this big idea is that nature represents a significant source of expertise and humans have much to learn from the billions of years of evolution of the Earth's living systems. For example, **biomimicry** (Benyus, 1997) refers to the practice of creating designs and processes that are fashioned after natural materials and systems. Similarly, a number of new ethnosciences that combine indigenous knowledge and Western scientific methods have emerged in recent years, including ethnobiology, ethonoecology, and ethnobotany (Rist & Dahdhouh-Guebas, 2006).

Another element of this big idea has to do with developing an affinity for and understanding of nature that disrupts dominant discourses, such as "nature as something that needs to be conquered," "nature as an unlimited store of riches and resources," and "nature as amusement park and playground." Instead, a sustainability worldview involves a more intimate response to nature along the lines of what E. O. Wilson (1993) described as **biophilia**, "an innately emotional affiliation of humans to other living organisms" (p. 31). This perspective leads to both a deep respect for nature in all of its manifest forms, as well as a profound curiosity about the human-nature relationship and the way that natural systems operate. This perspective also can lead to a desire for a more direct, personal engagement with the natural world.

For many individuals, development of a personal connection with nature can be a threshold experience that transforms their understanding of their relationship with and place in the natural world. Learning in and from nature also help learners integrate otherwise abstract theoretical concepts into a more active and personal understanding. Education aimed at helping learners develop this connection can take place anywhere and does not need to entail an expedition to pristine wilderness. In fact, at the core of this big idea is the understanding that nature is everywhere and that each of has direct access to nature each time we take a breath or look at the sky or feel the sun's warmth on our skin.

Local to Global

This idea relates to the interdependent nature of global political, economic, and social systems and the manner in which our local actions and decisions are inextricably connected with a broader global context. The term **glocal** is sometimes used to capture this sense of interdependence and simultaneity between local and global concerns. Glocal issues are often transboundary and may require a conception of citizenship that considers the interconnectedness of local decisions with outcomes on the opposite side of the world. This big idea also involves the notion of a **global ethic**. This perspective sees humans as citizens of the world, with shared values and goals that transcend culture, religion, and national identities. A global ethic is based on a respect for human rights and self-determination that transcend specific local, national, or regional agendas. This perspective involves an openness toward divergent cultural experiences and diverse ways of knowing and experiencing.

Other aspects of this big idea pertain to the global nature of information, media, and the exchange of ideas. Global markets and globalized consumerism can, on one hand, cause an acceleration of cultural contamination in which local wisdom and culture are displaced by a mass-marketed corporate common denominator of products, images and ideas. On the other hand, social media and mobile technologies create new ways for individuals to share and amplify highly personalized and very local concerns with a global community.

Interconnectedness

Interconnectedness refers to the manner in which a group of objects interact with one another to form a complex whole that operates as system. In the context of sustainability, we often focus on interconnectedness as a property of interwoven systems of humans and nature, referred to as *social-ecological systems*. Interconnectedness also can refer to phenomena that might be less readily thought of as systems. For example, ideas, people, communities, issues, and solutions also can be interconnected. Terms closely related to interconnectedness include interrelatedness, interdependence, mutuality, reciprocity, and networked.

The idea of interconnectedness frequently is associated with sustainability, particularly in reference to the manner in which the environment, society, and economic systems are inextricably linked. For example, extraction industries frequently damage local ecosystems but may create living wage jobs for local residents. At the same time, the environmental impacts of extraction and processing typically are experienced more acutely by poor and marginalized communities and may deprive future generations of the ability to live healthy, fulfilling lives.

Interconnectedness often involves the manner in which it is sometimes impossible to fully understand a system until we see how the elements within the system interconnect with one another or how the system interacts with other systems. For example, organisms in an ecosystem often evolve complex relationships with one another and with their nonorganic surroundings. It is sometimes necessary to examine an entire ecosystem to understand the individuals within that community. Similarly, we often gain new insights into local issues when we see how they are connected to a larger global context.

Many people find it difficult to understand very large-scale, complexly interconnected systems such as those associated with climate change, biodiversity, or globalized economic systems. Teachers can support the development of a sustainability worldview by providing opportunities for learners to engage with complex, interconnected phenomena and to embrace the uncertainty and ambiguity that arise from our innate inability to fully comprehend large interconnected systems. The primary tool for investigating interconnectedness is **systems thinking**, which is a strategy for representing complex interdependences and interrelationships. Systems thinking looks at the way systems behave and change over time and the various feedback loops and forces that affect interconnected processes. We will explore systems thinking in detail in Chapter 9.

EXTEND YOUR PROFESSIONAL KNOWLEDGE 4.1

The UNESCO World Conference on Education for Sustainable Development was held in Aichi Nagoya Japan in November 2014. This meeting marked the end of the United Nations Decade of Education for Sustainable Development (UNDESD) and the beginning of the next phase of education for sustainability worldwide. Visit the World Conference website at:

www.unesco.org/new/en/unesco-world-conference-on-esd-2014/.

1. Download the final report of the UNDESD titled *Shaping the Future We Want*.
2. In the report, look up the type of education (e.g., formal, nonformal, technical, etc.) and grade level (e.g., early childhood, high school, higher ed., etc.) that most interests you.
3. Download the UNESCO Roadmap for the Global Action Programme on Education for Sustainable Development at the same site.
4. Think about how you can implement some of the ideas described in the reports in your own professional practice as a teacher. How can these reports help you refine your own sustainability worldview and practice as a teacher?

Note

1   This telegram seems to have been the source of a statement often attributed to Einstein: "The significant problems we face cannot be solved at the same level of thinking we were at when we created them." It is not clear that he ever made this exact statement, so this quote may be misattributed or apocryphal. However, the complete text of this telegram certainly expresses the sentiment embodied in the statement.

References

Bandura, A. (1977). Self-efficacy: Toward a unifying theory of behavioral change. *Psychological Review, 84,* 191–215.

Bandura, A. (1997). *Self-Efficacy: The Exercise of Control.* New York: Freeman.

Bandura, A. (2000). Exercise of human agency through collective efficacy. *Current Directions in Psychological Science, 9,* 75–78.

Benyus, J.M. (1997). *Biomimicry: Innovation Inspired by Nature.* New York: Morrow.

Do, Q.-T., & Iyer, L. (2010). Geography, poverty and conflict in Nepal. *Journal of Peace Research, 47,* 735.

Ennis, R.H. (1996). *Critical Thinking.* Upper Saddle River, NJ: Prentice Hall.

Galtung, J. (1996). *Peace by Peaceful Means: Peace and Conflict, Development and Civilization.* London: Sage.

Gardiner, H. (2014, November 19). As other try to clean air, India raises bet on coal. *International New York Times,* pp. 1, 4.

Homer-Dixon, T. (1991). On the threshold: Environmental changes as causes of acute conflict. *International Security, 16*(2).

Maathai, W. (2000). Interview: Wangari Maathai. *Robert F. Kennedy Center for Justice and Human Rights.* Retrieved from: http://rfkcenter.org/wangari-maathai-16?id=37&lang=en

Marzano, R.J., & Kendall, J.S. (2007). *The New Taxonomy of Educational Objectives* (2nd ed.). Thousand Oaks, CA: Corwin.

McKeown, R. (2006). *Education for Sustainable Development Toolkit.* Paris: UNESCO.

Meyer, J., & Land, R. (2006). Troublesome concepts and troublesome knowledge: An introduction. In J. Meyer & R. Land (Eds.), *Overcoming Barriers to Student Understanding: Threshold Concepts and Troublesome Knowledge.* New York: Routledge.

New York Times. (1946, May 25). Atomic Education Urged by Einstein: Scientists in Plea for $200,000 to Promote New Type of Essential Thinking, p. 13.

New York Times Magazine. (1946, June 23). The Real Problem Is in the Hearts of Men: Interview With Michael Amrine, p. SM4.

Nolet, V.W. (2007). Preparing sustainability literate teachers. *Teachers College Record, 111,* 409–442.

Perkins, D.N., & Salomon, G. (2012). Knowledge to go: A motivational and dispositional view of transfer. *Educational Psychologist, 47,* 248–258.

Rist, J., & Dahdhouh-Guebas, F. (2006). Ethnosciences—A step towards the integration of scientific and indigenous forms of knowledge in the management of natural resources for the future. *Environment, Development and Sustainability, 8,* 467–493.

Wiggins, G., & McTighe, J. (2005). *Understanding by Design* (2nd ed.). Alexandria, VA: ASCD.

Wilson, E.O. (1993). Biophilia and the conservation ethic. In E.O. Wilson & S. R. Kellert (Eds.), *The Biophilia Hypothesis.* Washington, DC: Island Press.

Wingspread Conference on the Precautionary Principle. (1998, January 26). The Science and Environmental Health Network. Retrieved from: www.sehn.org/wing.html

Zohar, A., Schoenfeld, S., & Alleson, I. (2010). Environmental peacebuilding strategies in the Middle East: The case of the Arava Institute for Environmental Studies. *Peace and Conflict Review, 5*(1).

SECTION II

Fostering a Sustainability Worldview

5

TEACHING FOR SUSTAINABILITY

We must not forget that our sisters and brothers are waiting for a bright peaceful future. So let us wage a global struggle against illiteracy, poverty and terrorism and let us pick up our books and pens. They are our most powerful weapons. One child, one teacher, one pen and one book can change the world. Education is the only solution.

—Malala Yousafzai, July 12, 2013

Imagine this scenario: You find yourself in an elevator with a member of the governing board for your school district. She asks:

"What is education for sustainability? Why should we make it a priority in our district?"

Your experience with this woman leads you to believe she is a thoughtful professional who wants the best for children in the district, but she has little background in education. You also know you have only a few minutes to answer her questions.

> How would you respond to the board member's questions?

Your first impulse might be to say:

> "The goal of education for sustainability is to help learners develop a sustainability worldview—a way of seeing and interacting with the world through the lens of sustainability."

But if the board member does not already know what you mean by "sustainability," you will need much more time than you have available to explain! So you might decide to say something like this:

> "Sustainability refers to a constellation of ideas associated with safeguarding the life support systems upon which humans and other species must

depend, now and in the future. The noun sustain*ability* refers to a desired outcome—ensuring that the systems needed to support life endure over time and are available for future generations. The adjective sustain*able* refers to practices or strategies that are intended to bring about sustain*ability*. We will achieve sustain*ability* by engaging in sustain*able* practices. Educa-tion *for* sustainability is aimed at helping people learn thinking skills and problem-solving strategies associated with sustainable practices."

If your response is along these lines, you might be relieved that you are able to provide such a cogent answer to the board member! However, you also might worry that your explanation falls short of communicating the true complexity of the day-to-day work of **teaching for sustainability**. As you read in Chapter 3, education for sustainability can involve a variety of strategies and take place in a variety of settings, including nonformal education, community settings, and the formal education that takes place in elementary and secondary schools and in technical and higher education. Teaching for sustainability is the process by which teachers turn the broad conceptual and often philosophical ideals of education for sustainability into specific elements of effective teaching practice. It is the transla-tion of sustainability principles, concepts, and processes into the daily professional practice of teaching. Teaching for sustainability is, as the old tire advertisement used to say, "where the rubber meets the road."

The minute-to-minute and day-to-day professional practice of teaching involves the design of learning environments that help all learners make progress toward meaningful goals. To facilitate this process, teachers apply information about human learning and motivation, individual and cultural differences, instructional strategies, long-term planning, assessment, policy, leadership, professional ethics, and strategies for collaboration and teamwork. To effectively integrate sustainability into your professional practice as a teacher, it also is essential for you to understand the elements of a sustainability worldview, introduced in Chapter 3. Those elements include values, knowledge, dispositions, agency, and a constellation of big ideas that serve as portals into a deeper inquiry into the sustainability knowledge domain.

This chapter is concerned with the day-to-day and minute-to-minute practice of teaching for sustainability. *Education* for sustainability is an ideal that refers to funda-mental transformation of the purpose and processes of education at a systems level. The day-to-day work of *teaching* for sustainability involves *your* worldview—your way of seeing the world—that will affect every element of your professional teach-ing practice. This chapter will help you begin this process of translating the ideal into the real by focusing on what it is that teachers need to know and be able to do in order to help students develop a sustainability worldview. We begin by examin-ing the various purposes of educating for sustainability. As a teacher, the onus will be on you to be clear about your goals and motivations when you seek to incor-porate sustainability into your professional practice. Until you know the "why," you will find it difficult to decide the "what" of teaching for sustainability. This is where we begin our examination of the sustainability knowledge domain.

CONSIDER THIS 5.1 WHAT IS YOUR REASON "WHY"?

Before you read the descriptions of the various purposes of education for sustainability in the sections that follow, write a paragraph or two that outlines your motivation to teach for sustainability. How do you incorporate your values into professional practice? What philosophical perspectives inform your practice?

Clarifying the Purposes of Educating for Sustainability

There are multiple goals and purposes associated with education for sustainability, and these vary from context to context. There is no single "correct" purpose, but it is important for you to understand the philosophical perspectives that underlie the various instructional and curricular approaches that are associated with education for sustainability. Ultimately, your day-to-day instructional decisions must be aligned with those larger philosophical aims.

Stephen Sterling has written extensively (2004, 2009) about the various purposes of education for sustainability, and he suggests that those purposes derive from two broad perspectives. Those perspectives are an instrumental view and an intrinsic view of education for sustainability. He notes that a third, critical perspective, based largely on socially critical theory, also has been influential in the sustainability discourse, but it is probably a hybrid of the other two. Sterling says that while these three perspectives (instrumental, intrinsic, and critical) are sometimes seen as competing alternatives, they are not mutually exclusive and often operate in tandem. Instead, they represent differences in emphasis. It is important to understand the implications of the three perspectives for your teaching practice, so they will be described briefly here.

Instrumental

The instrumental perspective on education for sustainability is a descendant of the pragmatism school of philosophy that emerged in the United States in the 1870s. Instrumentalism, which is often attributed to John Dewey (1904/1964), holds that a theory or concept is valued according to its utility for predicting or explaining a phenomenon. Instrumentalism is less concerned with the verifiable truth of a theory than with the extent to which the theory helps solve a problem. For instrumentalists, a statement is viewed as true if it is useful for guiding an action or inquiry. An instrumental perspective views education as a means to an end and is concerned with the function that education serves for an individual or society. As Sterling (2010) notes, an instrumental perspective on education for sustainability often involves a sense of urgency, and education is viewed as a strategy for remedying the problems that create unsustainability. Thus, when we view education for sustainability as being aimed at changing people's worldview to bring about more sustainable patterns of behavior, we are using an instrumentalist perspective.

Today, the instrumental perspective is by far the dominant approach to education for sustainability around the world, particularly in formal education settings such as elementary and high school and in higher education. For that matter, as the title implies, this book also is based in part on an instrumental perspective. However, there are some significant drawbacks with an instrumental perspective that must be acknowledged.

The main critique of this perspective is that it assumes a linear relationship between the effects of education and the desired outcome of larger social and policy changes associated with a sustainable future (e.g., healthy environment, social justice, and viable economies). This is a somewhat mechanistic view that underestimates the complexity of the relationship among education, attitudes, behaviors, and larger societal changes. It assumes that identification of a set of "inputs" such as specific curriculum content or pedagogical strategies can have a predictable "output" of a more sustainable future. One of results of this kind of thinking in recent years has been the proliferation of so-called adjectival education initiatives (Development Education Commission, 1999). These are education programs developed to address a specific problem or issue that often have an adjective before the word "education." Some examples of adjectival educations are shown in Box 5.1. Adjectival education initiatives can be helpful when they result in high-quality curriculum or teaching materials that provide timely, accurate, and unbiased information. However, often adjectival education programs are created by industry or advocacy groups that have a particular political or business agenda that is subtly or explicitly reflected in the materials. Even when adjectival education programs are developed by credible organizations, they can result in a disjointed and segmented approach to teaching about issues that fails to highlight common themes and underlying causes.

A second critique of the instrumental perspective is that the putative benefits of education for sustainability are in the distant future. Therefore, it can be difficult to assess the efficacy of various curricular or pedagogical approaches against a standard of desired outcome. The instrumental perspective leads to a "teach and hope" approach. We teach now and hope that, at some point in the future, a positive benefit accrues. This is not necessarily an insurmountable problem, but it means that the success of instrumental education for sustainability must be evaluated using indicator systems rather than direct measurement.

Intrinsic

The intrinsic view of education for sustainability focuses on the inherent values and experiences associated with an education rather than with the desired

BOX 5.1 EXAMPLES OF ADJECTIVAL EDUCATION

Environmental Education	Population Education	Development Education
Energy Education	HIV/AIDS Education	Permaculture Education
Citizenship Education	Consumer Education	Media Education
Outdoor Education	Conservation Education	Religious Education
Holocaust Education	Entrepreneurship Education	Horticulture Education
Sex Education	Human Rights Education	Values Education
Natural History Education	Vocational Education	Economics Education
Conflict Resolution Education	Disaster Prevention Education	Recycling Education
Civics Education	Anti-Violence Education	Biodiversity Education
Nutrition Education	Indian Education	Peace Education
Leadership Education	Character Education	Tsunami Education

outcomes that would accrue. Sterling (2004) notes that this perspective is based on an idealist view of the world and a constructivist view of the learner. The idealist school of philosophy, which gained ascendancy in the 19th century, is concerned with representing the world as it should or could be rather than describing the world as it is. Idealists in the 19th century believed that the only reality we can really know is made up of thoughts and ideas. In the 20th century, idealism focused more broadly on the importance of values and ideals over concrete goals or outcomes. This perspective has long informed environmental education programs in formal and nonformal settings where the idea that there is inherent value in learning in and from nature is foundational. Experiencing nature is viewed as a meaningful goal for its own sake. For example, experiential learning, outdoor education, and various "learning by doing" approaches are often based on the assertion that simply being and learning in nature is inherently a worthwhile learning outcome. For adherents to the intrinsic view, environmental and sustainability issues can provide a context for learning, but behavior change for the sake of a sustainable future is seen as less important than that learners develop critical thinking and experience an open-ended pursuit of learning for learning's sake (Foster, 2008; Jickling & Spork, 1998; Sterling, 2010). The intrinsic perspective is concerned with the quality of the educational experience and the extent to which that experience facilitates personal growth and development, critical inquiry, meaning making, and self-determination (Sterling, 2004).

The main critique of the intrinsic perspective is that it is overly optimistic and process oriented and not sufficiently focused on bringing about specific changes associated with sustainability. As was discussed in Chapter 2, the current school-aged generation and the next several generations will face complex and perhaps intractable problems of unprecedented magnitude and complexity. So there is a real urgency to try to ensure that education systems respond in a meaningful way to help prepare those future generations to meet those challenges, and it can be difficult to support approaches that do have at least some intent in that direction. Sterling (2010) has called the intrinsic perspective necessary but not sufficient because the attitudes and values changes that an intrinsic perspective promotes are elements of the outcomes that would be expected to accrue from an instrumental approach. A critique that the instrumental and intrinsic perspectives share is that they assume education in general and education for a purpose is inherently benign. This is not necessarily a safe assumption, particularly when education perpetuates existing power imbalances or props up the social and economic systems that promote unsustainability. Therefore, a critical perspective is also an essential element of education for sustainability.

Critical

The critical perspective, based largely on critical theory and critical pedagogy, is concerned primarily with undoing the effects of oppression and hegemonic relationships. This perspective, which gained ascendancy in academia during the late 1980s and 1990s, particularly in Germany, the United States, Great Britain, and Australia, includes elements of both the instrumental and intrinsic views. It is instrumental in that it aims to correct past injustices and to prevent future oppression. In this respect, there is very clearly an intended outcome, and education is viewed as being for a purpose. At the same time, the critical perspective holds that there is inherent value in understanding the racial, social, and economic antecedents to oppression and in gaining a first-hand appreciation of struggle, power imbalance, and the effects of history. In general, a critical perspective on education is concerned with the manner in which dominant paradigms create injustice and the extent to which our everyday thoughts and behavior are shaped by those dominant ideologies. Education based on a critical perspective is focused on helping people become aware of and overcome those patterns of dominance and injustice. The critical perspective is frequently concerned with empowering those directly affected by oppression and with pedagogies that promote agency and self-determination. Issues of gender, race, culture, language, and status often figure prominently in approaches based on this perspective.

The critical perspective on education for sustainability has a number of influences but probably is most directly informed by four sources: (a) Paulo Freire's work (2008) on critical pedagogy; (b) ecofeminism, which is asserts that the exploitation of women and the environment are both the result of historical domination by patriarchal hierarchies; (c) critical race theory, which is premised on the assertion that racism is an inherent characteristic of American society (Ladson-Billings, 1999); and (d) environmental justice, which focuses on the manner in which the impacts of environmental exploitation and damage tend to disproportionately affect poor, minority, and disadvantaged populations. These various perspectives often are addressed within the larger context of environmental ecojustice education (Martusewiscz, Edmonson, & Lupinacci, 2011). Critical theory also is directly informed by a Marxist analysis of the effects of capitalism on social relations and belief systems (Brookfield, 2005, pp. 18–20).

Like the instrumental and intrinsic perspectives, a critical perspective is a required but not sufficient element of education for sustainability. However, this perspective is not without problems. One of the challenges of a critical perspective is to avoid falling into the trap of essentialist or typological thinking. This is the belief that the characteristics attributed to a group are fixed traits and that each individual in the group is expected to exhibit those characteristics. For example, essentialist thinking would lead to the belief that all individuals of a particular race should be expected to have similar values or opinions or that all indigenous people have shared experiences and beliefs. Essentialist thinking also can lead to the idea that certain groups are oppressors and others are oppressed simply because of their gender or race. For example, the narrative of male dominance and white privilege has been a frequent theme in higher education in the United States during the last 20 years. This discourse has often had an American-centric perspective focused largely on historical impacts of the exploitation and colonization of the Americas and Africa by Europeans over the last 500 years. The pernicious effects of male dominance and racism are still evident around the world today, and the work of undoing the effects of racism and oppressive hierarchies of all kinds must continue. However, the demographic, economic, and social landscape has changed significantly in the last 20 years, and critical theory has lost much of its explanatory power. Monolithic conceptions of race- or gender-based privilege fail to capture the true complexity and global nature of power and privilege relationships in the 21st century. Today, anyone who behaves in a way that limits opportunities for other humans or species or for future generations to experience a safe and meaningful quality of life is an oppressor. Unsustainable behavior is hegemony that cuts across temporal, gender, race, class, cultural, and species lines.

Investigating Your Personal Perspectives on Education for Sustainability

Statistician George Edward Pelham Box famously said "essentially all models are wrong, but some are useful" (Box & Draper, 1987, p. 424). All models are wrong because it is impossible to anticipate and simulate every possible variable in any given situation, but sometimes even an incorrect model can help us to make sense of complicated real-world phenomena. The same argument can certainly be said of the three perspectives on the purpose of education for sustainability. The real-world instantiation of any philosophical perspective is never going to be as clear-cut as its academic description. Each of the perspectives is problematic because each, in its own way, fails to capture all of the nuances of meaning and intention associated with the "rubber meets the road" reality of teaching. However, the three perspectives can provide a point of reference to help you clarify your own thinking about the goals and desired outcomes of education for sustainability.

All teachers bring a set of personal beliefs and passions to their teaching. In the early years of their careers, teachers' beliefs about teaching, learning, pedagogical approaches, and the purposes of education often are based on an investigation of various theories and philosophers conducted during preservice preparation. Preservice teachers are often encouraged to develop a set of assertions that form a personal philosophy of teaching. Then, throughout their careers, teachers' perspectives often evolve in response to experience and the acquisition of wisdom of practice. In addition, teachers often hold a number of implicit beliefs that reflect local norms, personal values, and cognitive styles (Reber, 2011). Your personal and professional philosophies can inform your decision making as a teacher in both helpful and sometimes unhelpful ways, so it is useful to periodically reevaluate your beliefs. The three perspectives on education for sustainability described above can provide a rich context for investigation. Start by checking your current beliefs and assumptions. For example, how would you complete each of the statements in Box 5.2?

BOX 5.2 CHECK YOUR CURRENT BELIEFS AND ASSUMPTIONS

The elements of education for sustainability about which I am most passionate are . . .
The ultimate purpose of education for sustainability is . . .
This purpose will be achieved if . . .
My role as a teacher is . . .
My learners will benefit from education for sustainability if they . . .
Society will benefit from education for sustainability if . . .

As you reflect on your current perspectives, decide how your responses align with the three perspectives on education for sustainability. Think about your response to the questions in Box 5.3.

BOX 5.3 HOW DO YOUR BELIEFS ALIGN WITH THE THREE PERSPECTIVES?

How do your personal beliefs fit with each of the perspectives (instrumental, intrinsic, critical)?

What tensions or contradictions arise as you analyze your personal assertions about education for sustainability?

How is your professional practice as a teacher informed by your perspectives?

Which elements of the three perspectives on education for sustainability are absent from your own belief system?

How are your beliefs about education for sustainability informed by perspectives other than the three described above?

Ultimately, your personal perspective on education for sustainability will involve a blending of the three perspectives described above, and you should expect your beliefs to shift as your understanding of education for sustainability deepens over time. In fact, as you will see in the chapters that follow, one of the most salient characteristics of education for sustainability is that it involves a way of looking at the world that is informed by multiple perspectives and a broad knowledge domain.

The Professional Knowledge Domain Associated With Teaching for Sustainability

The work of translating complex bodies of information into meaningful instruction is an essential component of effective teaching. For example, one of the core propositions of the National Board for Professional Teaching Standards is that accomplished teachers "know the subjects they teach and know how to teach those subjects to students" (NBPTS, 2002). National Board Certified Teachers (NBCTs) are expected to have a deep understanding of the history, structure, and real-world applications of the subject they teach and to be able to anticipate the skills gaps and preconceptions learners may bring to the subject. Similarly, the Interstate Teacher Assessment and Support Consortium (InTASC) has articulated standards that describe what teachers should know and be able to do to ensure the achievement of all learners (CCSSO, 2011, 2013). InTASC Standard #4 specifies, "The teacher understands the central concepts, tools of inquiry, and structures of the discipline(s) he or she teaches and creates learning experiences that make the discipline accessible and meaningful for learners to assure mastery of the content." InTASC Standard #5 specifies, "The teacher understands how to connect concepts and use differing perspectives to engage learners in critical thinking, creativity, and collaborative problem solving related to authentic local and global issues."

The integration of content knowledge and teaching expertise to which the NBPTS and InTASC standards refer is called **pedagogical content knowledge**. Pedagogical content knowledge involves knowing how best to make the ideas, propositions, concepts, and process associated with a specific content domain accessible for learners (Shulman, 1986, 1987). Teachers who have developed pedagogical content knowledge know:

- What makes specific topics within a domain easy or difficult to learn;
- Areas where learners are likely to have developed preconceptions or "buggy" ideas that need to be untangled;
- How to best represent the information in the domain to make it accessible for learners; and
- How to link the content of the domain to learners' existing knowledge so that it can become meaningful and accessible (Grossman, Schoenfeld, & Lee, 2005; Shulman, 1987).

To make information accessible for learners, teachers need to understand how ideas within a domain build and interconnect. Therefore, teachers also need sufficient **domain knowledge** as a prerequisite for development of pedagogical content knowledge (Kleickmann et al., 2013; Shulman, 1986). Domain knowledge is the realm of knowledge that an *individual* has about a particular subject area or field of study (Alexander, Schallert, & Hare, 1991; Murphy & Alexander, 2002). Typically, the knowledge, skills, values, and dispositions that students are expected to learn represents only a subset of a teacher's pedagogical and domain knowledge. Experienced teachers typically possess a much broader repertoire of pedagogical knowledge and skills and a more comprehensive knowledge of the content domain than they deploy on a day-to-day basis. This relationship is illustrated in Figure 5.1.

Clearly, there is a close relationship among a teacher's pedagogical content knowledge, domain knowledge, and the content of the curriculum that learners are expected to understand. Simply put, a teacher cannot teach what she or he does not know—to be effective, a teacher must have a deep, flexible knowledge of the content of her or his discipline *and* be able to teach that content to all learners. Inevitably, then, your ability to effectively teach for sustainability will depend on development of your own sustainability worldview. When this occurs, a reciprocal relationship forms among a teacher's own sustainability worldview, pedagogical content knowledge, domain knowledge, and the students' developing sustainability worldview. This relationship is illustrated in Figure 5.2.

As was discussed in Chapter 4, the knowledge domain associated with a sustainability worldview includes a variety of big ideas that include principles, values, core concepts, and a variety of themes and topics. Teachers can support development of a sustainability worldview by using approaches that help learners holistically integrate and enact values, knowledge, and dispositions in meaningful,

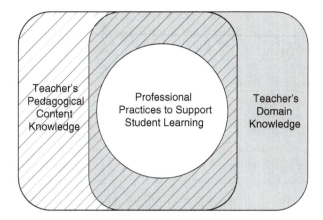

Figure 5.1 Relationship among pedagogical content knowledge, domain knowledge, and curriculum content

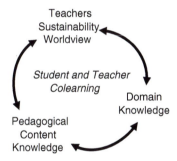

Figure 5.2 Reciprocal relationship between a teacher's pedagogical content knowledge and sustainability worldview

real-world contexts. The professional and pedagogical practices that accomplish this help learners:

- Develop universal values of care, compassion, respect;
- Seek positive and creative solutions to local and global sustainability challenges;
- Develop practical "how to" knowledge as well as theoretical knowledge that supports application of theory in real-world contexts;
- Tolerate and engage with complexity and ambiguity;
- Develop critical-thinking skills and strategies;
- Embrace multiple ways of knowing and doing that honor and respect diverse cultures, histories, and perspectives;
- Engage personally with the justice and equity dimensions of sustainability issues;

- Develop the disposition to ask questions, inquire, and investigate;
- Acquire collaboration and cooperation strategies; and
- Apply transdisciplinary knowledge and skills that integrates the arts, literature, storytelling media, and writing, as well as scientific and quantitative disciplines.

The remaining chapters in this book explore professional and pedagogical practices that promote this transformational approach to teaching. In particular, learner-centered strategies create opportunities for learners to grapple with the messy real world of ideas and issues, to test their own mental models and theories, and to reflect on their learning and evolving understanding of the world. Therefore, proficiency at designing and managing learner-centered strategies is an essential element of the pedagogical content knowledge associated with teaching for sustainability. With learner-centered strategies, the teacher no longer serves the role of "expert" or "sage on the stage" or transmits knowledge *to* students but rather serves as a facilitator and orchestrator who creates the conditions that enable learners to assume more direct control of their own development.

To effectively implement learner-centered strategies, it is important for teachers to understand the complexity and dynamism of issues and to bring a deep and flexible knowledge of big ideas, themes, and topics to the learning situation. The teacher must be able to help learners develop the capacity for critical reflection and systemic and futures thinking as well as develop the motivation to become personally engaged with sustainability issues.

Competencies That Support Teaching for Sustainability

Given this tight interconnectedness between teacher pedagogical content knowledge and student learning, it is important to identify competencies for teachers that can support student learning for sustainability. The framework articulated by the United Nations Economic Commission for Europe (UNECE, 2012) accomplishes this goal. The UNECE was established in 1947 to support the economic development of countries devastated by World War II and now includes 56 member states, including Canada and the United States. Today the UNECE promotes sustainable development and economic prosperity by helping the member states develop effective policies and apply best practices in a wide range of areas, including education for sustainability.

The UNECE framework goes beyond the competences that a teacher would need to be effective in a particular discipline and is not intended to be a set of minimum standards that should be met by all teachers. Rather, the framework is intended as a guide that describes what educators should know, what they should be able to do, how they should live and work with others, and how they should be able to effectively teach for sustainability. In essence, the UNECE framework describes the elements of a teacher's sustainability worldview as the larger context for the pedagogical content knowledge associated with the professional practice of teaching for sustainability.

The competencies are clustered into four broad categories intended to be representative of a wide range of learning experiences:

Learning to Know	refers to understanding the challenges facing society both locally and globally and the potential role of educators and learners. Competencies in this cluster begin with the sentence stem "The teacher understands. . . ."
Learning to Do	refers to developing practical skills and action competence in relation to education for sustainability Competencies in this cluster begin with the sentence stem "The teacher is able to. . . ."
Learning to Live Together	contributes to the development of partnerships and an appreciation of interdependence, pluralism, mutual understanding, and peace. Competencies in this cluster begin with the sentence stem "The teacher works with others in ways that. . . ."
Learning to Be	addresses the development of one's personal attributes and ability to act with greater autonomy, judgment, and personal responsibility in relation to sustainable development. Competencies in this cluster begin with the sentence stem "The teacher is someone who . . ."

Within these four categories, the competences are clustered around three essential characteristics of education for sustainability: *holistic approach, envisioning change,* and *achieving transformation.*

A Holistic Approach

Sustainability challenges often are simultaneously global and local, and changes in one part of the world can affect others many thousands of miles away today and far into the future. The solutions to these problems often involve complex dilemmas and widely varying perspectives. Teachers who are proficient at using holistic approaches promote creative ways of thinking and acting that reflect these complex interrelationships. Holistic educational approaches focus on creating a more balanced relationship among different dimensions of an individual's development (e.g., intellectual, physical, spiritual, emotional, social, and aesthetic), as well as the relationships between the individual and other people and the natural environment (Mahmoudi, Jafari, Nasrabadi, & Liaghatdar, 2012). The UNECE framework identifies three integrated components of holistic approaches. *Integrative thinking* attends to the interconnectedness and simultaneity of sustainability issues and challenges. The tools associated with **systems thinking**, which is addressed in Chapter 9, exemplify this aspect of holistic education. *Inclusivity* involves helping learners embrace a range of perspectives and approaches when exploring solutions to sustainability challenges. *Dealing with complexities* refers to the transdisciplinary nature of sustainability issues and the teacher's ability to create connections among the broad range of sustainability big ideas, themes, and topics.

Envisioning Change

Envisioning change attends to the temporal elements of a sustainability worldview. The three dimensions of teacher competencies related to the envisioning change cluster are *learning from the past*, *active engagement in the present*, and *exploring alternative futures*. Learning from the past pertains to a teacher's ability to help learners understand the historic basis of sustainability issues and analyze the root causes of those developments. Learning from the past involves understanding both successes and failures in cultural, social, economic, and environmental contexts. *Active engagement in the present* involves proficiency with strategies for helping students explore contemporary sustainability issues and search for solutions that address the needs of all people and other species in the present as well as those of future generations. *Exploring alternative futures* refers to approaches that involve learners in creating visions for a future that emphasize a positive future for people and nature, rather than a future that simply does less harm. This process draws upon scientific evidence and helps students uncover current beliefs and assumptions that underlie our choices and unsustainable behaviors. This component of the Envisioning Change competency cluster in the UNECE framework involves strategies for helping learners develop mind-sets and habits of mind that promote a positive future orientation and effective decision making. These strategies are discussed in Chapters 6 and 8.

Achieving Transformation

This competency cluster attends to a transformation of a teacher's own professional practice, as well as a transformation of the broader teaching profession. On a personal level, *transformation of what it means to be an educator* involves the willingness to examine one's own professional practices and engage in a reflective renewal process that moves toward practices associated with teaching for sustainability. For many teachers, the process of investigating and developing a sustainability worldview is itself transformative. Acting on behalf of the well-being of all, forever, can involve a wide range of changes in one's personal habits, consumption patterns, and day-to-day choices and decisions. This personal transformation, then, is almost certainly likely to inform a teacher's professional classroom practice in small and large ways. *Transformative pedagogy* includes a variety of learner-centered practices as well as pedagogies that encourage learners to engage in critical thinking and innovative solution seeking. A number of these pedagogical approaches are discussed in Chapter 7. When teachers engage in activities aimed at *transformation of education systems*, they are working within larger organizations and systems to help reorient the entire education system to address sustainability. Often this work can involve working within professional communities, in leadership roles, or through activism and advocacy activities.

The complete UNECE teacher competency framework is presented Figure 5.3.

Category: Learning to know

Cluster: *Holistic approach*
The teacher understands . . .

- The basics of systems thinking and ways in which natural, social, and economic systems function and how they may be interrelated
- The interdependent nature of relationships within the present generation and between generations, as well as those between rich and poor and between humans and nature
- Their personal worldview and cultural assumptions and seek to understand those of others
- The connection between sustainable futures and the way we think, live, and work
- Their own thinking and action in relation to sustainable development.

Cluster: *Envisioning change: Past, present, and future*
The teacher understands . . .

- The root causes of unsustainable development
- That sustainable development is an evolving concept
- The urgent need for change from unsustainable practices toward advancing quality of life, equity, solidarity, and environmental sustainability
- The importance of problem setting, critical reflection, visioning, and creative thinking in planning the future and effecting change
- The importance of preparedness for the unforeseen and a precautionary approach
- The importance of scientific evidence in supporting sustainable development.

Cluster: *Achieve transformation*
The teacher understands . . .

- Why there is a need to transform the education systems that support learning
- Why there is a need to transform the way we educate/learn
- Why it is important to prepare learners to meet new challenges
- The importance of building on the experience of learners as a basis for transformation
- How engagement in real-world issues enhances learning outcomes and helps learners to make a difference in practice.

Category: Learning to live together

Cluster: *Holistic approach*
The teacher works with others in ways that . . .

- Actively engage different groups across generations, cultures, places, and disciplines
- Facilitate the emergence of new worldviews that address sustainable development
- Encourage negotiation of alternative futures.

Cluster: *Envisioning change*
The teacher works with others in ways that . . .

- Facilitate the emergence of new worldviews that address sustainable development
- Encourage negotiation of alternative futures.

(continued)

Figure 5.3 (continued)

Cluster: *Achieve transformation*

The teacher works with others in ways that ...

- Challenge unsustainable practices across educational systems, including at the institutional level
- Help learners clarify their own and others worldviews through dialogue, and recognize that alternative frameworks exist.

Category: Learning to do

Cluster: *Holistic approach*

The teacher is able to ...

- Create opportunities for sharing ideas and experiences from different disciplines/places/cultures/generations without prejudice and preconceptions
- Work with different perspectives on dilemmas, issues, tensions, and conflicts
- Connect the learner to their local and global spheres of influence.

Cluster: *Envisioning change*

The teacher is able to ...

- Critically assess processes of change in society and envision sustainable futures
- Communicate a sense of urgency for change and inspire hope
- Facilitate the evaluation of potential consequences of different decisions and actions
- Use the natural, social, and built environment, including their own institution, as a context and source of learning.

Cluster: *Achieve transformation*

The teacher is able to ...

- Identify and put into action specific steps aimed at transforming the education systems that support learning
- Explain why there is a need to transform the way we educate/learn
- Implement pedagogies that prepare learners to meet new challenges
- Create learning opportunities that build on the experience of learners as a basis for transformation
- Show how engagement in real-world issues enhances learning outcomes and helps learners to make a difference in practice.

Category: Learning to be

Cluster: *Holistic approach*

The teacher is someone who ...

- Is inclusive of different disciplines, cultures, and perspectives, including indigenous knowledge and worldviews.

Cluster: *Envisioning change*

The teacher is someone who ...

- Is motivated to make a positive contribution to other people and their social and natural environment, locally and globally
- Is willing to take considered action even in situations of uncertainty.

Cluster: *Achieve transformation*

The teacher is someone who ...

- Is willing to challenge assumptions underlying unsustainable practice
- Is a facilitator and participant in the learning process
- Is a critically reflective practitioner
- Inspires creativity and innovation
- Engages with learners in ways that build positive relationships.

Figure 5.3 UNECE Competencies for Teachers in Education for Sustainability

Source: United Nations Economic Commission for Europe Strategy for Education for Sustainable Development, 2012.

Pedagogical Content Knowledge and Curriculum Standards

Perhaps as you have been reading this chapter and thinking about the professional competencies for teachers described in the UNECE framework, you have been wondering about the place of curriculum standards in the practice of teaching for sustainability. Content standards have assumed a central role in schools around the world in recent years, as policymakers have sought to tie high-stakes accountability to classroom practices. In the United States, for example, most states are using the Common Core standards (National Governors Association & Council of Chief State School Officers, 2010) to establish guidelines for English language arts and for literacy in history/social studies, science, and technical subjects. Similarly, more than half of the states are using the Next Generation Science Standards (NGSS Lead States, 2013) to establish expectations for science learning across grade levels. Many states are beginning to adopt the Smarter Balanced Assessment System (Smarter Balanced Assessment Consortium, n.d.) to assess student progress toward accomplishment of these standards and to evaluate school effectiveness in supporting student learning. While education policy is set at the state and local level, not at the national level, the widespread adoption of the Common Core and Next Generation standards and the Smarter Balanced Assessment system (Smarter Balanced Assessment Consortium, n.d.) are fast becoming a de facto national curriculum in the United States. The U.S. Department of Education has made it clear in a variety of policy statements that it intends to tie availability of federal funds for education to evidence that states and local schools are making meaningful progress toward helping all students meet acceptable standards on assessments such as Smarter Balanced that are tied to Common Core and NGSS standards.

Outside of the United States, the Programme for International Student Assessment (PISA) is being implemented in about 65 countries around the world. This is an international assessment that is intended to evaluate education systems worldwide by testing the skills and knowledge of 15-year-old students. The PISA program, which is operated by the Organisation for Economic Co-operation and Development (OECD, 2012) does include content standards, but large-scale assessments such as PISA and Smarter Balanced can drive curriculum changes as school districts and ministries of education seek to reorient instruction to better prepare students to perform the kind of higher level thinking demanded on high-stakes tests. There is considerable evidence from around the world that countries pay close attention to their international rankings on PISA scores and are treating PISA-based a high-stakes test, in much the same way that the states in the United States treat standards-based assessments.

In many countries, national, state, and provincial curriculum frameworks include significant sustainability-related content. For example, the province of Manitoba in Canada has developed an extensive set of sustainability goals and indicators across grade levels. Similarly, the national curricula in Australia, New Zealand, and Finland include significant sustainability content, and China has begun to incorporate education for sustainable development content into the national curriculum. However, for the most part there is a disconnect between these various sustainability curriculum frameworks and the PISA assessment. PISA typically contains items that use sustainability-related themes, but PISA does not include a "sustainability subtest" that assesses specific sustainability knowledge. Similarly, in the United States, the Common Core and NGSS standards include topics and themes that pertain to climate change, biodiversity, and globalization, for example, but there is not a separate sustainability strand. The Smarter Balanced assessment system also does not assess "sustainability knowledge."

In this high-stakes, standards-based environment, the goal of trying to find a place for sustainability-related content in an already crowded curriculum can seem daunting. However, a large body of research on effective education for sustainability programs around the world (cf. Buckler & Creech, 2014; Hopkins & Shi, 2014; Tilbury, 2011; Wals, 2012) indicates that the situation is not nearly as bleak as many teachers believe. Here are some implications that follow from this body of research:

1. Generally, teaching for sustainability focuses on thinking and problem solving rather than specific content. Focus on the thinking and dispositions that underlie a sustainability worldview. Helping learners become better thinkers will help them do better on standards-based tests.
2. There is no need for new sustainability-focused content standards. Existing content standards framework such as the Common Core and NGSS and many national curriculum frameworks provide ample opportunity for teachers to help learners make connections among issues and think about issues through the lens of sustainability.
3. Sustainability big ideas can create a robust framework for exploration of content standards and application of critical-thinking, problem-solving, and systems-thinking strategies that are called for on standards-based tests.
4. The research has consistently shown that sustainability creates a powerful, real-world context for application of theoretical knowledge. Create opportunities for learners to apply standards while exploring real-world and locally relevant issues that have a sustainability focus.
5. A focus on sustainability-related issues and big ideas often brings about non-curricular outcomes that in turn can positively affect school performance. A focus on sustainability can increase student engagement and attendance rates. These outcomes in turn ultimately can lead to increased performance on standards-based tests as well as longer-term goals, such as graduation rates.
6. All learners need basic academic skills, communication skills, media literacy, numeracy and mathematics skills, science literacy, and collaboration skills. These core academic skills are foundational to a sustainability worldview as well as to success in standards-based curricula. Investigation of sustainability big ideas can provide powerful opportunities for learners to apply and extend these foundation skills, while at the same time exploring their own sustainability worldview.

EXTEND YOUR PROFESSIONAL KNOWLEDGE 5.1

1. Download the curriculum standards for your country, state, or province.

   OR

2. Download the Common Core Standards at www.corestandards.org/read-the-standards/.

   OR

3. Download the Next Generation Science Standards at www.nextgenscience.org/framework-k%E2%80%9312-science-education.

4. Look at the standards for one grade level in one of the standards frameworks.

5. Identify areas where one or more of the sustainability big ideas discussed in this chapter can provide opportunities for learners to apply content standards.

6. Develop an activity or lesson plan that would help learners investigate a sustainability issue or big idea and also apply standards-based skills and knowledge.

References

Alexander, P.A., Schallert, D.L., & Hare, V.C. (1991). Coming to terms: How researchers in learning and literacy talk about knowledge. *Review of Educational Research, 61,* 315–343.

Buckler, C., & Creech, H. (2014). *Shaping the Future We Want: UN Decade of Education for Sustainable Development (2005–2014) Final Report.* Paris: UNESCO.

Box, G.E.P., & Draper, N.R. (1987). *Empirical Model Building and Response Surfaces.* New York: Wiley.

Brookfield, S.D. (2005). *The Power of Critical Theory: Liberating Adult Learning and Teaching.* San Francisco, CA: Jossey-Bass.

Council of Chief State School Officers. (2011). *Interstate Teacher Assessment and Support Consortium (InTASC) Model Core Teaching Standards: A Resource for State Dialogue.* Washington, DC: Author.

Development Education Commission. (1999). *Essential Learning for Everyone, Civil Society, World Citizenship and the Role of Education.* Bray and Birmingham, 80:20 and Birmingham DEC.

Dewey, J. (1964). The relationship of theory to practice in education. In R. D. Archambault (Ed.), *John Dewey on Education: Selected Writings.* Chicago, IL: University of Chicago Press. (Original work published 1904)

Foster, J. (2008). *The Sustainability Mirage—Illusion and Reality in the Coming War on Climate Change.* London: Earthscan.

Freire, P. (2008). *Education for Critical Consciousness.* London: Continuum.

Grossman, P., Schoenfeld, A., & Lee., C. (2005). Teaching subject matter. In L. Darling-Hammond & J. Bransford (Eds.), *Preparing Teachers for a Changing World. National Academy of Education Committee on Teacher Education.* San Francisco, CA: Jossey-Bass.

Hopkins, C., & Shi, G. (2014, November 7–14). *The contributions of education for sustainable development (ESD) to quality education: A synthesis report.* Paper presented at the 8th Biennial Meeting of the UNESCO International Network to Reorient Teacher Education to Address Sustainable Development, Okayama, Japan.

Jickling, B., & Spork, H. (1998). Education for the environment: A critique. *Environmental Education Research, 4,* 309–327.

Kleickmann, T., Richter, D., Kunter, M., Elsner, J., Besser, M., Krauss, S., & Baumer, J. (2013). Teacher's content knowledge and pedagogical content knowledge: The role of structural differences in teacher education. *Journal of Teacher Education, 64,* 90–106.

Ladson-Billings, G.L. (1999). Preparing teachers for diverse student populations: A critical race theory perspective. *Review of Research in Education, 24,* 211–247.

Mahmoudi, S., Jafari, E., Nasrabadi, H.A., & Liaghatdar, M.J. (2012). Holistic education: An approach for the 21st century. *International Education Studies, 5,* 178–186.

Martusewiscz, R.A., Edmonson, J., & Lupinacci, J. (2011). *Ecojustice Education: Toward Diverse, Democratic, and Sustainable Communities.* New York: Routledge.

Murphy, P.K., & Alexander, P.A. (2002). What counts? The predictive powers of subject-matter knowledge, strategic processing, and interest in domain-specific performance. *Journal of Experimental Education, 70,* 197–214.

National Board for Professional Teacher Standards. (2002). *What Teachers Should Know and Be Able to Do: National Board for Professional Teaching Standards.* Alexandria, VA: Author.

National Governors Association Center for Best Practices & Council of Chief State School Officers. (2010). *Common Core State Standards.* Washington, DC: Author.

NGSS Lead States. (2013). *Next Generation Science Standards: For States, by States.* Washington, DC: National Academies Press.

Organization for Economic and Cultural Development (2012). *PISA 2012 Technical Report.* Paris: OECD Publishing.

Reber, J. (2011). The under-examined life: A proposal for critically evaluating teachers' and students' philosophies of teaching. *College Teaching, 59,* 102–110.

Shulman, L. (1986). Those who understand: Knowledge growth in teaching. *Educational Researcher, 15,* 4–14.

Shulman, L.S. (1987). Knowledge and teaching: Foundations of the new reform. *Harvard Educational Review, 57*(1), 1–21.

Smarter Balanced Assessment Consortium (not dated). *A Summary of Core Components.* Retrieved from http://www.smarterbalanced.org/about/

Sterling, S. (2004). An analysis of the development of sustainability education internationally: Evolution, interpretation and transformative potential. In J. Blewitt & C. Cullingford (Eds.), *The Sustainability Curriculum: The Challenge for Higher Education* (pp. 43–62). London: Earthscan.

Sterling, S. (2010). Learning for resilience, or the resilient learner? Towards a necessary reconciliation in a paradigm of sustainable education. *Environmental Education Research, 16,* 511–528.

Tilbury, D. (2011). *Education for sustainable development: An expert review of processes and learning.* Paris: UNESCO.

United Nations Economic Commission for Europe (UNECE). (2012). *Learning for the Future: Competences in Education for Sustainable Development.* Geneva Switzerland: Author.

Wals, A. (2012). *Shaping the Education of Tomorrow: Full-length Report on the UN Decade of Education for Sustainable Development.* Paris: UNESCO.

Yousafzi, M. (2013, July 12). Remarks by Malala Yousafzi: Youth takeover ("Malala Day") at the United Nations, New York.

6

LEARNING THAT SUPPORTS A SUSTAINABILITY WORLDVIEW

We know in our bones that the real problems facing our planet can only be met by the ingenuity, experience and buy-in—the contagious excitement—of billions of us.
—Frances Moore Lappé, 2007, p. 115

The term **adaptation** refers to the process by which something is made suitable for its purpose or situation. Think of a well-tailored suit that fits perfectly or a successful movie based on a popular book. Evolutionary biologists describe adaptation as the characteristics of living organisms that enable them to survive and reproduce in a particular environment (LaFrenier, 2010, p. 3). For example, hummingbirds have long beaks and tongues that enable them to reach into a variety of types of blossoms, and they are able to hover in flight so they can reach flowers that would be otherwise inaccessible. People often think of adaptations as the physical attributes of an organism; however, many species also have evolved a variety of behavioral and mental abilities that also contribute to their survivability. This has been particularly true for humans.

Beginning about 3.5 million years ago, the Earth's climate began a general cooling trend that included increased temperature and humidity fluctuations. This trend probably accelerated the process of human evolution when the demands of finding food and staying warm became more challenging. As our hominid ancestors in the genus *Homo* encountered novel adaptation demands, they evolved a number of characteristics that improved species survivability. For example, we evolved a more efficient form of bipedal locomotion so we could travel longer distances and use less energy getting around. We also evolved improved senses, manual dexterity, and eye-hand coordination and so were able to make use of a wide variety of tools.

Arguably, our most important adaptation was a nervous system built around a large, complex brain. This larger, more complex brain eventually allowed *Homo sapiens* to develop language and sophisticated cultural behaviors, create and use tools, and to become effective at making decisions and solving difficult problems. However, the thing that our large brain allows us to do better than any other species is learn and then share what we've learned with others.

Our ability to learn has enabled us to live everywhere on the planet and to exploit whatever environment we inhabit for food, water, shelter, and energy. We learned how to capture and domesticate other species, and we have developed complex strategies for social contracts and trade. From an evolutionary standpoint, humans have been a wildly successful species—at least up to now. However, we have reached a critical point in the evolution of our species. The crucial question for humanity is this: Will the very adaptations that have led to our previous evolutionary success now lead to our demise and perhaps eventual extinction? Or can those adaptations help us continue to thrive?

Of course, the premise of education for sustainability is that we *can* ultimately learn how to create the conditions that foster well-being for all forever. Yet while our previous adaptations occurred on the order of thousands of years, we now need to learn new survival strategies in a much shorter time frame, perhaps only a few hundred or even a few dozen years. Can our evolved capacity to learn and share what we've learned help us speed up evolution by helping us learn new ways of thinking and behaving?

BOX 6.1 BRAIN (ENERGY) DRAIN

A bigger brain turned out to be an expensive upgrade. Our brain represents only about 2% of total body weight but uses about 20% of the energy our bodies consume. Nature is a scrupulous accountant so for humans to afford an organ that requires such a large share of the bodily energy budget, efficiencies had to be found somewhere else in the system. There are a number of hypotheses about the evolutionary trade-offs that permitted humans to power that bigger brain. For example, one idea is that *Homo* evolved a smaller, more specialized gut that uses less energy, making a larger proportion of the energy we consume available for the brain. We compensated for that smaller, more finicky digestive system by learning to control fire and cook our food, which allowed us to eat meat and other high-energy foods that would otherwise be difficult to digest. Along with the ability to procure and digest higher energy food, we also evolved a greater capacity for storing fat for later use. This combination of adaptations allowed early humans to spend less time foraging for food and more time putting that powerful brain to use solving problems and making decisions.

The overarching goal of education for sustainability is to help learners develop a sustainability worldview—a 21st-century version of what Einstein referred to as a "new type of thinking." This new type of thinking is necessary for people to be able to deal effectively with the uncertainty and complexity embodied in the various challenges humanity faces today and will face in the future. At the same time, a sustainability worldview also is focused on creating conditions that will prevent future problems. Teachers can promote the new type of thinking represented by a sustainability worldview by providing opportunities for students to be become better learners, thinkers, problem solvers, and decision makers.

There are several thinking capabilities that are of particular importance to development of a sustainability worldview. These are:

- Adaptive expertise: The ability to flexibly and creatively apply knowledge in new and unique contexts;
- Critical thinking: Reasoned and reflective thinking to analyze arguments, understand underlying assumptions, judge the credibility of sources, and ultimately to decide what to believe or do;
- Decision making: The process of using knowledge and judgment to select a behavior from among multiple courses of action;
- Systems thinking: A strategy for seeing systems and seeking to understand their behavior; a framework for seeing interrelationships and patterns of change over time; and
- Character strengths: The values and dispositions that contribute to our sense of wellbeing and happiness. We can use our character strengths to enhance our ability to learn, make decisions, and solve problems.

This list is not a taxonomy or a hierarchy of thinking skills and strategies. Rather, these are various ways of using information and thinking about issues that are consistent with the principles, values, and knowledge base associated with sustainability. In this chapter, we will examine the underlying learning processes associated with the development of adaptive expertise. Also, because learning does not occur in isolation from culture and context, we will examine the influences of these factors as well as strategies for promoting a positive future orientation and for learning associated with values. Critical thinking, decision making, systems thinking, and well-being will be examined in later chapters.

Adaptive Expertise

The various challenges often associated with sustainability often are characterized as **wicked problems**. Wicked problems are difficult to define, do not have a clear solution, have multiple causes, are symptoms of other problems, or are unique (Rittel & Webber, 1973). In contrast, tame problems can be defined clearly, and a solution path can be readily identified and implemented. Tame problems can be useful instructional tools in content classes because they allow learners to focus on isolated features, procedures, or processes. Often, students are taught how to solve tame problems by applying a general problem-solving strategy that follows a predetermined set of steps such as the procedure shown in Figure 6.1.

While practice with a general problem-solving strategy *may* help students get better at solving well-defined problems found in traditional subject areas or on standardized tests, tame problem solving does not transfer readily to the real world outside of school. After years of encountering tame school-based problems, people often leave school with two misconceptions that interfere with their ability to deal with real-world, wicked problems: the belief that all problems can be solved and that for any problem, there is a single correct solution.

In the real world, some problems simply cannot be solved. We address these problems by searching for a combination of conditions that is more good and less bad. For example, the loss of an aquifer due to pollution, overextraction, or climate change is not a problem that can be "fixed." Any workaround is going to be a less than satisfactory compromise that will fall far short of qualifying as an actual solution to the loss of a finite and irreplaceable resource. Some problems are unstable or recurrent. As soon as we address one dimension of the problem, another issue pops up, so we end up "re-solving" the problem over and over. Issues involving inequality, changeable or unstable leadership, or scarce resources can follow a cyclical or stepwise pattern; each time a critical threshold is crossed, the

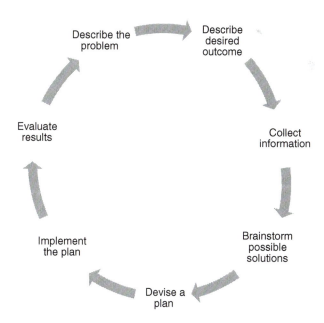

Figure 6.1 General strategy for solving tame problems

problem resurfaces. Some problems have multiple solutions that must be evaluated according to the needs of various stakeholders, and sometimes the best solution for one group is the worst solution for another. The best way to resolve this kind of dilemma might be to find an outcome that ends up making everyone equally unhappy but no one feeling like the loser.

CONSIDER THIS 6.1 WICKED PROBLEMS IN OUR OWN LIVES

Wicked problems can be found in any area of our lives. They can involve personal, family, professional, or community issues. Think about a wicked problem with which you are personally familiar.

- What makes it a wicked problem? Does the problem have any of these characteristics:
  - It is unstable or changes frequently;
  - It involves multiple subproblems that must be solved before the larger one can be tackled;
  - It involves a cyclical pattern so the problem keeps recurring;
  - It involves a scarce or diminishing resource; or
  - It involves stakeholders who have competing goals and interests.
- What are some possible "workarounds" that, while not perfect solutions, create a situation that is less bad and more good?
- How will you know when the problem is "fixed"?

Yet even though wicked problems are complicated, messy, ambiguous, and sometimes fraught with interpersonal conflict, they usually can be tamed, and sometimes we can solve them. However, successful engagement with wicked problems require new ways of thinking beyond "one size fits all" general problem-solving strategies. To this end, for example, Brown, Harris, and Russell (Brown, 2010) have proposed a conceptual framework for dealing with the uncertainty and complexity associated with wicked problems. That framework calls for thinking characterized by:

- *Adaptability*: The ability to change one's mind and course of action when presented with new information. This is not willy-nilly change for change sake, but a purposeful, systematic flexibility in the service of an optimal outcome.
- *Transdisciplinarity*: The ability to apply knowledge and modes of inquiry from multiple disciplines, cultures, and traditions.
- *Inquiry in communities*: The ability to participate as a member of a community that shares a set of norms, language, and goals. Collaborative inquiry attends to value of the knowledge held by the community as a whole.

- *Collective learning:* The recognition that learning and knowledge are situated in larger social contexts. Collective learning often involves an iterative process of question asking focused on values ("what should be?"), information gathering ("what is?"), idea generation ("what could be?"), and testing our ideas ("what can be?) (Brown, 2010).

An educational experience that focuses on the memorization of facts and procedures or the generation of "correct" test answers simply will not prepare students to engage in the kind of collaborative, adaptive, highly flexible thinking necessary to solve wicked problems. Students need to be able to understand and guide their own thinking processes, build and improve upon it, and participate in inquiry communities to make decisions in the face of uncertainty. We can prepare students to engage with the complexity and uncertainty of wicked problems by helping them develop **adaptive expertise**, sometimes referred to as **adaptive competence** (Hatano & Oura, 2003; Bransford, Brown, & Cockling, 1999). This is the ability to "apply meaningfully learned knowledge and skills flexibly, and creatively in a variety of contexts" (De Corte, 2011/12, p. 33). Adaptive expertise can be developed in any knowledge domain, including the content areas typically addressed in formal schooling as well as the more specific domain associated with a sustainability worldview. Transdisciplinary adaptive expertise would involve the ability to apply knowledge from multiple domains flexibly and creatively in a variety of contexts.

Adaptive expertise can be contrasted with routine expertise, which refers to the ability to complete school tasks quickly and accurately but without understanding. Routine experts may get good at a set of core competencies and then continue to apply those same skills with greater and greater fluency and efficiency. However, the range of contexts in which they can apply their expertise is limited, so routine experts often experience difficulty when called upon to apply their competency to new situations or problems. For example, a student may become skilled at plugging variables into a calculator to solve homework problems involving multiplication of expressions with exponents but not be able solve a real-world problem dealing with exponential decay, such as calculating the projected half-life of a pesticide.

Compared to novices (i.e., individuals with little or no background knowledge related to a particular problem) or routine experts, adaptive experts are able to apply their competence in more contextually specific ways, modify their procedures, and even invent new procedures to fit new contexts. Adaptive experts are more likely to continually expand and modify their core competencies in response to new challenges and contexts and are better able to transfer knowledge and skills to new contexts to solve unique problems.

Helping learners develop adaptive expertise has been described as the "gold standard for learning" (Bransford, Derry, Berliner, Hammersmith, & Beckett, 2005), and it should be the aim of education for sustainability. Although development of true expertise in a domain often takes years of experience and practice, teachers can help move all learners toward adaptive expertise by promoting **learning with understanding** (Richhart, Church, & Morrison, 2011).

Learning With Understanding

Learning with understanding is active knowledge construction that leads to meaningful and authentic use of information. Learning with understanding implies flexibility, versatility, and applicability. It helps students see meaningful patterns of information; transfer knowledge and abilities to novel situations; and successfully engage in a variety of thinking processes, including those associated with a sustainability worldview listed at the beginning of this chapter. Learning with understanding might be thought of as the opposite of rote learning, which is often characterized as remembering facts. While learners need to be able to apply facts and concepts across disciplines and in unique contexts to develop novel solutions and strategies, instruction that focuses primarily on recall of specific facts and completion of assignments cannot prepare students to actively engage with the various wicked real-world problems that are the focus of sustainability.

Over the last 30 years, the research on learning and cognition has provided a number of insights about how people learn and the ways teachers can facilitate learning with understanding that moves students toward adaptive expertise (cf. Bransford et al., 1999; Bransford, Derry, Berliner, Hammerness, & Beckett, 2005; Ambrose et al., 2010). Much of that research has focused on the differences between content area experts and novices. Generally, our aim as teachers is not for our students to become experts but rather to help all learners move along a continuum of proficiency so that their thinking and problem solving becomes more like that of experts and less like that of novices. The study of expertise has resulted in a number of key principles about how learning occurs. Knowledge of these principles can help teachers better promote learning with understanding (Ambrose et al., 2010; Bransford et al., 1999):

1. **Students bring a broad range of prior knowledge to a learning situation.** A learner's initial understandings, or **preconceptions**, can include beliefs, skills, facts, and concepts, and it can both help and interfere with new learning. Preconceptions can be helpful when teachers activate students' prior knowledge and link new information to the information students already have. At the same time, by providing opportunities for students to reveal their preconceptions, teachers are able to identify inaccuracies and fill in the gaps. When students' preconceptions are inaccurate or incomplete, they may interfere with development of deeper understanding.

2. **The manner in which learners organize and store information has a direct impact on their ability to retrieve it and apply it.** Learners must have a deep foundation of factual knowledge about a topic, but this information must be stored in a way that facilitates retrieval and use of it for problem

solving and decision making. Experts organize information in knowledge networks in which the nodes are core concepts and big ideas. When information is stored in rich networks with many connections among ideas, it can be retrieved and used more efficiently and automatically.

3. **Learning can be optimized when students use metacognitive strategies to monitor, evaluate, and take control of their acquisition and use of knowledge.** Metacognition helps learners monitor for inconsistencies in their knowledge structures and decide when additional information is needed. Metacognition can entail more than simply reflecting on what one has learned after the fact. When students are actively monitoring their learning before, during, and after learning, they can become skilled users of knowledge and control their learning in the future.

4. **When students have opportunities to learn and use knowledge in a variety of contexts and to engage in authentic intellectual work, they are more likely to transfer learning to novel situations later.** Transfer and flexible use of knowledge are arguably the most important goals for education. Learners must be able to transfer what they learn to future classes as well as to their personal, professional, and civic lives after they leave school. However, transfer is not an automatic process. Transfer of learning is an active process that is enhanced by learning with understanding. Students are more likely to develop flexible understanding of why, when, and how to use knowledge in novel situations if they are encouraged to extract underlying principles, core concepts, and big ideas during initial learning activities.

5. **Student motivation involves the dynamic interaction of social, emotional, and cognitive factors**. Effective learning environments treat knowledge acquisition and motivation as interactive elements that strengthen or weaken one another. Motivation directly influences the direction, intensity, and persistence with which students approach learning. Classroom climate in particular can impede learning or help energize student learning. Culturally and gender-sensitive classrooms and culturally relevant modes of inquiry and knowing can greatly enhance student motivation, particularly historically marginalized students. We will examine culturally responsive teaching strategies in more detail later in this chapter.

The research about how people learn has had a transformative impact on professional teaching practice, and it has direct implications for the professional practice of teaching for sustainability. For example, Darling-Hammond (2008) notes that this research has shown that teachers who are most effective at supporting the process of learning for understanding consistently:

- Promote active learning that engages learners in meaningful activities and prompts them to think about, apply, and test out what they are learning;
- Make explicit connections to students' prior knowledge and provide opportunities for students to surface and test their preconceptions;

- Provide opportunities for students to interact with ambitious and meaningful tasks based on how knowledge is used in real-world contexts;
- Support students' use of metacognitive thinking and strategies to evaluate and guide their own learning; and
- Use ongoing formative assessments to diagnose student understandings and to provide step-by-step scaffolding to guide student learning.

A number of instructional approaches that have these features will be explored in detail in the next chapter.

Approaches that allow learners to engage with real-world problems also can provide opportunities for students to use a variety of *thinking routines* that can be applied across content disciplines and contexts. These are simple strategies, used over and over again, to help direct and guide student thinking (Richhart, Church, & Morrison, 2011). Thinking routines are designed to be incorporated into a teacher's ongoing practice. For example, many teachers use the K-W-L thinking routine (Ogle, 1986) in which students describe what they already **K**now, **W**ant to know, and then later, have **L**earned about a topic. Thinking routines are intended to prompt actions or "moves" that are integral to understanding (Richhart, Palmer, Church, & Tishman, 2006). Richhart and his colleagues at the Harvard Project Zero (Richhart et al., 2011, p. 11) have identified eight thinking moves that can support learning with understanding when teachers provide opportunities for learners to acquire, refine, and apply them in various activities and assignments. These eight thinking moves are:

1. Observing closely and describing what is there;
2. Building explanations and interpretations;
3. Reasoning with evidence;
4. Making connections among ideas;
5. Considering different viewpoints and perspectives;
6. Capturing the heart and forming conclusions;
7. Wondering and asking questions; and
8. Uncovering complexity and going beneath the surface of things.

In their book *Making Thinking Visible*, Richhart et al. (2011) provide step-by-step guidelines for implementing 20 thinking routines that can easily be integrated into the ongoing practice of teaching for sustainability.

Transfer

Before we go any further, we need to take a moment to examine a BIG assumption. This might even be the BIGGEST assumption underlying the entire enterprise of formal education around the world today and throughout history. (This is a really big assumption!)

> Educators often *assume* that what students learn at one time and place will be available to them at some other time and place and that they will use it.

This process that educators are assuming is going to happen is called **transfer**. Transfer can be broadly conceptualized as any situation in which a learner uses what he or she has learned previously.[1] The reason educators place so much faith in transfer is that much of the time this big assumption turns out to be accurate. People often do transfer what they learn in early grades to later school studies, and they do often apply what they learn in school to nonschool contexts. Often, but not always.

The problem with this big assumption is that thinking abilities are not nearly as transferable as many educators would like to believe. Transfer is far from automatic, and it frequently fails. Most teachers are very familiar with the problem of students seeming to have learned something in one context but failing to use it later on. This is a vexing problem for educators, particularly in the context of education for sustainability, which is often concerned with teaching people things now that they will use at some uncertain time in the future to solve problems that have not yet been fully identified. This is why helping students develop adaptive expertise is so important. The ability to apply knowledge and skills flexibly and creatively in a variety of contexts is essential for engaging with wicked real-world problems and with the goal of creating the conditions of well-being now and in the future.

Often we think of knowledge, skills, and procedures as the "what" that is being transferred. However, transfer can involve a variety of constructs, including emotions, dispositions, and learning strategies (Engle, 2012). The "what" being transferred can refer to almost anything that is learned. Sometimes transfer is productive, such as when we use information that was learned previously in a new situation. However, sometimes transfer is unproductive, such as when a negative emotion associated with one situation interferes with learning in a new context or when a solution that worked with one type of problem is inappropriately applied to a different type of problem.

In traditional descriptions of transfer, several conditions must be met for transfer to occur. First, the information to be transferred must have been learned in a way that makes it accessible for use in the new situation. Second, there must be enough similarity between the initial learning situation and the transfer situation for the learned information to be applicable. Third, the learner must recognize that similarity and recognize the applicability of the learned information in the new situation. However, recent expanded theories of transfer indicate that transfer is situational and may be mediated by a variety of external factors such as interactions with the environment, peers, and teachers, suggesting that transfer is far more complex and subtle than was previously thought (Schwartz, Bransford, & Sears, 2005).

There are two types of transfer with which to be concerned: **near transfer** and **far transfer** (Larsen-Freeman, 2013; Perkins & Salomon, 2001). This distance metaphor refers to the degree to which the transfer task resembles the learning situation. Near transfer involves use of well-practiced routines or knowledge in a situation that is similar to the context in which it was learned, such as someone who learns how to read a bar chart in a mathematics class and then uses that skill in a world issues class. Far transfer occurs when the situation in which information is used is very different than the context in which it was learned. Far transfer depends on deliberate, mindful abstraction of knowledge from one context for application in another, such as when someone learns about ecosystems in a biology class and then recognizes the characteristics of an ecosystem in the interdependencies and interaction patterns among people and groups in her own community.

Far transfer can be either **forward reaching** or **backward reaching**. In forward reaching far transfer, a learner abstracts what is learned in one context for use in a later situation (Perkins & Salomon, 2001). For example, a student applies a general problem-solving strategy learned in an algebra class later when working with a community group advocating for more bicycle trails in the city. Backward reaching far transfer occurs when a learner abstracts the characteristics of the current situation and then searches through previous experiences to find knowledge, strategies, or routines that can be applied. For example, when investigating the availability of healthy affordable food in the local community, a student recalls a protocol for asking clarifying questions that was used in her English/language arts class and subsequently incorporates those questions on an interview guide that she uses in her community work.

Instruction that focuses on learning with understanding can aid transfer because it supports the development of flexible, well-organized knowledge structures. It is much easier to access information that is part of a rich network than it is to access something that is stored in a list of disconnected facts. Also, when information is stored in interconnected networks, the learner is better able to recognize similarities among seemingly unrelated contexts and to see recurrent patterns and processes even when those features are subtle or abstract. Teachers can aid in the development of well-organized knowledge networks by helping students see the interconnectedness of ideas within a discipline and by providing many examples in which an idea or concept is applied in diverse contexts. Teachers can also support development of organized knowledge structures by linking new information to learners' prior knowledge and by making the organization of information explicit during instruction. Instructional strategies such as brainstorming, anticipation guides, graphic organizers, and explicit prompting and questioning can surface preconceptions, activate prior knowledge, and help students see how new information relates to previous learning.

Teachers also can directly foster transfer through use of **hugging** and **bridging** (Perkins & Salomon, 2001). Hugging incorporating features of the desired transfer context into the original learning situation. The idea is to facilitate forward reaching transfer by making the learning experience resemble the situations in which the information is likely to be used later. Simulation and modeling can help here; however, it is generally preferable for students to work directly in authentic contexts. Inquiry-based approaches that allow students to grapple with real-world problems are extremely valuable for this purpose.

Bridging refers to the process of mediating backward reaching transfer by making conceptual links between new learning and other applications of this information. Bridging focuses more on helping students develop metacognitive strategies and routines that prompt transfer than on students' direct experience of the similarities among contexts. Directly prompting students to look for general principles that are similar across transfer contexts, encouraging students' metacognitive reflection, and use of analogies are all examples of bridging strategies.

Positive Future Orientation

Education for sustainability is, by definition, focused on the future and thus reliant on effective transfer. However, there are a number of other factors in addition to the success of near and far transfer that affect people's **future orientation**. Future orientation refers to thinking about and acting upon the future. Being future oriented entails having hopes and goals for the future, developing a plan or strategy to meet those goals, and then believing that there is a reasonable chance you will be able to carry out those plans (Nurmi, 1989). Future orientation is a multidimensional construct that includes cognitive, motivational, and affective components (Seginer, 2009). Future orientation is influenced by family and cultural factors (Rarasati, Hakim, & Yuniarti, 2012) as well as by the characteristics of one's immediate community or surroundings (Joireman, Schaffer, Balliet, & Strathman, 2012). Europeans and North Americans tend to be somewhat more future oriented than Chinese (Guo, Ji, Spina, & Zhang, 2012) or Japanese people (Caprara et al., 2012), but individual differences can be found across cultures.

During adolescence, future orientation develops rapidly as people form goals and plans concerning education and career. In general, adolescents who have a hopeful outlook on the future are more likely to make a successful transition to adulthood than those who do not (Arenett, 2000; Nurmi, 1989). However, future orientation seems to be particularly important for at-risk youth. Adolescents with a pessimistic outlook on their future tend to be more likely to engage in problem behaviors (Chen & Vazsonyi, 2013). On the other hand, Stoddard, Zimmerman, and Bauermeister (2011) reported that African American adolescents who demonstrated early risk factors for dropping out of high school but who had higher levels of future orientation are less likely to engage in violent behavior over time.

One dimension of future orientation that has particular relevance in the context of education for sustainability has to do with the extent to which individuals balance current behaviors with future consequences. People vary considerably on this construct, which is known as Consideration of Future Consequences (CFC) (Stratham, Gleicher, Boniger, & Edwards, 1994). At one end of the continuum, we find people who are willing to sacrifice present well-being for future gains. These people believe that future benefits can make certain behaviors desirable, even if they result in discomfort or cost in the short term. On the other end of the continuum, we find people who are focused on their current well-being and are not particularly concerned with future consequences. The willingness to make short-term sacrifices for future benefits is positively correlated with a number of desirable behaviors, such as altruism, healthy eating, exercise, and savings. An individual's level of concern for future consequences is fairly stable over time, but it is context dependent. For example, Carmi (Carmi & Bartal, 2014; Carmi, 2012) found that when people were asked to weigh the risks associated with future environmental threats, such as climate change, against other more immediate threats, such as terrorism or armed conflict, they tended to prioritize the more immediate threats, regardless of the actual risk associated with those threats or the potential for those threats to actually occur.

As with every human trait, the propensity to consider future consequences of current behaviors varies from person to person. The good news is that future orientation is changeable and can be influenced by education. There are a number of ways a positive future orientation can help your students develop a sustainability worldview, but it is important to remember that development of a positive future orientation is not an automatic process. Here are five ways you can help your students develop a positive future orientation.

1. **Help learners see, not just imagine, what a positive future looks like.** Provide clear messages that help students understand what a positive future orientation entails. Expose your students to a wide range of images of positive futures, for themselves and for the larger society. Encourage students to explore personal as well as career goals that are consistent with creating a safe and just space for humanity and other species, and help them broaden their perceptions of what is possible for themselves personally as well as in larger societal contexts. Provide culturally relevant examples that go beyond career and school outcomes and popular media tropes of fame and fortune, and encourage students to explore life paths that are not confined to simplistic gender, race, or cultural stereotypes.

2. **Support learners in development of plans that are likely to result in positive future outcomes.** All children, but particularly adolescents, should be encouraged and guided in development of a future orientation that focuses on positive personal outcomes as well as the larger aims of sustainability. Learners should have opportunities to explore their own fears and concerns, as well as their beliefs interests, hopes, and aspirations. At the same time, provide opportunities for learners to develop realistic goals and plans. These opportunities need to become part of the ongoing learning process and not be relegated to "career exploration" discussions. To develop a

future orientation on a personal level, students need routine opportunities to explore the questions "What do I want?"; "What do I need to do to get there?"; and "Where are my support systems?"

3. **Help learners see that a positive future is a realistic and attainable goal.** In the context of sustainability, learners need to see that a positive future is completely attainable and that it DOES NOT involve a postapocalyptic world in which a select few rise from the ashes to rebuild nor does a positive future require extraordinary heroics to "save the planet." Provide opportunities for students to connect their own current behaviors with positive future outcomes and to develop a sense of the possible. They need to see that a positive future is feasible but it will require focus, diligence, and hard work.

4. **Help learners become better decision makers.** While people can learn strategies and thinking habits that can lead to a positive future orientation, all humans are susceptible to errors of inference. Help students learn strategies and thinking habits that prepare them make realistic assessments of short- and long-term risks so that they can become more effective decision makers. These ideas will be explored in detail in Chapter 8.

5. **Help learners develop agency to bring about a positive future.** A positive future orientation is hopeful but also involves agency. Help your students develop a sense of agency with sustainability issues through thinking strategies and skills that allow them to act directly to create a positive personal and collective future. Make sure your instruction moves beyond teaching *about* sustainability issues and themes to also include strategies and skills that build agency. Your students need to have opportunities to put their own ideas into practice, to learn "hands-on" as well as "minds-on" skills. Project-based learning and service learning, which will be discussed in the next chapter, provide opportunities for students to grapple with real-world issues and at the same time gain a sense of their own abilities and dispositions.

CONSIDER THIS 6.2 YOUR POSITIVE FUTURE

How do you think about your own future? Do you generally have a positive outlook on the future? As you have been thinking about your own sustainability worldview, have you found that your outlook on the future has changed? How could helping your students develop a sustainability worldview help them also develop a more positive future orientation?

Learning and Values

As was discussed in Chapter 3, values are at the center of a sustainability worldview and the larger project of education for sustainability. They influence our political beliefs, our purchasing and consumption decisions, our career choices, the amount of resources we use, and our feelings of personal well-being (Schwartz, 2011).

However, educators often are uncomfortable with the idea of teaching values. Teachers may worry about engaging in a form of indoctrination if they promote values associated with a dominant or colonizing culture, or they may perceive values and moral education as being the purview of religion or family. These concerns are sometimes well founded and often shared by families and religious leaders who prefer to retain responsibility for the moral and values education of children. Therefore, for much of the 20th century, public education around the world was generally viewed as a values-neutral enterprise focused on cognitive notions of academic attainment. Any focus on values was largely restricted to those thought to be associated with good citizenship and civic engagement (Lovat & Toomey, 2009).

Recently, ideas about the role of values in learning have begun to be reassessed as broader definitions of learning have highlighted the importance of affective, social, and emotional domains. As noted earlier in this chapter, learning is now understood as a dynamic process that involves the whole person in deeper forms of intellectual engagement, including communicative capacity, empathy, and self-reflection. At the same time, key characteristics of the learning environment are now understood to be crucial for student attainment, especially for students from poor and otherwise disadvantaged backgrounds. In particular, a trusting and caring environment, positive relationships among students and teachers, and a commitment to meeting the needs of all students are essential (Lovat, Clement, Dally, & Toomey, 2010; Pugh & Telhaj, 2008).

The recent interest in values education has direct implications for education aimed at helping learners develop a sustainability worldview. For example, **positive education** that focuses on character strengths and well-being is at the nexus of values education and academic attainment as well as education for sustainability. We will examine this work in detail in Chapter 10. Recent research has also revealed intriguing findings regarding the relationship of values and decision making. For example, studies across cultures and over time have consistently shown that people try to maintain consistency between their behaviors and values that they consider important (Bardi & Schwartz, 2003; Roccas & Sagiv, 2010; Rokeach, 1973). However, as will be explored in Chapter 8, people do not always act in ways that are consistent with their values. People often make decisions on the basis of inaccurate perceptions and emotional reactions rather than on the basis of a deliberate consideration of the short- and long-term impacts of the decision.

Given the prominent role that values play in education for sustainability, one of the challenges for teachers interested in helping learners develop a sustainability worldview is to avoid approaches that promote uncritical acceptance of a set of a particular values, even those values embedded in documents such as the Universal Declaration of Human Rights and the Earth Charter. Feeling the press of what Martin Luther King (1967) described as the "fierce urgency of now," the temptation may be strong to overtly promote a particular set of values. The risk is that well-meaning values education could, under these circumstances, become superficial, moralizing or, worse, coercive propagandizing.

The goal of values education in the context of education for sustainability is to engage learners in thoughtful consideration of their own values and beliefs and investigation of the values that underlie a sustainability worldview. Teachers can facilitate this process and militate against moralizing and propagandizing by tying values education to the process of critical thinking. A number of instructional strategies for helping learners become effective critical thinkers are described in Chapter 8. Providing opportunities for learners to investigate and critically analyze various values principles, such as those in the Earth Charter, while using critical-thinking processes allows them to draw their own conclusions about the importance and relevance of a particular value for themselves.

Use of classroom dialogues and conversations can also help learners socially construct their understanding and embrace of values. This process moves away from the common I-R-E classroom discussion sequence in which the teacher intiates a discussion with a question, students respond, and then the teacher evaluates. Instead, in dialogic teaching, teachers and learners both make substantial and significant contributions to a conversation so that the learners' thinking on particular ideas or topics is moved forward (Mercer & Littleton, 2007).

In **dialogic teaching**, extended interactions may occur between the teacher and learners. These interactions are intended to allow learners to explore ideas and think together about difficult topics, threshold concepts, and wicked problems that have a values component. The teacher uses these discussions as an opportunity to model communication elements such as inquiry, negotiation, and critical thinking. The teacher facilitates a group discussion through use of norms and rules for participation, turn taking, and respect. Learners participate in a variety of ways, including offering academic knowledge, providing an open and honest reflection, revising their own proposals or ideas, sharing experiences, or establishing practical commitments (Alvarez, 2014).

EXTEND YOUR PROFESSIONAL KNOWLEDGE 6.1

1. Go to Creative Change Educational Solutions (www.creativechange. net/home/).
   a. Investigate the various curriculum resources that are accessible through the website (you will need to create a login ID and password).
   b. Think about how you might be able to use these materials to help your students develop a positive future orientation and sustainability worldview.
2. *Teaching and Learning for a Sustainable Future* is a UNESCO program that provides professional development for teachers, curriculum developers, and education policymakers.

(continued)

Box (continued)

> a. Go to the program website atwww.unesco.org/education/tlsf/mods/
>   theme_gs/mod0a.html.
> b. Investigate the various modules and activities. Think about how you
>   might incorporate some of these activities into your own professional
>   practice.
> c. Look at the *Teaching and Learning Strategies* tab to find more ideas
>   and suggestions for engaging learners in sustainability issues.

Note

1   The discussion of transfer here is based largely on traditional theories of transfer and research validated teaching practices. Recent research is pointing to an expanded and more complex conception of transfer and the factors that affect it. It is likely that expanded theories of transfer will eventually have implications for classroom practices, but a coherent body of practice based on newer notions of transfer has not yet been validated.

References

Alvarez, C.A. (2014). Dialogue in the classroom: The ideal method for values education in multicultural contexts. *Procedia—Social and Behavioral Sciences, 132*, 336–342.

Ambrose, S., Bridges, M., DiPietro, M., Lovett, M., Norman, M., & Mayer, R. (2010). *How Learning Works: Seven Research-Based Principles for Smart Teaching*. San Francisco, CA: Jossey-Bass.

Arnett, J.J. (2000). High hopes in a grim world: Emerging adults' views of their futures and "Generation X." *Youth & Society, 31*, 267–286.

Bardi, A., & Schwartz, S. H. (2003). Values and behaviour: Strength and structure of relations. *Personality and Social Psychology Bulletin, 29*, 1207–1220.

Bransford, J., Brown, A.L., & Cockling, R.C. (1999). *How People Learn: Brain, Mind, Experience, and School*. Washington, DC: National Academy Press.

Bransford, J., Derry, S., Berliner, D. C., Hammerness, K., & Beckett, K.L. (2005). Theories of learning and their role in teaching. In L. Darling-Hammond & J. Bransford (Eds.), *Preparing Teachers for a Changing World: What Teachers Should Learn and Be Able to Do* (pp. 40–87). San Francisco, CA: Jossey-Bass.

Brown, V. A. (2010). Collective inquiry and its wicked problems. In V.A. Brown, J.A. Harris, & J.Y. Russell (Eds.), *Tackling Wicked Problems Through the Transdisciplinary Imagination*. London: Earthscan.

Caprara, G.V., Alessandri, G., Trommsdorff, G., Heikamp, T., Yamaguchi, S., & Suzuki, F. (2012). Positive orientation across three cultures. *Journal of Cross-Cultural Psychology, 43*, 77–83.

Carmi, N. (2012). Caring about tomorrow: Future orientation, environmental attitudes and behaviors. *Environmental Education Research, 19*, 430–444.

Carmi, N., & Bartal, E. (2014). Perception of environmental threat in the shadow of war: The effect of future orientation. *Human and Ecological Risk Assessment: An International Journal, 20*, 872–886.

Chen, P., & Vazsonyi, A. T. (2013). Future orientation, school contexts, and problem behaviors: A multilevel study. *Journal of Youth and Adolescence, 42*, 67–81.

Darling-Hammond, L. (2008). *Powerful Learning: What We Know About Teaching for Understanding.* San Francisco, CA: Jossey-Bass.

De Corte, E. (2011/12). Constructive, self-regulated, situated, and collaborative learning: An approach for the acquisition of adaptive competence. *Journal of Education, 192*(2–3), 33–47.

Engle, R. (2012). The resurgence of research into transfer: An introduction to the final articles of the transfer strand. *Journal of the Learning Sciences, 21*, 347–352.

Guo, T., Ji, L. J., Spina, R., & Zhang, Z. (2012). Culture, temporal focus, and values of the past and the future. *Personality and Social Psychology Bulletin, 38*, 1030–1040.

Hatano, G., & Oura, Y. (2003). Commentary: Reconceptualizing school learning using insight from expertise research. *Educational Researcher, 32*(8), 26–29.

Joireman, J., Schaffer, M., Balliet, D., & Strathman, A. (2012). Promotion orientation explains why future-oriented people exercise and eat healthy: Evidence from the two-factor consideration of future consequences-14 scale. *Personality and Social Psychology Bulletin, 38*, 1272–1287.

King, M. L. (1967, April 4). *Beyond Vietnam: A Time to Break the Silence.* Speech delivered at the Riverside Church, New York.

LaFrenier, P. (2010). *Adaptive Origins: Evolution and Human Development.* New York: Psychology Press.

Lappé, F. M. (2007). *Getting a Grip: Clarity, Creativity, and Courage in a World Gone Mad.* Cambridge, MA: Small Planet Media.

Larsen-Freeman, D. (2013). Transfer of learning. *Language Learning, 63*(1), 107–129.

Lovat, T., Clement, N., Dally, K., & Toomey, R. (2010). Values education as holistic development for all sectors: Researching for effective pedagogy. *Oxford Review of Education, 36*(6), 713–729.

Lovat, T., & Toomey, R. (Eds.). (2009). *Values Education and Quality Teaching: The Double Helix Effect.* Dordrecht: Springer-Verlag.

Mercer, N., & Littleton, K. (2007). *Dialogue and the Development of Children's Thinking.* Routledge: London.

Nurmi, J. E. (1989). Development of orientation to the future during early adolescence: A four-year longitudinal study and two cross cultural comparisons. *International Journal of Psychology, 24*, 195–214.

Ogle, D. M. (1986). K-W-L: A teaching model that develops active reading of expository text. *Reading Teacher, 39*(6), 564–570.

Perkins, D., & Salomon, G. (2001). Teaching for transfer. In A. L. Costa (Ed.), *Developing Minds: A Resource Book for Teaching Thinking* (pp. 370–378). Alexandria, VA: ASCD.

Pugh, G., & Telhaj, S. (2008). Faith schools, social capital and academic attainment: Evidence from TIMSS-R mathematics scores in Flemish secondary schools. *British Educational Research Journal, 34*(2), 235–267.

Rarasati, N., Hakim, M. A., & Yuniarti, K. W. (2012). Javanese adolescents' future orientation and support for its effort: An indigenous psychological analysis. *World Academy of Science, Engineering and Technology, 66*, 597–601.

Richhart, R., Church, M., & Morrison, K. (2011). *Making Thinking Visible How to Promote Engagement, Understanding, and Independence for All Learners.* San Francisco, CA: Jossey Bass.

Ritchhart, R., Palmer, P., Church, M., & Tishman, S. (2006, April). *Thinking routines: Establishing patterns of thinking in the classroom.* Paper presented at the annual conference of the American Educational Research Association (AERA), San Francisco, CA.

Rittel, H., & Webber, M. (1973). Dilemmas in a general theory of planning. *Policy Science, 4,* 155–169.

Roccas, S., & Sagiv, L. (2010). Personal values and behaviour: Taking the cultural context into account. *Social and Personality Psychology Compass, 4,* 30–41.

Rokeach, M. (1973). *The Nature of Human Values.* New York: Free Press.

Schwartz, D.L., Bransford, J., & Sears, D. (2005). Efficiency and innovation in transfer. In J. Mestre (Ed.), *Transfer of Learning from a Modern Multidisciplinary Perspective* (pp. 1–51). Greenwich, CT: Information Age.

Schwartz, S. (2011). Studying values: Personal adventure, future directions. *Journal of Cross-Cultural Psychology, 42,* 307–319.

Seginer, R. (2009). Future orientation in times of threat and challenge: How resilient adolescents construct their future. *International Journal of Behavioral Development, 32,* 272–282.

Stoddard, S.A., Zimmerman, M.A., & Bauermeister, J.A. (2011). Thinking about the future as a way to succeed in the present: A longitudinal study of future orientation and violent behaviors among African American youth. *American Journal of Community Psychology, 48,* 238–246.

Strathman, A. Gleicher, F., David S. Boninger, D.S., & Edwards, C.S. (1994). The Consideration of Future Consequences: Weighing Immediate and Distant Outcomes of Behavior. *Journal of Personality and Social Psychology, 66,* 742–752.

7

POWERFUL PEDAGOGIES

It's not just about hope and ideas, it's about action. . . . Our duty is to have a dream, but to work everyday for reality.

—Shirin Ebadi, 2008

Often, when people think about education for sustainability, what comes to mind is a long list of topics and issues. As a result, teachers sometimes believe that they are unable to incorporate education for sustainability into their daily teaching practice because they are being held accountable to an already overcrowded curriculum to which new content cannot possibly be added. However, one of the most significant findings to emerge over the last decade is that education for sustainability is as much about pedagogy as it is about content. The instructional practices associated with education for education for sustainability have the potential to improve educational outcomes for all students. Far from getting in the way of the work to which teachers are held accountable, the practices associated with the day-to-day work of teaching for sustainability have the potential to help teachers get better at this work.

In fact, the use of **high-leverage instructional practices** is one of the most important and defining characteristics of effective education for sustainability. These are practices that teachers use frequently and, when implemented effectively, can help teachers manage differences among students and advance the learning of all students (Ball, Sleep, Boerst, & Bass 2009; Windschitl et al., 2010). High-leverage instructional practices are useful across subject areas, grade levels, and teaching contexts and, when coupled with reflective and formative strategies, also can support a teacher's continued professional growth (Hatch & Grossman, 2009). Teachers implement high-leverage instructional practices when they:

- Make content explicit by using language and examples carefully, providing clear explanations, and highlighting core ideas.
- Pose carefully phrased questions that elicit, probe, and advance students' thinking about the content.
- Lead whole-class discussions that build collective knowledge and allow students to practice listening, speaking, and interpreting.
- Recognizing and identify common patterns of student thinking and choosing effective strategies to support and extend deeper understanding of principles and concepts.

An **instructional approach** is an integrated *set* of instructional practices that structures the ways in which teachers and students interact with one other, with instructional materials, and with the information to be learned (Corcoran & Silander, 2009). Instructional approaches can be valuable when they bundle together a group of instructional practices that build on one another to enhance learning and facilitate effective implementation of those practices. Generally, an instructional approach can be named, described, observed, replicated, and evaluated. Some examples that we will explore in this chapter include "place-based learning," "project-based learning," "collaborative learning," and "service learning."

The scholarly literature and the broader sustainability discourse reference a bewildering assortment of procedures characterized as "approaches" that have similar names, overlapping purposes, and many shared attributes. Therefore, it can be helpful to think of instructional approaches as belonging to families. The individual members of a family may have unique characteristics, but they all bear a common family resemblance. For example, there are meaningful distinctions between the approaches called project-based learning and problem-based learning, but both are members of the family of approaches called inquiry-based learning (Barron & Darling-Hammond, 2008).

A number of learning processes often associated with education for sustainability were identified in the Wals (2012) and Tilbury (2011) reports discussed in Chapter 3. Those reports indicated that education for sustainability often involves learning that is highly collaborative, active, participatory, and learner centered. Education for sustainability also often involves exploration of real-world problems, learning that occurs outside of traditional classroom settings, and purposeful engagement with communities. This kind of learning can be promoted by five families of approaches:

- Collaborative small-group learning
- Inquiry-based learning
- Experiential learning

- Service learning
- Place-based learning.

We can think of the approaches associated with these five families as high-leverage instructional approaches to teaching for sustainability because they promote improved learning outcomes for all students and because they can promote the kind of learning and thinking associated with a sustainability worldview. We will examine the defining characteristics and commonly encountered members of each of these families of approaches shortly.

Several features common to all five families help make them high-leverage approaches to education for sustainability. First, they all involve **learner-centered teaching** (Weimer, 2013). This is an active learning strategy in which the role of the teacher shifts from deliverer of content to facilitator of learning and the learners assume greater responsibility for and control over their own learning. In her extensive exploration of learner-centered teaching, Weimer (2013, p. 15) described it as a way of teaching that engages students in the hard messy work of learning by giving them control over the learning process. Learner-centered teaching promotes learning for understanding through collaboration and reflection.

Second, all of the families of approaches discussed in this chapter share a common ancestry in John Dewey's writings on the process of inquiry in the role of education in social reform. They also have common roots in more recent constructivist theory. In all five families of approaches, learning is assumed to be an active process in which knowledge is constructed rather than transmitted. Learners actively engage with ideas and issues by creating something, solving problems, performing, writing, or speaking.

Third, these approaches generally focus on outcomes that have value beyond school. Learners engage with real-world problems, questions, and designs that exist outside of the artificial world of classrooms. They see that their contributions have value for some purpose other than the assignment of a grade or fulfillment of a course requirement.

Because they share these features, the five families of approaches are highly complementary and synergistic. For example, experiential learning and inquiry-based learning typically involve some form of collaborative learning. Also, it can be beneficial to shift between approaches as learner needs and priorities change during different phases of the learning process. Thus, a process that begins as experiential learning may transition into a more explicitly project-based approach as learners interact with and problematize a particular situation or issue. Indeed, service learning and place-based learning are actually hybrid models that blend approaches from two or more families. For example, in some contexts, place-based learning can be simultaneously experiential, inquiry based, highly collaborative, and also involve some element of service learning (Smith & Sobel, 2010). This is certainly true of many of the "Smart by Nature" school garden projects described by Stone (2009) and are particularly applicable to the practice of teaching for sustainability.

We turn now to a more detailed examination of the five families of approaches.

Collaborative Small-Group Learning

Collaborative learning refers to a wide variety of arrangements in which learners work together to accomplish learning goals. Most teachers are very familiar with this family of approaches and employ some form of collaborative small-group work on a regular basis. Collaborative small-group learning can be employed in any subject area and at any level, from preschool to university, and as noted earlier, it also is a central feature in the other three families of approaches discussed in this chapter.

As the name implies, all of the variants in this family of approaches involve learners collaborating in some form of structured small group to accomplish individual and group goals. A key feature of this family of approaches is that learners support one another's learning as they work together to accomplish tasks. The approaches in this family emphasize the development of social and collaboration skills in addition to other cognitive or project-related outcomes. Individual learners are expected to participate actively in all group activities, to contribute to group discussions, and to assist with the smooth conduct of group work.

An extensive body of research over the last five decades has demonstrated that working in small groups can enhance problem-solving performance and at the same time provide opportunities for learners to refine their social and language skills as they communicate with one another to share explanations, clarify meanings, and ask questions, particularly when productive interactions are supported by instructional scaffolding (Johnson & Johnson, 2009). Interactive, collaborative group work can help learners develop a sense of shared purpose and an understanding of the value of helping and supporting one another's learning (Gillies, 2003; Gillies & Ashman, 1998). Collaborative group work has consistently been shown to be especially beneficial for racial, ethnic, and linguistic minority learners (Gay, 2002; Ladson-Billings, 1995). For all of these reasons, collaborative group-based learning is an essential feature of education for sustainability.

It is important to distinguish simply working in groups from collaborative learning. Learning can be enhanced when learners work in *carefully planned and well-managed* group configurations as opposed to ad hoc arrangements where learners simply "huddle up" to work on a project together. In order to transform mere group work into collaborative learning, the teacher must act as a facilitator to help learners assume responsibility for their own learning and contribute to the social construction of knowledge. Thus, the success of collaborative group-based learning is dependent on the teacher's ability to accomplish several key tasks (Dillenbourg, 1999):

1. *Set up the initial conditions.* The teacher needs to assume direct responsibility for specifying the conditions that will most likely lead to group success. Often this involves establishment of group size, assignment of members to groups, establishing the rules for group processes and timelines, and clearly specifying the desired outcomes to be accomplished and products to be delivered. When

greater learner autonomy and responsibility is desired, the teacher should scaffold learner's participation in decisions related to setting initial conditions by ensuring that decision criteria and rubrics are employed.

2. *Scaffold effective interactions and collaborative behavior.* The teacher should clearly identify the characteristics of effective collaboration and provide effective models and examples of interactions that reflect those characteristics. Often it is desirable for the learners to participate in the process of developing criteria and rubrics that can scaffold effective collaborative learning and group work. By assuming direct responsibility for the formation of the "rules of engagement" for collaborative work, learners become more invested in adhering to group norms and the success of the group.

3. *Monitor and regulate interactions.* To ensure that all learners benefit, participate, and are heard, the teacher needs to actively monitor and intervene as needed to be sure groups function effectively and continue to address the established standards for collaborative work. When group members are expected to self-regulate their collaborative effectiveness, it is important for the teacher to be sure that they are using tools such as rubrics and checklists effectively and that norms for collaboration and collegiality are being followed.

While all collaborative learning approaches can be considered constructivist in orientation and generally learner centered, they can vary on a number of dimensions, including the extent to which the teacher configures and manages the groups, the intended outcomes for the group work, and the group permanency. Groups can be as small as two individuals working in a dyad or as large as a six-member team, although the benefits associated with group-based learning fade when groups get too large—smaller groups promote active participation of all members and can work more quickly.

The key to success with all collaborative learning approaches is for learners to engage in productive collaboration in which all learners in the group are mutually engaged. As Barron and Darling-Hammond (2008) note,

> [I]f a collaboration is going well (1) many students will be involved in the discussion as contributors and responders; (2) the contributions are coordinated rather than consisting of many independent unrelated conversational turns; (3) there are few instances of off-task behavior; and (4) students attend to each other and to their work in common, as indicated by eye gaze and body position. (p. 27)

Collaborative or Cooperative?

The terms **collaborative** and **cooperative** are often used interchangeably to refer to a wide variety of group-based learning configurations, so the distinctions between these two approaches can sometimes be unclear. The term **collaborative learning** is the broader, superordinate term, while "cooperative learning" refers to a specific set of instructional practices usually associated with the work of Johnson and Johnson (1999), Kagan (1994), and Slavin (1983). Generally, cooperative learning is classroom based and somewhat more teacher directed than other collaborative-learning approaches. It also tends to focus more directly on teacher-selected instructional goals that address foundational social skills or core content. In contrast, collaborative learning usually assumes that learners have mastered the necessary social skills and prior knowledge needed to contribute to group effectiveness. Collaborative learning tends to be less teacher directed, more goal oriented, and less developmental than cooperative learning.

Cooperative learning can be used to help surface preconceptions, focus learners' attention on specific elements of a lesson or project, provide an opportunity for learners to clarify or solidify their understanding of complex ideas, or to ensure that learners have an opportunity to process and work with information learned during a lesson or activity. Some examples of commonly used cooperative learning strategies include *Think-Pair-Share, Jigsaw II, Numbered Heads Together*, and *Roundtable*. These and numerous other cooperative learning strategies have been described extensively and frequently in the professional literature, so they will not be reviewed here.

BOX 7.1 COLLABORATIVE SMALL-GROUP LEARNING FAMILY TRAITS

- Learning occurs in small groups with two to six members
- May entail different degrees of teacher directedness but generally is learner centered; teacher sets up initial conditions and then serves as facilitator
- Can be employed in any discipline and at any level, pre-K to adult
- Duration of groups can range from brief (within one class session) to extended (several weeks)
- Often is an essential element of other instructional approaches
- Focuses on development of social skills and group collaboration skills as well as academic knowledge and skills.

Inquiry-Based Learning

The family of **inquiry-based learning** approaches prompt learners to assume direct responsibility for their own learning by pursuing an inquiry into an authentic, real-world problem. Learners work in small collaborative groups to investigate questions, solve problems, complete projects, or design something. The premise of inquiry-based learning is that when learners engage with a real-world problem, project, or design challenge that is meaningful to them, they are presented with an immediate and compelling context for learning and for using information in more authentic and expert-like ways.

The three inquiry-based learning approaches most commonly encountered are project-based learning, problem-based learning, and design-based learning (Barron & Darling-Hammond, 2008). These approaches bear many more similarities than difference, although each has distinctive characteristics that will be explored shortly. As with the other approaches discussed in this chapter, with inquiry-based learning, the teacher is responsible for establishing the initial conditions and parameters of the inquiry process, facilitating effective collaborative work and group process, and monitoring and intervening as needed to ensure effective group functioning. However, inquiry-based learning is intended to be highly learner centered and often involves student or community-generated projects; high rates of collaboration; and an open-ended process in which learning is guided by the parameters of the specific project, problem, or design being implemented. In this respect, the teacher's role is clearly facilitative rather than central to the learning process.

Inquiry-based learning's focus on authentic, meaningful problems makes this family of approaches ideally suited for use in education for sustainability. Often, the problems and design challenges addressed in inquiry-based learning involve pressing, real-world issues that are also being investigated by disciplinary experts and professionals. This real-world context can be highly motivating for learners and can prompt **productive disciplinary engagement** that is marked by four characteristics (Engle & Conant, 2002):

First, learners are encouraged to **problematize** what they are studying. This means they are to ask questions, challenge assumptions, and make alternative proposals. Information previously assumed to be factual is recast as a claim that must be examined and that needs to be supported by evidence and explanation. Problematizing does not entail simply looking up information on the Internet or asking an expert but instead prompts learners to challenge the accuracy and meaning of authoritative sources by assembling a compelling body of evidence based on their own investigation.

Second, productive disciplinary engagement means learners are granted authority as "experts" in the area they are investigating. This means they have a direct and primary role in defining and investigating the problem, and the other members of the learning community, including the teacher, identify them with their claims and explanations. In other words, they become the local authority on their particular topic or problem. Often, this authority rests with a particular collaborative small group within the larger class, but it also could apply to individual learners or to an entire class or a larger community of learners that extends beyond the class.

Third, learners are held accountable to the others in the local community and to the norms of the discipline. This means their work must be responsive to intellectual standards regarding sources of evidence and the basis for claims. They would be expected to investigate relevant sources of information and to consult with others in the course of investigating a problem and to accurately cite sources. They also would be expected to respect the social and disciplinary norms of the community and to support the learning of others in the community.

Fourth, learners must be provided with sufficient resources to pursue their investigations. This means they need to have sufficient time allocated for group work; access to technology, books, and other reference sources; and support for field-based, outside-of-the-classroom work, as needed. It is particularly important for learners to have access to models of discipline-based practices and sources. For example, if a group is working on a design for a water filter to be used in a rural village, it might be important for them to be able to communicate directly with people in that village or to consult with a public health specialist or an engineer.

BOX 7.2 INQUIRY-BASED LEARNING FAMILY TRAITS

- Learner centered, teacher sets up initial conditions and then serves as facilitator, but learners are responsible for their own learning
- Entails collaborative small-group learning
- Learners pursue a challenge or inquiry that focuses on a meaningful real-world problem or issue
- Requires extended engagement with a challenge (problem, project, design, etc.); generally more than a single class session
- Requires application and transfer of previous learning as well as acquisition of new knowledge and skills
- The project, problem, or design *is* the curriculum, not simply an activity or assignment within a unit or lesson
- Often entails work outside of the traditional classrooms and across multiple disciplines
- Immerses learners in the culture and norms of a discipline or profession. Often involves application of authentic disciplinary tools and strategies.

The features in common to all members of the inquiry-based learning family are summarized in Box 7.2. As this list suggests, there is a strong family resemblance among the members of the inquiry-based learning family. In all of these approaches, learners are presented with a "challenge" that becomes the focus of an extended inquiry. This inquiry then becomes the "curriculum" for the class or classes in which the approach is being implemented, not a peripheral assignment or activity. The key differences among the approaches primarily have to do with the nature of the challenge and the expected outcomes of the inquiry (Larmer, 2014; Savery, 2006).

In problem-based learning, the challenge takes the form of an ill-structured but somewhat well-defined problem (Savery, 2006). Typically, the problem is based within a particular content area or discipline; frequently, it is posed by the teacher. Problem-based learning is used frequently in professional schools in fields such as medicine, architecture, engineering, and business and increasingly disciplinary high school and university-level classes, for example, in mathematics and the sciences. Learners work in collaborative groups to develop a reasoned response to the problem (if not an actual solution) and then present the results of their inquiry in a report or presentation. The problem to be investigated usually takes the form of an authentic case or dilemma that is typically encountered by professionals working in the field or discipline. The response or solution is expected to use discipline-based or professional knowledge and procedures to focus on the parameters of the specific problem. In this respect, problem-based learning tends to be somewhat more narrowly constrained than project-based learning.

With project-based learning, the "project" that forms the challenge also may take the form of a problem or dilemma, but it often is messier, more open ended, and more interdisciplinary than the challenges encountered in problem-based learning. The outcome of a project-based learning inquiry typically is more involved and multidimensional than the case analysis or solution descriptions generated in problem-based learning. As a result, project-based learning tends to be of longer duration and involve application of a broader knowledge base than problem-based learning. For example, a project-based learning inquiry focusing on storm water runoff in a community might culminate in a report presented to city planners, a presentation at a neighborhood association meeting, and a proposal for a public education campaign. A problem-based inquiry addressing the same problem might be more narrowly focused on the challenge of estimating the maximum capacity that would be necessary for a drainage system that could handle the runoff of several properties in a particular neighborhood.

In design-based learning, the task is to design, if not to create, a physical object that addresses a particular challenge or dilemma. Frequently, design-based learning focuses on science, technology, engineering, or math (STEM) related projects such as, for example, to design a robot that can perform certain tasks or a bridge that can withstand a particular weight load. However, increasingly, design-based learning is being applied to sustainability-related projects that have real-world implications. For example, a design-based learning activity might focus on the redesign and "upcycling" of materials that might otherwise be discarded or recycled.

Most likely, inquiry-based learning would be consistent with an instrumental perspective on education for sustainability, particularly when the inquiry is project or design focused and addresses a real-world need or challenge. When the inquiry focuses on a hypothetical or simulated problem, for example a case analysis used only for instructional purpose, as opposed to a "live" real-world issue, inquiry-based learning would more likely be consistent with an intrinsic perspective on education for sustainability.

CONSIDER THIS 7.1 PROBLEMATIZING SUSTAINABILITY

Identify two or three issues and challenges in your community that could be the basis for inquiry-based learning for your students.

1. How could inquiry-based learning related to these issues create opportunities for your students to practice the elements of a sustainability worldview (values, knowledge, dispositions, agency)?
2. How could inquiry-based learning based on these issues involve sustainability big ideas?

Experiential Learning

Experiential learning is a process that engages learners in direct experiences accompanied by focused reflection for the purpose of increasing knowledge, developing skills, clarifying values, and developing one's capacity to contribute to their community (Association of Experiential Education, 2014). Generally, experiential learning is consistent with the intrinsic perspective on education for sustainability described in Chapter 5. The purpose of experience in this context is not to provide learners opportunities to practice a specific set of skills but rather to serve as a mechanism for broader transformative learning.

Experiential learning is an amalgamative philosophy of education based on the work of Kurt Lewin, John Dewey, Jean Piaget, Carl Rogers, and Paulo Freire, among others. Most current applications of experiential learning are based on six propositions that follow from the work of these earlier theorists. These propositions form the basis of a theory of experiential that has been most fully articulated by David Kolb (Kolb, 1984; Kolb & Kolb, 2005):

1. *Learning is best conceived as a process, not in terms of outcomes.* Ideas are not fixed but are formed and revised based on interactions with the environment.
2. *All learning is relearning.* Learning is best facilitated by a process that provides students opportunities to surface preconceptions and beliefs so they can be examined, tested, revised, and integrated with new learning.
3. *Learning requires a resolution of conflicts between dialectically opposed modes of adaption to the world.* The process of learning involves moving between reflection and action and the resolution of tensions and conflicts that arise between our abstract constructions of the world and the concrete reality of experience.
4. *Learning is a holistic process of adaptation to the world.* It is not just a cognitive process in which one acquires knowledge passively but involves the whole person—thinking, feeling, perceiving, and doing.
5. *Learning results from a synergistic transaction of the person and the environment.* The learner is not merely interacting with the environment mechanistically, but instead both the environment and the learner undergo change. The learner's

personal characteristics, behaviors, and environmental influences operate in a
reciprocal relationship.
6. *Learning is the process of creating knowledge.* Learning is seen as a social and constructivist process in which knowledge is created and shared in communities
rather than transmitted from teacher to student.

Experiential learning should not be confused with unassisted discovery learning in which learners are expected to develop conceptual understanding while
receiving little, if any, assistance from the teacher. While "discovery" of new insights
or understandings is an underlying goal of experiential learning, the teacher is
expected to play a direct role in assisting or enhancing this process. Minimally,
experiential education involves at least two components—learners engage in
the experience and then reflect on it. However, often experiential learning is
described as occurring in cycles in which the learners:

1. Engage in the experience;
2. Review and reflect on the experience; and
3. Plan for the next experience, which ideally would entail some form of transfer to new or more challenging contexts.

Additional steps in this process can involve more in-depth analysis of the experience, sharing one's findings and reflections with others, or making explicit generalizations to other contexts.

Experiential learning typically involves the following features, implemented
through some form of collaborative learning:

*   The teacher carefully chooses or structures a set of authentic experiences that
require learners to take initiative, make decisions, and be accountable for results.
Often, the learners are directly involved in this selection process because the experiences should be personally significant or appealing to them. Also, the experience
should involve the whole person. Experiences that engage all of the senses can be
far more salient and transformative than those that merely engage the intellect.
*   Once the experience is selected, the teacher functions as a facilitator for the
learning process by posing problems and guiding questions and by safeguard-
ing learners' physical and emotional safety. In many situations, the teacher is
a coparticipant or "guide alongside" in the experience and engages in her or
his own reflective process along with the learners.
*   Learners actively engage in a process of posing questions, investigating,
experimenting, and constructing meaning. Curiosity, experimentation, creativity, risk taking, and problem solving are encouraged and supported in
this process, as the experience itself serves as the source for new inquiry and
learning. The teacher can support this process by helping learners clarify
assumptions and expectations, explore alternatives, and pose new questions.

- Before, during, and after the experience, learners are encouraged to engage in reflection and critical analysis. Learners should be supported in exploring their own values and investigate the ways their beliefs and understandings have changed as a result of the experience.
- As the learners are engaged with the experience, the teacher also needs to be aware of her or his biases, beliefs, and preconceptions and the influence these may have on the learning process. Again, as a coparticipating guide alongside, the teacher can lend insights about her or his own perceptions and changing thinking.

Experiential learning is an implicit element of both the Montessori and Reggio Emilia approaches (Edward, 2002) as well as many independent schools conceived as alternatives to the more regulated and structured public school curricula. Similarly, many youth development organizations, including 4-H and the various scouting organizations such as Girl Guides, Girl Scouts, and Boy Scouts, employ an experiential-learning approach.

Experiential learning frequently is used in nonformal environmental and outdoor education programs where the experiences can range from brief encounters with nature in an urban park to extended wilderness adventures. It is particularly well suited for the investigation of environmental subjects because human behaviors are involved in most environmental issues. The pairing of direct, hands-on experiences in nature with the process of reflection can help learners become more acutely aware of their own interaction with the natural world and the impact of their behaviors.

However, experiential learning does not need to be nature focused, and there is almost no limit on what can serve as an experience or the settings in which it can occur. For example, the performing or visual arts can provide opportunities for powerful experiences that can serve as the basis for transformative learning. Dramatic productions, spoken word events, mural projects, or film/video projects all can serve as the basis for experiential learning.

CONSIDER THIS 7.2 FOOD DESERT

A number of students in your school live in a food desert. Their neighborhood is served only by fast food restaurants and convenience stores, so few healthy, fresh, affordable food options are available for families that do not have access to private transportation. The nearest grocery store that sells fresh food is five miles away. The neighborhood is bordered by multilane highways with no sidewalks or bicycle lanes. The public bus stops in the neighborhood about once an hour. The students have noticed that many of their family members suffer from obesity, diabetes, and heart disease. The

students want to develop a project to help bring healthy food to their neighborhood, and they have asked for your help.

1. Do you think these students are addressing a wicked problem? Why or
    why not? Is there more than one problem involved?
2. How could this issue become the basis for inquiry-based teaching?
3. What are some options the students could consider as they engage with
    this issue?
4. How might you provide opportunities for students to make use of eight
    high-leverage thinking moves, described in Chapter 6, as they engage
    with this project?

Service Learning

Service learning is the intentional combination of meaningful community-based
service with academic learning so that the learners and community partners benefit equally. Learners receive academic credit for participating in an organized
service activity that meets a community need and, through reflection on the activity, develop a deeper understanding of academic coursework that is linked to
the service-learning experience. This meaningful community-based engagement
gives learners a better understanding of themselves and the broader contexts that
surround various societal issues and challenges.

As noted earlier, service learning is a hybrid model. It is based largely on Kolb's
(1984) conception of experiential learning but includes elements of inquiry-based
learning. The assumption in service learning is that the learner provides more
than just enthusiasm and an extra set of hands but also contributes know-how,
creativity, and problem-solving abilities. Through development of a reciprocal,
mutually beneficial relationship between the learner and community partner, a
well-designed service-learning activity can be a transformative experience that
challenges learners to rethink their perspectives and assumptions and to believe
that they can make a difference (Sessa, Grabowski, & Shashidhar, 2013).

Service learning can involve a wide variety of partners including
community-based organizations, business, families, and individual community
members. The partnership is intended to be mutually beneficial, collaborative, and to meet a community need. Service learning can involve collaborative
small-group learning in which a group works together to provide a service to a
community partner; however, service learning often involves an individual learner
working independently with the community partner over an extended period of
time. Under these circumstances, the learner can become more directly engaged
in the culture and the norms of the community partner, and a much richer collaboration can develop between the service learner and the community partner.

Service learning has been studied extensively over the past two decades in both
higher education and at the elementary and secondary levels. This body of research

indicates that service learning is particularly well suited for use in education for sustainability (Community Works Institute, 2010). Well-designed service-learning experiences help can improve learners' abilities to evaluate differing perspectives and complex situations, think critically, understand social issues, and exercise better judgment and decision making (Felten & Clayton, 2011). Learners enact a sustainability worldview as they grapple directly with various sustainability issues and big ideas at the community level and engage directly with positive solutions and strategies for addressing sustainability-related challenges.

The research on service learning has helped elucidate its key characteristics as well as the conditions under which it is most effective. Depending on the nature of the service project and the needs of the community partner, a service-learning experience usually includes five core components (Berger-Kaye, 2010, pp. 16–18):

1. *Investigation.* The individuals who are to engage in a service-learning experience begin by researching the community of interest to identify needs and challenges. Through this process, the learners choose the issues they want to address and identify community partners with whom they would like to work. The investigation stage of service learning also includes an assets assessment in which learners identify their own interests, skills, and talents and think about how these assets can be applied in a service experience. At the same time, it can be useful to conduct an inventory in the community to similarly identify the pool of talents, skills, and more tangible assets that can be mobilized. A variety of research and reporting processes are often employed during this stage, including surveys, neighborhood inventories, and development of indicator systems that can be used later to assess progress and success. For example, the *Healthy Neighborhood Healthy Kids Guide* from Shelburne Farms (Tillman, 2007) is an outstanding resource for facilitating this process.

2. *Planning and Preparation.* Having identified needs and assets, the learners research and explore in more depth the issues that surfaced during the investigation stage. The goal of this stage is to gather information and resourc es that will enable the learners to directly engage in productive service. Learners may examine a variety of primary source documents, conduct interviews, or identify various resources that can help them investigate the issues they hope to address through service learning.

3. *Action.* Having completed their preparation and planning, the learners begin to work actively to address the issues or needs previously identified. Depending on the project, the plan may be carried out in a single day or may extend for as long as an entire academic year. This stage often involves a continuation of the learning processes begun during the investigation and preparation stages as learners refine and apply their knowledge and skills. At the same time, they often develop a much deeper understanding of community contexts and perspectives as they work side by side with community partners and agencies. Also, the process of translating a plan into tangible action leads to a more complex and elaborated understanding of the issues they may have previously only known about through academic research and reading.

4. ***Reflection.*** The process of reflection continually occurs throughout the investigation, planning, and action phases. Through reflection, learners connect the knowledge and skills learned through the service activity to their own personal growth and developing sustainability worldview. They place their tangible and sometimes challenging experiences in a broader community and global context and begin to see that their own actions can have a direct and lasting impact. At the same time, the reflection process helps learners think about the effectiveness of their planning processes as well as their effectiveness in working with the community partner. Through reflection, learners identify areas in which they want to grow further personally and think about what elements of their plans they might change another time.

5. ***Demonstration/Celebration.*** During this final stage of the process, learners share what they have learned and accomplished with interested stakeholders. Demonstrations can take a variety of forms including presentations, exhibits, performances, letters, written reports, etc. Typically, the demonstration process involves sharing information with the community partner as well as classmates, teachers, and other interested members of the community such as the media and policymakers. Often, the demonstration process includes a celebration of accomplishments as well as the process and partnership itself.

Service learning can be a powerful process for linking traditional curriculum goals and standards to sustainability principles and concepts and for helping learners develop and enact a sustainability worldview.

Place-Based Learning

Place-based learning uses the local community as the integrating context for learning. Often with place-based learning, the local community is construed as including the natural and built environments, the people and other species that live there, cultural and historical aspects, and sociopolitical situations. Place-based learning is a hybrid model that includes elements of inquiry-based learning, experiential learning, and service learning. This approach prompts learners to "engage the local" by generating questions, investigating issues, and seeking solutions to local problems (Demarest, 2014). This process of asking questions about one's place can be a transformative experience as learners begin to see themselves and understand broader social and global issues in the context of their local place. At the same time, inquiring about one's place can inspire learners to action and development of service-learning projects aimed at addressing the problems and issues that surfaced. Those problems can take the form of environmental issues, human equity and justice issues, or social and economic issues. By entering into the inquiry through the lens of one's local place, learners often see the interconnectedness among these issues in ways that they are not evident when those issues are examined in isolation or as academic subjects.

In many respects, place-based learning is more of a philosophical approach to teaching than a specific set of procedures or a curriculum framework. The key to place-based learning is to prompt learners to ask questions about their local community and then to let those questions direct future inquiry. Here is how to get started:

1. Prime the pump with a vivid learning experience tied to the local community. This could take many forms including a field trip, a guest speaker, a primary source document from a local museum or historical society, or a discussion about a current issue or event in the community.
2. Prompt learners to explore their local community by posing questions that require them to think about their own relationship to place. For example
   a. How does this place make you feel?
   b. What is worth preserving here?
   c. What would happen if . . . ?
   d. What is at risk here?
   e. Is this a place where you want to spend time?
3. Once learners start thinking about the local community through the lens of place-based questions, engage them in their own inquiry about the community. This process can employ the strategies associated with experiential learning (experience, reflect, plan for the next experience); service learning (investigate, plan, act, reflect, demonstrate), or inquiry-based learning (problematize the local place, investigate, develop a project, share results).
4. As a "guide on the side," help learners think about all the dimensions of their local place. Create opportunities for them to work in small collaborative groups and to engage in meaningful reflection about their experiences.
5. Help learners see the explicit links among local issues and sustainability big ideas. Use the local place as a context for exploring threshold concepts such as interconnectedness and intergenerational equity. Connect their exploration of local place to Earth Charter principles such as those pertaining to protecting and caring for the community of life (1–4); ecological integrity (5–8); social and economic justice (9–12); and democracy, nonviolence, and peace (13–16).

EXTEND YOUR PROFESSIONAL KNOWLEDGE 7.1

Return to the *Facing the Future* website (www.facingthefuture.org/).

1. Click on the Issues and Solutions tab and find *Take Action! Project Database* link.
2. Investigate the various projects listed in the database.
3. How could you use these resources to help your students engage with sustainability issues? Think about ways that you could employ learner-centered strategies to help your students explore these projects.

References

Association of Experiential Education. (2014, August). What is experiential education? Retrieved from: www.aee.org/about/whatIsEE

Ball, D.L., Sleep, L., Boerst, T.A., & Bass, H. (2009). Combining the development of practice and the practice of development in teacher education. *Elementary School Journal, 109,* 458–474.

Barron, B., & Darling-Hammond, L. (2008). How can we teach for meaningful learning? In L. Darling-Hammond (Ed.). *Powerful Pedagogy: What We Know About Teaching for Understanding.* San Francisco, CA: John Wiley & Sons.

Berger-Kaye, C. (2010). *The Complete Guide to Service Learning.* Minneapolis MN: Free Spirit.

Community Works Institute. (2010). *Connecting Service-Learning to the Curriculum: A Workbook for Teachers and Administrators.* Shelburne, VT: Author.

Corcoran, T., & Silander, M. (2009). Instruction in high schools: The evidence and the challenge. *Future of Children, 19*(1), 157–183.

Demarest, A. (2014). Our Curriculum Matters: What Is Place-Based Education? Retrieved from: www.ourcurriculummatters.com

Dillenbourg, P. (1999). What do you mean by collaborative learning? In P. Dillenbourg (Ed.), *Collaborative Learning: Cognitive and Computational Approaches.* New York: Pergamon.

Ebadi, S. (2008). *The Nobel Women's Initiative 2008 Annual Report.* Ottawa: Author.

Edward, C.P. (2002). Three approaches from Europe: Waldorf, Montessori, and Reggio Emilia. *Early Childhood Research & Practice, 4,* 17–24.

Engle, R.A., & Connant, F.R. (2002). Guiding principles for fostering productive disciplinary engagement: Explaining an emergent argument in a community of learners classroom. *Cognition and Instruction, 20,* 399–483.

Felten, P., & Clayton, P.H. (2011). Service learning. *New Directions for Teaching and Learning, 128,* 75–84.

Gay, G. (2002). Preparing for culturally responsive teaching. *Journal of Teacher Education, 53,* 106–116.

Gillies, R.M. (2003). The behaviours, interactions, and perceptions of junior high school students during small-group learning. *Journal of Educational Psychology, 95,* 137–147.

Gillies, R.M., & Ashman, A.F. (1998). Behavior and interactions of children in cooperative groups in lower and middle elementary grades. *Journal of Educational Psychology, 90,* 746–757.

Hatch, T., & Grossman, P. (2009). Learning to look beyond the boundaries of representation: Using technology to examine teaching (Overview for a digital exhibition: learning from the practice of teaching). *Journal of Teacher Education, 60,* 70–85.

Johnson, D.W., & Johnson, R. (1999). *Learning Together and Alone: Cooperative, Competitive, and Individualistic Learning* (5th ed.). Boston, MA: Allyn & Bacon.

Johnson, D.W., & Johnson, R.T. (2009). An educational psychology success story: Social interdependence theory and cooperative learning. *Educational Researcher, 38,* 365–379.

Kagan, S. (1994). *Cooperative Learning.* San Juan Capistrano, CA: Kagan Cooperative Learning.

Kolb, A.Y., & Kolb, D.A. (2005). Learning styles and learning spaces: Enhancing experiential learning in higher education. *Academy of Management Learning & Education, 4,* 193–212.

Kolb, D.A. (1984). *Experiential Learning: Experience as the Source of Learning and Development.* Englewood Cliffs, NJ: Prentice Hall.

Ladson-Billings, G. (1995). Toward a theory of culturally relevant pedagogy. *American Educational Research Journal, 32*(3), 465–491.

Larmer, J. (2014). Boosting the power of projects. *Educational Leadership, 72*, 42–46.

Savery, J.R. (2006). Overview of problem-based learning: Definitions and distinctions. *Interdisciplinary Journal of Problem-based Learning, 1*(1).

Sessa, V.I., Grabowski, S., & Shashidhar, A. (2013). Service-learning pedagogy, civic engagement, and academic engagement: Multiple bidirectional relationships in college freshmen. *International Journal of Research on Service-Learning and Community Engagement, 1*, 23–46.

Slavin, R.E. (1983). *Cooperative Learning*. New York: Longman.

Smith, G.A., & Sobel, D. (2010). *Place- and Community-Based Education in Schools*. New York: Routledge.

Stone, M.K. (2009). *Smart by Nature: Schooling for Sustainability*. Healdsburg, CA: Watershed Media.

Tilbury, D. (2011). Education for sustainable development: An expert review of processes and learning. Paris: UNESCO.

Tillman, T. (2007). *Healthy Neighborhoods/Healthy Kids Project Guide*. Shelburne VT: Shelburne Farms.

Wals, A.J.E. (2012). *Shaping the Education of Tomorrow: 2012 Full-Length Report on the UN Decade of Education for Sustainable Development*. Paris: UNESCO.

Weimer, M. (2013). *Learner Centered Teaching: Five Changes to Practice*. San Francisco, CA: Jossey-Bass.

Windschitl, M., Thomson, J., Braaten, M., Stroupe, D., Chew, C., & Write, B. (2010, April). *The beginner's repertoire: A core set of instructional practices for teacher preparation*. Paper presented at the annual meeting of the American Educational Research Association, Denver, CO.

SECTION III

Learning and Thinking for Sustainability

8

CRITICAL THINKING AND DECISION MAKING

If the world were merely seductive, that would be easy. If it were merely challenging, that would be no problem. But I arise in the morning torn between a desire to improve (or save) the world and a desire to enjoy (or savor) the world. This makes it hard to plan the day.

—E.B. White, 1969

Every day, each of us commits a small act of oppression, a small act of theft, or even a small act of murder when we make decisions that diminish opportunities for others to enjoy a safe and just life, now or in the future. Challenges such as climate change, racism, war, overconsumption, and inequity are not the inevitable result of mysterious forces beyond our control. These challenges are actually the result of human decisions—the decisions each of us makes every day. Climate change is occurring because many people in the world have decided that it is an acceptable cost for the privilege of turning the ignition key on a gas-guzzling automobile or consuming a hamburger made of feedlot-raised beef. Racism occurs because many people have decided that it is an acceptable cost for the comfortable path of silence and inaction. Crushing poverty occurs because many people have decided that hunger, privation, and death are acceptable costs for the privilege of overconsumption and profligate consumerism.

If we hope to improve the quality of our collective decision making, we need to first improve the quality of our individual decision making. Unfortunately, people often do not realize that the choices they make on a day-to-day basis really do have profound impacts. For that matter, many people do not even realize they are making those choices. However, the combined effect of many small decisions can add up to big collective impacts, and some of our collective decisions will have profound implications for generations to come. The decisions we make about the variables that directly affect our own lives interconnect with larger, planetary systems. Yet, it is not too difficult to see that our individual decisions about the food we eat, the clothes we wear, how we dispose of our waste, where we live, and how we transport ourselves have local, global, environmental, social, and economic impacts.

The good news is that we can all learn how to make better, wiser decisions, even under challenging circumstances. This is why **critical thinking** and **decision making** are crucial elements of a sustainability worldview. When we see interconnectedness, we begin to see that our own decisions matter. When we come to understand that we choose our beliefs, we choose our behaviors, and we choose our way of being in the world, we can begin to act in ways that are less harmful, more peaceful, and more likely to preserve opportunities for a healthy and satisfying life for others around the planet now and in the future.

Perhaps more importantly, children can begin learning at an early age how their decisions affect others, how to learn from their own experiences, and how to make wise choices. As a teacher at any grade level, you can help your students learn to make better decisions about their own lives and the way they contribute to their larger communities. At the same time, as you refine your own sustainability worldview, you will find it helpful to understand the processes that affect your own decision making in the classroom as well as in your life outside of schools.

Critical thinking and decision making are intertwined processes. In its simplest sense, critical thinking is the process of conducting an objective and reasoned analysis in order to make a judgment or decide what to believe. Decision making is the process of using knowledge to select a behavior from among multiple courses of action that initially appear equal. However there are a number of complexities lurking below the surface of these simple definitions. First, critical thinking is not an abstract exercise—it is thinking *about* something and for a purpose and usually leads to a decision. Therefore, we might thinking of critical thinking as part of the decision making process. Second, the quality of one's critical thinking and decision making depend to great extent on the flexibility and organization of one's background knowledge. Learning with understanding and development of adaptive competence are essential supports for effective critical thinking and decision making. At the same time, critical thinking and decision making are informed by values and beliefs as much as by facts and concepts. Indeed, frequently, critical thinking focuses on clarification of one's own biases and assumptions. Third, critical thinking and decision making are susceptible to a variety of errors of inference that often operate below our level of awareness. As a result, even when we think we're being careful and thoughtful, we sometimes exercise poor judgment or make poor decisions without even realizing that we are doing so. It is only later, in hindsight, that we realize we could have chosen differently or that we have not weighed all options or arguments effectively. Finally, as with other thinking processes, individuals vary in their ability to think critically, but critical thinking is an intentional cognitive process that can be learned and practiced. In this chapter, we will explore the cognitive processes that underlie effective critical thinking and decision making and examine ways you can help the learners with whom you work become better at these thinking processes that are so vital to a sustainability worldview.

Critical Thinking

Descriptions of critical thinking tend to derive from two compatible but slightly different perspectives: those that focus on the *critical* part of critical thinking and those that focus on the *thinking* part of critical thinking. Descriptions that focus on *critical* thinking generally are associated with the critical perspective discussed in Chapter 5. This perspective, based on critical theory, has its roots in enlightenment goal of **critical reasoning**—reasoning for the purpose of creating a harmonious and benevolent society. According to this perspective, critical thinking is a tool of social inquiry focused on transforming societies so that they become less dominating and more democratic. The aim of critical thinking from this perspective is to "explain what is wrong with current social reality, identify the actors to change it, and provide both clear norms for criticism and achievable practical goals for social transformation" (Bohman, 2013, p. 23). Contemporary notions of critical thinking often focus on the dispositions associated with "being a critical thinker" in addition to the underlying thinking skills involved in the process of "engaging in critical thinking."

As discussed in Chapter 5, critical theory has had considerable influence in the broader environmental and social activism communities and is the most prominent perspective in fields such as environmental justice, eco-feminism, multi-cultural education, and education for social justice. Thus conceptions of critical thinking within the sustainability discourse often reflect a critical perspective. For example, the Wals (2012) study describes critical thinking-based learning as a process that:

> [E]xposes and questions the assumptions and values people, organizations and communities live by and challenges their merit from a particular normative point of view (e.g. animal well-being, eco-centrism, human dignity, sustainability) to encourage reflection, debate and rethinking those assumptions and values. (p. 29)

Descriptions that focus on critical *thinking* generally refer to a multicomponent phenomenon that includes a variety of dispositions, values, and cognitive skills possessed by critical thinkers. For example, Beyer's (1995) list of essential elements of critical thinking includes:

*   Dispositions (habitual ways of behaving or habits of mind);
*   Applying criteria to make judgments;
*   The ability to form a reasoned argument that is supported by evidence;

- Making inferences and drawing conclusions from facts and assumptions;
- Examining issues from multiple points of view; and
- Making use of variety of procedures such as asking questions, making judgments, and identifying assumptions.

According to Beyer, critical thinking involves "the complex and often simultaneous interaction of these elements in the search for the most accurate understanding of an object, condition, event, action, or other phenomenon" (p. 10).

Similarly, Leicester (2010) identifies three types of reflection associated with critical thinking, each of which involves multiple aspects.

Questioning reflection is focused on developing a complete understanding of the various dimensions of an issue. Aspects of questioning reflection include:

- Recognizing and questioning assumptions and implicit values;
- Being cautious about generalization;
- Noticing the context in which an issue is set;
- Exploring alternatives and alternative points of view;
- Adopting a reflective, critical stance as a regular practice; and
- Forming your own informed point of view.

Rational reflection is focused on the use of evidence and logic to explore an issue. Aspects of rational reflection include:

- Respecting and seeking worthwhile knowledge and understanding;
- Understanding primary and secondary sources of knowledge;
- Seeking evidence for one's belief;
- Recognizing valid and invalid arguments;
- Becoming lifelong learners.

Meta-analytic reflection is focused on the analytics and tools that critical thinkers use. These include:

- Conceptual analysis;
- Meta level analyses (metacognition, self-assessment, analysis of our own assumptions, etc.);
- Creating logical classifications;
- Making insightful comparisons.

Helping Learners Become Better Critical Thinkers

You can see that a sustainability worldview entails both the *critical* and the *thinking* dimensions of critical thinking, so it is important to provide learners with opportunities to employ a critical perspective as well as systematic information gathering and analysis strategies while engaging with issues. Leicester (2010) suggests that learning to be a critical thinker involves a process in which one learns to become increasingly critical:

> We learn to practice and improve the habits and tools of critical thought and we learn to become self-conscious (reflective and reflexive) about our own learning and thinking, so that a critical stance towards it enables self-improvement in the ability to be analytic. (p. 3)

Just as with other complex thinking processes, proficiency with critical thinking requires effectively scaffolded instruction; practice that includes reflection, self-assessment and teacher feedback; and opportunities for application and transfer, including far transfer. Critical thinking should not be relegated to stand-alone courses or specialized programs but instead should be infused into all content classes as a mode of inquiry to support deeper learning. Teachers can support students' development as critical thinkers by providing ample opportunities for practice with the various component abilities of critical thinking and by creating opportunities for students to integrate those various abilities in authentic, real-world contexts. The framework proposed by Ennis (2001), shown in Figure 8.1, outlines the content of a critical-thinking curriculum that could be infused into other classes and across grade levels.

Along with component abilities such as those outlined in Figure 8.1, most contemporary descriptions of the characteristics of critical thinkers include dispositions. For example, according to Ennis (2001), critical thinkers care that their beliefs are true and decisions justified, care about presenting a position honestly and clearly, and are concerned for the dignity and worth of every person. Other qualities often mentioned include skepticism, fair-mindedness, open-mindedness, respect for evidence and reason, and a willingness to change a position or point of view (e.g., Beyer, 1995; Brookfield, 2011; Leicester, 2010).

Core critical-thinking abilities	
Ability	**Description**
Elementary classification skills	
Focus on a question	Identifying and formulating questions as well as the criteria for judging possible answers
Analyze arguments	• Identifying conclusions; • Identifying stated and unstated reasons; • Identifying and handling irrelevance; and • Seeing the structure of an argument
Ask and answer clarifying and challenging questions	Asking for examples, seeking clarification of main points or ideas, inquiring about unstated meanings, etc.

Assess the basis for a decision	
Judge the credibility of a source	Evaluating according to criteria such as expertise, reputation, conflict of interest, triangulation with other sources, etc.
Make observations and judge observation reports	Application of criteria to judge the credibility of an observation such as level of inference, first hand versus hearsay, corroboration of observations with other evidence, etc.

Evaluate and make inferences	
Deduce whether an argument is deductively valid	Understand the elementary, logical arguments relating to sets and groups, and conditional arguments, such as "only," "if and only if," "unless," etc.
Induce whether an argument is inductively valid	• Awareness of issues involved when generalizing from a particular instance to broader contexts, such as sample size and context. • Evaluation of causal and explanatory claims, intended meanings, historical claims, and unstated reasons. • Often includes investigation, data collection, or experimentation.
Make and evaluate value judgments	• Investigate and understand background information and consequences of accepting claims at face value. • Look for alternative principles or explanations when weighing claims and arguments.

Advanced clarification	
Define terms and judge definitions	Evaluate the various dimensions of definitions to assess veracity and quality. Understand the attributes of definitions and assess qualities such as persuasiveness, content, and purpose.
Attribute unstated assumptions	Determine when an assumption is not being stated, and assess the source or attribution of that assumption.

Additional notable abilities	
Engage in suppositional thinking	The ability to reason or argue from positions or perspectives with which one disagrees without letting that disagreement interfere with thinking. The ability to see an argument from someone else's point of view.
Integrate the other critical-thinking abilities and dispositions to make or defend a decision	Effectively apply multiple critical-thinking abilities at the same time to arrive at a conclusion or complex decision.

Auxiliary critical thinking abilities	
Proceed in an orderly manner appropriate to the situation	Use a thoughtful problem-solving process and metacognition to monitor and evaluate one's thinking and decision making.
Sensitivity to the feelings, level of knowledge, and degree of sophistication of others	Take into consideration the feelings of others and adjusting one's speech and behavior to be considerate of others
Employ appropriate rhetorical strategies	Read the situation and match one's speech, tone, rhetoric, and emotional content to the context.

Figure 8.1. Core critical-thinking abilities
Source: Adapted from Ennis (2001). Used with permission.

As these descriptions of component abilities and dispositions suggest, critical thinking is a complex process. Here are some general guidelines for helping your students become better critical thinkers in the context of a sustainability worldview.

1. Provide regular and systematic opportunities for students to practice the components of critical thinking in a variety of contexts including traditional content areas as well as in broader contexts related to sustainability.
2. Make critical thinking a routine part of the classroom climate so that students see critical thinking as an everyday practice. Establish routines and protocols that help students challenge and clarify assumptions, argue issues with supporting evidence, reflect on their own biases, disagree respectfully and constructively, and grapple with challenging dilemmas.
3. Help students see how the component abilities contribute to a broader competency called "critical thinking." Clearly identify component abilities and dispositions as elements of critical thinking, and help students begin to see themselves as "critical thinkers." Create opportunities for students to discern the conditions under which critical thinking is useful and appropriate and to see how the various component abilities and dispositions interact.
4. Sustainability-related scenarios, case studies, and real-world problems provide fertile ground for practice and application of critical-thinking abilities. Help students see the dispositions and abilities associated with critical thinking as elements of a broader sustainability worldview. Provide opportunities for students to apply various Earth Charter principles as well as core concepts such as **interconnectedness**, **universal responsibility**, and **respect for limits** while grappling with real-world issues.
5. Model critical thinking and make your own thinking visible to students in your daily professional practice. Help students also see how critical thinking is a component of your own sustainability worldview. Learn how to ask challenging and thought-provoking questions that model critical thinking to provide opportunities for students to practice critical thinking. Provide constructive and supportive feedback for students as they practice critical thinking in a variety of contexts.

CONSIDER THIS 8.1 PLASTIC BOTTLES AND WATER FILTERS

As you read the two scenarios below, think about the ways that each problem provides opportunities for students to apply critical-thinking and problem-solving skills in a real-world context. If you were advising these students, what steps would you recommend they follow in each scenario? How might you scaffold their use of the critical-thinking abilities described in Figure 8.1?

Scenario 1: Plastic Bottles

Your school district has a contract with soft drink distributor that has installed vending machines that sell bottled water and high sugar content energy drinks and in the cafeteria. A group of students want to launch a campaign to ban bottled water and unhealthy drinks from the school. The students have asked for your help.

Scenario 2: Water Filters

After studying about the worldwide water crisis, some students in one of your classes contacted students at a school in Tanzania. Your students discovered that their Tanzanian friends do not have a reliable supply of potable water in their community and often need to haul water by hand from a well located several miles away. The village cannot afford to drill a deep well or build a water treatment facility. If the people in the village had access to personal water filters, they could use water from a source that is closer to their village but that is often contaminated. Your students and the students in Tanzania want to work together to launch a social entrepreneurship project to support the local manufacture of ceramic water filters. The students have asked for your help.

Decision Making

Each of us makes dozens of decisions each day. Many of these decisions are fairly simple and are based on information acquired directly from the environment through our senses (e.g., what to have for breakfast, which bus to catch, whether to go the gym after work, etc.). However, experience tells us that decision making often entails much more than simply reacting to our immediate desires and environmental stimuli. Even the routine decisions we make every day can involve complexity, uncertainty, missing information, real or imagined risk, messy interpersonal situations, or strong emotions. The more of these elements a situation involves, the more difficult it is to arrive at a satisfactory decision. Consider, for example, the thinking process that underlies a decision as simple as deciding what kind of beverage to choose for your morning break. As illustrated in Figure 8.2, this decision can quickly become quite complicated if you want to consider factors such as the health benefits and the environmental, social, and economic impacts of your choice.

Complex decisions often also involve information that has been learned and stored in memory in the form of **explicit knowledge** or **tacit knowledge**. Explicit knowledge is knowledge that can be learned directly from others, in school, or from books or media. Tacit knowledge is informal knowledge that is usually acquired through life experiences. For example, in the decision illustrated in Figure 8.2, you might apply explicit knowledge about Fair Trade Certification processes or about the health effects of various artificial sweeteners. At the same time, you might apply tacit knowledge about your own body's reaction to too much caffeine or the quality of the coffee at various coffee shops in your neighborhood. This is information you would gain from direct experience.

CONSIDER THIS 8.2 SKETCH A DECISION TREE

1. Are there expressions or ideas in the Decision Tree illustrated in Figure 8.2 with which you are unfamiliar? Investigation of the unfamiliar terms in the figure could deepen your understanding of the interconnectedness of the issues involved.

2. Try sketching out a decision tree for a consumer decision you make on a regular basis that you have not previously examined through the lens of a sustainability worldview. With a friend or colleague, discuss the considerations that you had not previously factored into this decision and think together about the way the decision involves interconnected systems.

Many of our day-to-day decisions involve wicked problems. As you recall from Chapter 6, wicked problems involve complex issues that cannot be easily defined and for which there is no easy solution. Indeed, the solution to a wicked problem often generates a whole new set of problems. With wicked problems, the aim of decision making is usually not to make a "correct" decision but rather to make a decision that is "more good" and "less bad." Under these circumstances, we are less likely to rely on explicit knowledge and more likely to depend on tacit knowledge associated with the qualities of good judgment and wisdom.

Judgment involves discernment, good sense, and discretion and pertains to the cognitive, social, and emotional processes that are engaged when one makes a decision (Cauffman & Woolard, 2005, p. 282). Judgment is situational and often refers to an intrapersonal context. A person could exercise good judgment in one context and poor judgment in another. For example, someone might exercise

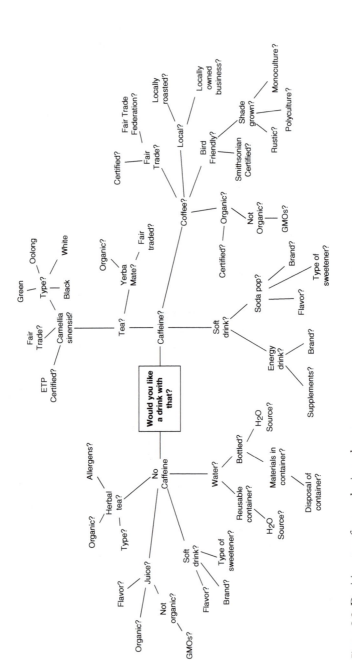

Figure 8.2 Decision tree for purchasing a beverage

regularly and follow a healthy diet but make poor decisions about romantic relationships.

Wisdom refers to a more stable quality that one might display repeatedly over time and that is applied in a broader, less personal sociocultural context. Wisdom is not just about maximizing one's own self-interest but about balancing self-interest (intrapersonal) with the interests of others (interpersonal) as well as the larger context in which one lives (extrapersonal), such as one's community or country or environment or planet (Sternberg, 2003). More formally, wisdom involves skilled application of intelligence, creativity, knowledge gained from experience, and the ability to tolerate uncertainty to achieve a common good (Strohm Kitchener & Brenner, 1990). Taking this idea one step further, Schwartz and Sharpe (2010, p. 8) describe **practical wisdom** as the ability to translate wise decision making into meaningful action. A practical, wise decision maker knows how to translate the will to do the right thing with the skill to get the right thing done.

Effective decision making for sustainability entails using sound judgment and the skilled application of knowledge, including knowledge gained from experience, to make decisions that attend to the creation of a safe and just space for humanity and other species now and in the future. This is decision making is informed by the practical wisdom associated with a sustainability worldview. It involves seeing the ways our individual decisions are interconnected with larger community and global contexts, balancing our current needs and wants with future consequences, the intention of creating positive outcomes in our own lives and the lives of others, and the skills and ability to act on those intentions.

While it is easy to describe what effective decision making for sustainability looks like, it is far more difficult to engage in this kind of thinking in our own lives and even more difficult to help others learn how to do it. Why is this so? The answer to this question has to do with the kinds of decisions our brains evolved to do well and the psychology that underlies our day-to-day decision making.

The Psychology of Decision Making

Contemporary research on judgment and decision making dates to the 1970s and often involved cognitive processes associated with thinking and learning. Typically, this work was conducted in laboratory settings and focused on somewhat artificial problem solving and reasoning tasks. Much of this work grew out of interests in machine learning and artificial intelligence and coincided with the rapid advancements in computing that occurred in the second half of the last century. More recently, the focus of this research has shifted to the study of social, emotional, and cognitive dimension of human decision making in naturally occurring settings and often has attended to the effects of uncertainty and risk in the context of real-world problems. Here are some things we have learned from that research:

1. We are not always consciously aware of the mental processes that underlie our decisions; as a result, we often commit errors of judgment and decision making without realizing we are doing so. However, we can learn to identify and exert control over the processes that affect our ability to make wise decisions, and we can learn strategies for making better decisions and for acting more wisely.
2. Sometimes, our ability to make effective decisions is limited because we have too little or too much information. In these situations, when our ability to reason (or rationality) is "bounded" by the information we have at hand and our mental-processing abilities, we often opt for a solution that is satisfying and minimally sufficient but may not be optimal.
3. People often employ mental shortcuts when making decisions based on limited or uncertain information. Much of the time, these shortcuts are helpful, but sometimes they get in the way of effective decision making because they result in biased judgments and logical fallacies.
4. Context matters. Effective decision making requires adaptation to specific circumstances and ecologies. In particular, an individual's perception of risk plays an important role in decision making ability.
5. Intelligence does not necessarily equate to wise decision making. Even very intelligent and well-educated people make unwise decisions with disturbing regularity.

Two Systems for Making Decisions

Compared to other mammals, and particularly primates, the human brain is much larger and uses considerably more energy—about 20% of the energy our bodies consume. As a result, the evolution of *Homo sapiens* involved a variety of physiological and sensory adaptations that made a larger amount of the body's total energy budget available to the brain. We also evolved more energy efficient and effective ways to use our brains. One of those adaptations is a two-system approach to judgment and decision making. These two systems have been described in a variety of ways, including *associative* and *rule based* (Sloman, 1996), *implicit* and *explicit* (Evans, 2003), *System 1* and *System 2* (Kahneman, 2011; Stanovich & West, 2000), or *experiential* and *analytic*, the descriptors used in this chapter (Slovic, Finucane, Peters, & MacGregor, 2004). The two systems differ from one another in the speed with which they process information, the level of conscious control we exert over them, and the kind of information they handle. The two systems also differ in the amount of energy they require. In general, mental operations that require higher levels of conscious control and awareness consume more energy than operations that operate below the level of consciousness.

The **experiential system** is an automatic processing mode that includes instinctive and involuntary behaviors as well as patterns of behaviors that have been learned to automaticity. The experiential system operates in the background, and most of the time it operates without effort or conscious allocation of attention. For example, humans have in common with most vertebrates innate abilities to perceive sounds, detect movement, respond to stimuli in our immediate environment, and react to potential dangers. These are all experiential system capabilities.

The experiential system also involves emotion and intuitive thinking. We use intuitive thinking when we read social situations, make certain moves when playing chess or some video games, or when we make snap decisions based on "gut feelings." These are all processes that require less conscious control and therefore consume lower amounts energy.

BOX 8.1 AFFECTIVE RESPONSES ALSO CAN MOVE TO THE EXPERIENTIAL SYSTEM

With practice, complex activities that require our undivided attention when we are first learning them also can come under the control of the experiential system. Remember when you were first learning how to drive a car or play a difficult piece on the piano or speak a new language? Perhaps you can complete one or more of these activities effortlessly today. However, when you were first learning the activity, you probably found it difficult, uncomfortable, and, after a while, fatiguing. Perhaps you also recall that the process of learning these complex behavior patterns involved an emotional reaction such as frustration, fear, elation, or relief. Often the affective component associated with the early-learning process remains linked with the behavior under the control of the experiential system. So, even a very experienced and careful driver may feel a twinge of anxiety when faced with the need to parallel park many years after successfully passing the driver's license road test.

The **analytic system** involves deliberation, reasoning, and problem solving and therefore requires more energy than the experiential system. The analytic system comes into play when we are making a choice or decision, or performing tasks that require concentration. Examples of analytic system activities include searching for a friend in a crowded subway station, sending a text message, computing the tip for a restaurant waitperson who has just provided excellent service for your party of five, filling out a job application form, and driving on a busy or unfamiliar street. Where experiential system activities are largely associative—stimulus-response—the analytic system involves more complex, open-ended problem solving. Also, because the analytic system activities are not automatic and require intentional allocation of attention and thought, they are slower, more deliberate, and energy intensive.

BOX 8.2 TO THINK WITH THE ANALYTIC SYSTEM IS HUMAN

Many primates may have developed a simple version of the analytic thinking system. This is evidenced by the ability of chimpanzees and gorillas to learn to communicate fairly complicated and abstract ideas through the use of sign language or communication boards. However, the analytic system thinking seems to be unique to humans. Unlike most other species, humans are able to construct fairly complicated thinking and behavior patterns, based largely on simple associations that become automatic through practice. At first, these complicated thinking and behavior patterns require conscious control and considerable attention, so they start out in the analytic system. However, eventually, these complex patterns of learned behavior move under the control of the experiential system and operate in much the same fashion as instincts and involuntary reactions. For example, we learn to sight-read letter-sound associations and familiar words, complete simple math fact problems, and detect the emotion communicated in a friend's voice inflection, all without conscious effort. This ability to move complicated (and therefore energy consuming) analytic system thinking to the more automatic (and therefore more energy efficient) experiential system is one of the evolutionary adaptations that allowed humans to use their energy-consuming brains more efficiently. This adaptation allows us to leave the analytic system in "energy saving mode" while the experiential system handles most of the routine, moment-to-moment thinking that gets us through the day.

To summarize:

The experiential system:

- Is automatic and fast;
- Renders snap answers and gut reactions;
- Operates below our level of conscious awareness;
- Operates at a concrete, associative, or stimulus–response level;
- Processes perceptions and emotions as well as cognitive content;
- Involves intuitive responses and social judgments; and
- Can include complex collections of behaviors that have been learned to automaticity.

In contrast, the analytic system:

- Is slower and more deliberative;
- Requires conscious effort;

- Operates at an abstract, deductive level;
- Manages unfamiliar tasks and application of rules; and
- Generally does not involve affective content.

Bounded Rationality and Heuristics

If each we had unlimited energy, mental ability, and time, we would always engage the analytic system before we make a decision. The analytic system would lead us to consider all pertinent information, weigh the consequences of the various decision alternatives, and then direct us to make the choice that has the highest probability of being the best course of action. Unfortunately, humans usually make decisions under less than ideal conditions—with limited information, under time constraints, or under conditions of complexity that surpass our mental computational abilities. Decision making under these less than optimal conditions is known as **bounded rationality** (Simon, 1956). Bounded rationality has two components: the finite limits of our mental abilities (e.g., memory, perception, and mental agility) and the characteristics of the environment in which a decision is being made. The environment includes physical variables that introduce complexity to the decision process, as well as our own goals, needs, and drives. Factors such as fatigue, emotion, time constraint, and perceived risk can add to the complexity of the decision making process and also affect our decision making capacity. For example, texting while driving is inherently dangerous and foolish because our rationality is bounded by our innate inability to attend simultaneously to two very different but equally demanding tasks that require engagement of the analytic system.

Humans evolved under conditions of bounded rationality. Early humans needed to make very difficult decisions about potential threats, food sources, kin relationships, weather conditions, and trade negotiations, often based on very little information or under extreme time constraints. To cope with the limitations imposed by bounded rationality, humans evolved a number of mental shortcuts that allow us to fill in the gaps when information is missing or to simplify complex decisions. These shortcuts take the form of **heuristics**, which are simple rules of thumb that allow us employ a minimum of time, computational power, or information to make decisions in real-world environments (Gigerenzer, Todd, and the ABC Research Group, 1999). Heuristics are fast, efficient strategies that usually operate below our conscious control in the experiential system. Heuristics facilitate decision making by compensating for the problems of bounded rationality: not enough information, too much information, or not enough computational capacity.

For example, the **recognition heuristic** is simple: when making a choice, we are more likely to choose something if we recognize it. More formally, if one of two alternatives is recognized and the other is not, the recognized choice is valued more highly (Goldstein & Gigerenzer, 2002). Similarly, when presented with an array of choices, we tend to prioritize items in order of recognition. The recognition heuristic is also known as the **availability heuristic** and has been researched extensively under that name. We will explore this heuristic in more detail shortly.

Advertisers and political candidates routinely exploit recognition-based heuristics with advertising campaigns that provide very little substantive information about a product or candidate but are intended simply to build brand or name recognition. They accomplish this objective by pairing their product with distinctive logos, phrases, or music and by bombarding consumers or voters with a high number of advertisements across media platforms. This strategy works particularly well when there is relatively little meaningful difference among alternatives (for example, political candidates from the same party in a primary election or brands of coffee) or when the comparison criteria are complex and subtle (for example, insurance policies, computers, or automobiles).

Most of the time heuristics serve us quite well, and, in some instances, they can be more accurate than sophisticated computational strategies (Gigerenzer & Gaissmaier, 2011). However, there is a hitch: heuristics only work some of the time. They do not guarantee a correct answer, and, frequently, heuristics can lead to biased and inaccurate decision making.

The pioneering work of cognitive psychologists Daniel Kahneman and Amos Tversky offers intriguing insights into various inference and judgment errors to which we are prone when we rely on heuristics (Tversky & Kahneman, 1974). Much of Kahneman and Tversky's work has involved investigation of three classes of heuristics that account for a wide variety of errors of judgment and decision making: the **representativeness heuristic**, the **availability heuristic**, and the **affect heuristic**. As you will see, the error patterns associated with these heuristics are particularly relevant in the context of education for sustainability.

Representativeness Heuristic

When we rely on the representativeness heuristic, we tend to choose an alternative if we think it is "typical" or if it fits with our expectations. We all experience (and sometimes employ) the representativeness heuristic when we encounter decision making based on stereotypes. For example, when presented with pictures of two women, one of whom is wearing a fleece vest, quick-dry pants, and hiking shoes and the other wearing a blazer, dress slacks, and high-heeled shoes, you might believe that you could predict which of the two women is a financial analyst and which is an environmentalist.

The decision error associated with representativeness is the belief that similarity on one dimension is the same as similarity on all dimensions. People often rely on the representativeness heuristic when estimating the likelihood of an event. As a result, they may ignore the real probability of an event and instead base their decision on their belief about what "should" happen. Here are some examples of flawed reasoning prompted by the representativeness heuristic:

- Business and investment decisions often are overly influenced by short-term trends than by long-term data. The 2008 global economic crisis was caused in part because many people believed that rapid short-term rises in housing prices were typical and therefore took out risky loans on which they later defaulted.

- The macro process of global warming triggers a variety of climatic changes, including increased precipitation that can cause record snowfall in higher latitudes. Short-term local fluctuations in weather tend to influence people's understanding of the long-term impacts of climate change. So, for example, when cooler weather or higher than usual precipitation occurs for several years in a row, people may believe that this pattern is representative of the local weather but not attend to longer-term warming trends.

- Media images of successful black men often feature professional athletes and entertainers, although these two professions account for a small percentage of successful black men. Young black boys may tend to show a preference for careers in sports or entertainment if they believe that these images are representative of successful black men.

- Industrial food producers have developed strains of vegetables and fruits that can be transported long distances and remain visually appealing long after harvest. People who buy this type of food may come to believe that unblemished fruits and vegetables that are available year-round is typical and, therefore, better than less-attractive, locally produced, seasonally available food. This fallacy fails to consider the energy and climate impacts of industrially produced food, the economic benefits of local agriculture, or the health benefits of fresh, organically produced food.

Availability Heuristic

When the availability heuristic is employed, alternatives that are more easily recognized, recalled, or imagined are more likely to be selected. Earlier, this heuristic was introduced as the recognition heuristic. The availability heuristic compensates for the problem of too little information by "filling in the gaps" with information readily available in memory. Events that are dramatic or vivid may make a more lasting impression and therefore, be easier to recall later. Similarly, recent events or events with which one has personal experience are more likely to be recalled than events that happened in the past or to others. The decision error associated with the availability heuristic is the belief that things that come easily to mind are more common and, therefore, more accurate reflections of the real world. Here are some examples of flawed reasoning prompted by the availability heuristic:

- Individuals who regularly patronize large, nationally owned businesses may believe that locally owned businesses are not viable in their community. Examples of busy, "big box" stores are readily available in memory, but examples of successful small businesses may be harder to recall.

- When people see a variety of wild animals (e.g., deer, raccoons, birds, squirrels) and non-native plants in urban areas and suburban areas, they may doubt that biodiversity is at risk worldwide. Readily available memories of encounters with a variety of local species can cause people to underestimate threats to biodiversity elsewhere.

- The election of Barack Obama as president led many people to believe that racism is no longer a problem in the United States.
- Ready access to clean water at the turn of a tap leads many people to believe that water is an unlimited resource that does not need to be conserved.
- Vivid news reports focused on particularly gruesome but low-incidence crimes or acts of terrorism can lead people to believe that they are at greater risk than they really are.

The availability heuristic makes our judgment and decision making particularly vulnerable to media and sensationalist news reporting. An event that receives extensive media coverage is more likely to be considered important or probable than other events that may actually be more significant or likely. For example, in the months following the attacks of September 11, 2001, in New York and Washington, DC, many people in the United States chose to travel by automobile instead of by airplane, even though the risk of injury or fatality is much greater for automobiles than airplanes. In fact, in the year after the attacks, there were 42,815 highway deaths in the United States compared with just 1,379 deaths worldwide from airplane crashes (Gigerenzer, 2004). The images of the attacks on the World Trade Center and Pentagon were vivid, widely publicized, frightening, and readily available in the memory of anyone deciding whether to fly or drive during the years following the event. Unfortunately, this kind of flawed reasoning can translate into public policy. In the United States, the odds of being involved in a fatal automobile accident are about 400 times greater than the odds of being killed by a terrorist, yet the budget for Homeland Security is about 50 times that of the National Transportation Safety Administration, which is responsible for oversight of highway and vehicle safety.

Affect Heuristic

The affect heuristic substitutes positive or negative feelings for accurate information to guide a decision process. The notion of affect refers to the general quality of feeling "good" or "bad" about a situation (Slovic, 2010). Of course, "goodness" or "badness" can refer to a wide range of emotional responses, but the affect heuristic seems to be less sensitive to the specific type of emotion involved and more tuned to the intensity of feeling that a decision or choice evokes. Affective responses are associated with the experiential thinking system, so they are rapid and automatic and often preempt a more deliberate weighing of pros and cons or consideration of factual information. The affect heuristic underlies the "gut reaction" approach to decision making.

Affect-guided decision making is not necessarily a bad thing. Sometimes our initial emotional reaction in a situation is based on subtle cues that are not immediately evident at a conscious level. For example, firefighters, police, military personnel, and medical first responders often report that they rely on their "instincts" to make rapid, difficult decisions. Although, in reality, what they recognize as "instinct" is probably an automatic and rapid affective response that arises in the experiential thinking system and is based on strong associations between a store of tacit knowledge gained from experience as well as explicit knowledge gained from extensive training and practice.

As with the other heuristics, there are times when the affect heuristic interferes with effective decision making. All of our perceptions involve at least some affective component, and affective reactions are often our first response to a situation (Zajonc, 1980). So even when we believe we are behaving in a rational manner, our decision making is being informed at least in part by affect. As a result, we can delude ourselves about the objectivity of our decision making. Of course, advertisers and marketers take full advantage of this phenomenon by linking their products to images that evoke strong emotions such as pride, happiness, security, envy, sexual desire, or belongingness.

Affect seems to be particularly important in the assessment of risk and benefit. When assessing the risks and benefits associated with an issue, people are more influenced by how they feel about the issue than by what they think about it (Finucane, Alhakami, Slovic, & Johnson, 2000). When someone has a positive feeling about an issue, they tend to overestimate the benefits and underestimate the risks. If they have a negative feeling about the issue, they underestimate the benefits and overestimate the risks. In other words, we tend to treat risk as a feeling rather than as a quantifiable probability.

It is easy to see how this "risk as feeling" phenomenon could influence people's thinking about issues like climate change, food safety, or terrorism. For example, automobiles are often seen as symbols of status, independence, power, and freedom. Positive feelings associated with automobiles leads to an overestimation of the benefits of automobile ownership and use and an underestimation of the risks associated with greenhouse gas emissions and climate change. Similarly, positive feelings associated with convenient, tasty "comfort foods" can lead to an underestimation of the risks associated with genetically modified foods or with high fat, high sugar diets.

Accurate information about the probability of an event occurring can help attenuate the influence of affect on risk assessment, but the relationship is complicated. Events that are more highly dreaded are seen as a greater risk hazard than less dreaded events, even when the actual probability of a highly dreaded event is very low. For example, in the United States, the probability of being involved in a terrorist attack is extremely low, but because it is highly dreaded, people tend to believe that the risk associated with terrorism is high. On the other hand, while there is nearly a 100% probability that every human and every other species on the planet will experience significant effects from climate change, many Americans view it as a low-hazard and, therefore, low-risk event.

CONSIDER THIS 8.3 TUNING INTO THE TWO SYSTEMS

1. For the next few days, as you encounter various forms of marketing or advertising, see if you can identify the ways the advertisement attempts to exploit the characteristics of the experiential and analytic systems. Which heuristics does the advertisement invoke?

2. Think about your assessment of the risk associated with various events you read about in the news or situations you encounter in your day-to-day life over the next week. Focus on engaging your analytic system to separate your emotional response to the situation from an accurate assessment of the actual risk involved. Notice whether your decision making changes as a result.

Practices That Promote Effective Decision Making for Sustainability

A wide variety of professional development programs, curricula, and decision making protocols have been developed over the years to help everyone from school children to business executives to policymakers become better decision makers. However, you do not need to hire an expensive consultant or buy a specialized curriculum to help your students learn how to make better, more sensible decisions. We each have the ability to make better decisions already at our disposal. All we need to do is get better at engaging the slower, deliberate, analytic system and to view our various decisions, big and small, through the lens of a sustainability worldview. Here are some research-validated strategies that will help the learners in your classes begin today to make better decisions (Marzano & Kendall, 2007; Swartz, 2001):

1. Help learners become fluent at applying core sustainability concepts and principles to everyday decisions. Scaffold this process by including these big ideas in the criteria for assignments and in-class activities. For example, ask them to consider ideas such as interconnectedness, intergenerational equity, and just societies on a routine basis. Model this process by helping learners see how you incorporate these ideas in your own day-to-day decision making.

2. Provide regular opportunities for learners to practice making meaningful decisions. Learner-centered pedagogies such as those discussed in Chapter 7 provide real-world opportunities for learners to make decisions that are important to them personally but also have consequences beyond the mere completion of an assignment.

3. Support learners' decision making with protocols that prompt learners to engage their analytic system and to reflect on both the cognitive and affective

aspects of their learning and thinking during the decision making process. Use questioning that goes beyond "How did you feel?" to help learners see how their emotional reactions can sometimes influence their effectiveness as decision makers.

4. Help learners develop strategies that prompt them to engage the analytic system. A protocol for doing this typically includes these steps:

    a. Prompt learners to clarify the parameters of the decision with questions such as

        "What is the decision I am making?"
        "Why is this decision necessary?"

    b. Identify the options and alternatives in the decision you are being asked to make.

    c. Identify the consequences of effective and poor decisions and clarify the criteria for making a good decision. For example, you might prompt learners to complete these paired sentences:

        "If I make a good decision, _____ will happen."
        "If I make a poor decision, _____ will happen."

    d. Identify the decision path that will best satisfy the "good decision" criteria but not the "poor decision" criteria.

5. Help learners understand the true complexity and broader impacts of their routine decisions. Encourage them to develop schematics such as the decision tree illustrated in Figure 8.2 to analyze the impacts of their decisions.

6. Help learners combine effective critical thinking with effective decision making.

Finally, one of the most powerful resources for making effective decisions is systems thinking. Systems thinking involves a variety of thinking tools that attend to the characteristics and behaviors of systems and allow us to better identify trends over time, causal relationships, and runaway feedback loops. We will examine systems thinking in detail in the next chapter.

EXTEND YOUR PROFESSIONAL KNOWLEDGE 8.1

1. Visit **The Critical Thinking Community** at (www.criticalthinking.org//). This is a nonprofit organization focused on cultivating change in education and society through critical thinking. Their website includes an extensive library of downloadable resources and videos for K-12 teachers.

    a. Under the Library tab, choose the *K-12 Instruction Strategies & Samples* link.

(continued)

Box (continued)

> b. Download one of the handbooks and examine the examples of lesson plans.
> c. Design a lesson or series of lessons that incorporate critical thinking in the investigation of a sustainability issue. Think about how to include one or more of the sustainability big ideas in the lessons.
> 2. Visit **Edutopia** at (www.edutopia.org/).
>   This site includes lesson plans, lesson topics, and examples of ways to incorporate inquiry-based learning and critical thinking into your professional practice. This site also includes links to other resources.
>   a. Under the *Browse Topics* tab, choose *All Topics A-Z*.
>   b. Click on *Critical Thinking* and then expand the Resources list.
>   c. Investigate the resources related to Socratic Seminars. Look at the videos and example lessons.
>   d. Plan a lesson that prompts your students to investigate a sustainability issue in your community using a Socratic Seminar.

References

Beyer, B.K. (1995). *Critical Thinking*. Bloomington, IN: Phi Delta Kappa Educational Foundation.

Bohman, J. (2013). Critical Theory. *The Stanford Encyclopedia of Philosophy* (E.N. Zalta, Ed.). Retrieved from: http://plato.stanford.edu/archives/spr2013/entries/critical-theory/

Brookfield, S.D. (2011). *Teaching for Critical Thinking: Tools and Techniques to Help Students Question Their Assumptions*. San Francisco, CA: Wiley/Jossey-Bass.

Cauffman, E., & Woolard, J. (2005). Crime, competence, and culpability: Adolescent judgment in the justice system. In J. E. Jacobs & P. A. Klaczynski (Eds.), *The Development of Judgment and Decision Making in Children and Adolescents* (pp. 279–302). New York: Psychology Press.

Ennis, R.H. (2001). Goals for a critical thinking curriculum and its assessment. In A. L. Costa (Ed.), *Developing Minds: A Resource Book for Teaching Thinking* (pp. 44–46). Alexandria, VA: ASCD.

Evans, J. St. B.T. (2003). In two minds: Dual-process accounts of reasoning. *Trends in Cognitive Sciences, 7*, 454–459.

Finucane, M.L., Alhakami, A., Slovic, P., & Johnson, S.M. (2000). The affect heuristic in judgments of risks and benefits. *Journal of Behavioral Decision Making, 13*, 1–17.

Gigerenzer, G. (2004). Dread risk, September 11, and fatal traffic accidents. *Psychological Science, 15*, 286–287.

Gigerenzer, G., & Gaissmaier, W. (2011). Heuristic decision making. *Annual Review of Psychology, 62*, 451–482.

Gigerenzer, G., Todd, P. M., & the ABC Research Group. (1999). *Simple Heuristics That Make Us Smart*. Oxford: Oxford University Press.

Goldstein D. G., & Gigerenzer, G. (2002). Models of ecological rationality: The recognition heuristic. *Psychological Review, 109*, 75–90.

Kahneman, D. (2011). *Thinking, Fast and Slow*. New York: Farrar, Straus & Giroux.

Leicester, M. (2010). *Teaching Critical Thinking Skills*. London: Continuum.

Marzano, R.J., & Kendall, J.S. (2007). *The New Taxonomy of Educational Objectives*. Thousand Oaks, CA: Corwin.

Schwartz, B., & Sharpe, K. (2010). *Practical Wisdom: The Right Way to Do the Right Things*. New York: Penguin.

Simon, H.A. (1956). Rational choice and the structure of the environment. *Psychological Review, 63*, 129–138.

Sloman, S. (1996). The empirical case for two systems of reasoning. *Psychological Bulletin, 119*, 3–22.

Slovic, P. (2010). *The Feeling of Risk: New Perspectives on Risk Perception*. New York: Earthscan.

Slovic, P., Finucane, M.L., Peters, E., Macgregor, D.G. (2004). Risk as analysis and risk as feelings: Some thoughts about affect, reason, risk, and rationality. *Risk Analysis, 24*, 311–322.

Stanovich, K.E. & West, R. F. (2000). Individual differences in reasoning: Implications for the rationality debate? *Behavioral And Brain Sciences, 23*, 645–726.

Sternberg, R. (2003). The balance theory of wisdom. In *Wisdom, Intelligence, and Creativity Synthesized* (pp. 152–173). Cambridge: Cambridge University Press.

Strohm Kitchener, K., & Brenner, H.G. (1990). Wisdom and reflective judgment: Knowing in the face of uncertainty. In R. Sternberg (Ed.), *Wisdom: Its Nature, Origins, and Development*. Cambridge: Cambridge University Press.

Swartz, R.J. (2001). Thinking about decisions. In A. L. Costa (Ed.), *Developing Minds: A Resource Book for Teaching Thinking* (pp. 58–66). Alexandria VA: ASCD.

Tversky, A., & Kahneman, D. (1974). Judgment under uncertainty: Heuristics and biases. *Science, 185*, 1124–1131.

Wals, A. (2012). *Shaping the Education of Tomorrow: Full-Length Report on the UN Decade of Education for Sustainable Development*. Paris: UNESCO.

White, E.B. (1969, July 11). Notes and comments by author. Interview with Israel Shenker, *New York Times*. In White, M. (Ed.), *In the Words of E.B. White: Quotations from America's Most Companionable of Writers*. Ithaca, NY: Cornell University Press.

Zajonc, R.B. (1980). Feeling and thinking: Preferences need no inferences. *American Psychologist, 35*, 151–175.

9

SYSTEMS THINKING

Social systems are the external manifestations of cultural thinking patterns of profound human needs, emotions, strengths, and weaknesses. Changing them is not as simple as saying "now all change," or of trusting that he who knows the good shall do the good.

—Donella Meadows, 2008, p.167

Systems thinking is a strategy for seeing systems and seeking to understand their behavior. System thinking is an essential skill for the development of a sustainability worldview because, as Peter Senge (1990) noted, "(It) is a discipline for seeing wholes. It is a framework for seeing interrelationships rather than things, for seeing patterns of change rather than static 'snapshots'" (p.68). Helping your students learn to "see in wholes" can lead them to see whole people, whole schools, whole communities, whole ecosystems, whole economies, and, ultimately, the whole planet. When they learn to think in systems, it becomes much more difficult for them to believe that when they dispose of something, it goes to some magical place called "away." It is much more difficult for them to see their own patterns of consumption and assumption of economic privilege as disconnected with the needs of others. Systems thinking can help your students identify the variables that add to their own well-being—things like fulfilling relationships with friends, mastery of new skills, increasing responsibility and autonomy, and purposeful engagement in meaningful activities—and the things that detract from it—thoughtless consumerism, materialism, confusion of needs and wants, and disengagement from the greater world.

While there is not a specifically agreed upon definition of systems thinking, it is a process that generally involves application of the principles of systems dynamics first developed by Jay Forrester and his colleagues and students in the MIT Systems Dynamics Group in the 1960s. In recent years, systems thinking has been applied in a variety of contexts, particularly in the business and education sectors. Many of the tools and strategies associated with systems thinking are based on the work of Donella Meadows (Meadows, Randers, & Meadows, 2004; Meadows, 2008) and Peter Senge (Senge, 1990; 2000). The discussion that follows, based largely on Meadows's and Senge's work, will provide you with an introduction to the terminology and strategies associated with system thinking.

Systems thinking is an essential component of a sustainability worldview because it can help us understand very large, complex, or long-term processes. It can help us recognize whole systems, perceive the way the component parts of a system are interconnected, and understand the way a system behaves over time. A systems perspective helps us perceive interrelationships rather than happenstance collections of things and to recognize patterns of change rather than static events (Senge, 1990). Systems thinking is not difficult, but it does entail some specific vocabulary and application of a small set of system-thinking tools that will help you see how systems work. We will start our exploration of systems thinking by clarifying exactly we mean by the word "system."

What Is a System?

A **system** is an interconnected set of elements that has a coherent organization and a recognizable purpose or function (Meadows, 2008). Systems come in many shapes and sizes, and the term "system" can be applied to a wide variety of entities; however, all systems share a set of defining characteristics:

- A system has an identifiable set of parts. The parts of a system are sometimes called **components**. Each part has a specific function and characteristics that differentiate it from the other elements of the system. All of the components of a system must be present and operating for the system to perform optimally.
- A system has a **structure** that enables it to be a whole greater than the sum of its parts. A whole system functions differently than its various parts behave on their own. The structure of the system also determines its boundaries. Some systems have very clear and easy to discern structures. However, many systems are complex and include components and boundaries that are not easily detected.
- The parts of a system exhibit interconnectedness. A system's wholeness and integrity are maintained by the interaction of its component parts. The exact relationship of the various parts of a system can vary widely within any particular system and among systems; however, all systems exists because of the mutual interaction of their component parts.

- A system has an identifiable function or purpose that persists over time and under different conditions. Often, the function or purpose[1] of a system is its least obvious attribute. Sometimes, a system's function can only be discerned by observing its pattern of behavior over time.

CONSIDER THIS 9.1 CHARACTERISTICS OF A SYSTEM

Refer to the defining characteristics of a system and decide whether each of these items qualifies as a system.

- A cat named Rita
- The letters of the alphabet
- The eighth grade humanities team at Granite Island Middle School
- Water
- All of the species that live in and around a pond
- The streets in the northwest quadrant of Calgary, Alberta
- Sand on an ocean beach
- Traffic lined up at a highway tollbooth

Systems are everywhere, but we do not always recognize them. Living organisms, corporations, the climate, governments, oceans, automobiles, rivers, computers, soil, buildings, social media, and economies all are examples of systems. Often, we experience only a small part of much larger systems or see only a glimpse of complex, interconnected system processes. For example, think about camping in a wilderness forest—in a rainstorm. You experience a soggy tent, damp sleeping bag, and watery oatmeal for breakfast. You also see the puddles, feel the raindrops on your face, smell the sweet aroma of wet leaves and moss, and hear water softly dripping through the trees. These are the dimensions of rain that you sense directly. However, the rain is part of a larger weather system nested in an even larger climate system, which is nested in a still larger atmospheric system. You may know about these systems, but you do not experience them directly. Those systems overlap with the forest ecosystem and surface hydrologic system in the area surrounding your campsite, as well as local geologic, agricultural, and economic systems. If you also consider your camping equipment, clothing, transportation to and from the campsite, and the food you consume along the way, you soon see that every aspect of your trip to a pristine (if wet!) wilderness area is inextricably linked to many complex systems that reach around the entire planet. Seeing and understanding this kind of interconnectedness is the essence of systems thinking.

BOX 9.1 OVERLAPPING AND NESTED SYSTEMS

When systems are **nested**, one system serves a particular purpose within a larger system. When systems **overlap**, two or more systems share components. For example, the human circulatory system is nested inside the larger system that is the human body. That circulatory system also overlaps with the respiratory system, the digestive system, and the nervous system. Here are some more examples of overlapping and nested systems:

System	Overlaps with	Nested in
neighborhood association	town council	state government
grade-level team	school site council	school district
green heron	wetland habitat	mangrove ecosystem
rear wheel	drive train	bicycle
family	culture	community
chassis assembly line	manufacturing plant	corporation
El Niño	ocean atmosphere	climate
coffee growers cooperative	consumer preferences	Fair Trade practices

System Dynamics and Feedback

Every system exhibits its own **dynamics**, or unique pattern of behavior over time. A system's dynamics are determined by its structure and the way the components interconnect. In turn, a system's dynamics determine how it will respond to outside forces. A system can change, adapt, self-organize, self-repair, and sometimes transform into a completely different system. Box 9.2 presents four examples of systems that adapted or transformed in response to outside forces but maintained their original functions.

BOX 9.2 TRANSFORMED SYSTEMS

Good Eats

After the economy of the community changed, a mom and pop lunch wagon business successfully converted to a casual dining-style restaurant. Their loyal customer base followed them to their new business, and they attracted many new patrons, in large part because of the popularity of their locally sourced, healthy foods.

(continued)

Box 9.2 (continued)

Ecosystem Transformation

Warming climate has increased the range of bark beetles and a stand of insect-damaged white pines fueled an intense forest fire. After the fire, varieties of grasses and shrubs that had never before grown in the area began to appear.

Responsive Transition

In response to changing community demographics, an elementary school added more supports for English language learners (ELL). Teachers were provided incentives to earn ELL endorsements. Subsequently, test scores for ELL students in the school rose.

Growing a Healthy Community

A small group of neighbors in a poor community planted a garden in an empty lot. Soon more members of the community began spending time at the garden, and the garden program expanded. When neighbors became acquainted with one another, they organized monthly neighborhood potluck dinners. After a few years, the neighborhood garden program produced surplus food that was donated to the community food bank.

Generally, the components of a system interact with one another in response to the flow of information. In systems, information can take many forms. For example, in your home's heating system, the ambient air temperature is information for the thermostat. The thermostat sends information to the furnace in the form of electrical energy that signals the furnace to turn on or off. In the language of systems thinking, your home heating system, as well as the systems in the examples in Box 9.2, are responding to *feedback*. Feedback is information that is transmitted and returned to a system and provides signals about how the system is interacting with its environment (Richardson & Pugh, 1981).

CONSIDER THIS 9.2 COMPONENTS OF SYSTEMS AND FEEDBACK SOURCES

Look at the examples in Box 9.2 again. See if you can identify the components of each system and the various sources of feedback to which the systems responded.

Causal Loop Diagrams

A **causal loop** (also called a **feedback loop**) is created when a system's use of feedback has a direct impact on its own behavior. A home heating system causal loop is diagramed in Figure 9.1. As the diagram illustrates, the chain of cause and effect that includes the thermostat, furnace, and room temperature forms a circular or **closed loop**. A closed loop occurs when there is a closed pathway from information to action (Kirkwood, 1998; Richardson & Pugh, 1981).

Causal loop diagrams such as the one shown in Figure 9.1 are an important systems-thinking tool because they can show complex interconnected and causal relationships. The labels indicate the various elements in the system. The arrows in the causal loop diagram are read as "influence." To read the diagram, simply start with an element and follow the arrows (Senge, 1990). Here is the story told by the home heating system causal loop:

> The temperature setting on the thermostat influences the gap between the current temperature in the house and the desired temperature. When there is a gap, the furnace turns on and influences the ambient temperature in the house. When there is no longer a gap, the furnace turns off. As the house cools, the gap between the current temperature and desired temperature grows until, eventually, the thermostat signals the furnace to turn on again. The system repeatedly cycles through this process until the setting on the thermostat is changed.

Not all systems include feedback loops. For example, a deciduous tree is a complex system that responds to seasonal changes in amount and intensity of sunlight. In the fall, as days shorten, chlorophyll production and photosynthesis in the leaves cease, and sugars stop flowing from the leaves into the stems and trunk of the tree. Eventually, the leaves fall off, and the tree goes dormant for the winter. In the spring, when it is exposed to more sunlight each day, the tree wakes up and generates a new set of leaves that begin producing chlorophyll for use in photosynthesis. The tree is an example of an **open loop system**. An open loop system does not have a feedback process and has no ability to affect its own behavior. The tree responds to sunlight, but, as far as we can tell, the behavior of the tree has no

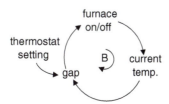

Figure 9.1 Causal loop diagram for thermostat controlled furnace

measureable effect on the sun's production of light energy or the rotation of the Earth around the sun that results in changes in day length.[2]

You may have noticed the letter "B" encircled by an arrow in the center of the causal loop diagram in Figure 9.1. This symbol indicates that this is a **balancing loop**. In a balancing loop, or, more formally, a **balancing feedback process**, the system maintains a state of equilibrium around a goal. If you were to characterize a balancing loop with an aphorism, it might be "the more things change, the more they stay the same." The goal of the heating system is to keep the ambient temperature of the house the same as the temperature setting on the thermostat. When you know the goal of a balancing feedback process, you can begin to identify the system components needed to maintain that goal.

CONSIDER THIS 9.3 COMPONENTS OF VERY DIFFERENT SYSTEMS

Here are the goals for four very different systems. Think about some of the major components for each of these systems, and sketch out a causal loop diagram for each system to show how those components interact.

1. Living wage green jobs for people in a community
2. Resilient habitat for native species in a watershed
3. An adequate education for all students in a school district
4. Healthy neighborhoods in a city

Instead of a balancing process, some systems operate with a reinforcing process. A **reinforcing loop** occurs whenever a system exhibits continuous or exponential growth. In a reinforcing loop, "the more things change, the more they keep changing." A causal loop diagram portraying a reinforcing loop is labeled by the letter "R" instead of a "B."

Reinforcing loops often figure prominently in issues related to sustainability such as climate change, biodiversity, community resilience, and local economies. For example, one of the results of global climate change is that the Arctic is warming at nearly twice the rate of the rest of the planet. One of the impacts of this rapid warming is that permanent polar ice and summer sea ice are melting. Ice, particularly ice that has snow on top of it, reflects significantly more solar energy back into space than water. This reflective property, called **albedo**, contributes to planetary cooling and can offset the effects of global climate change. As polar ice melts, the planet loses albedo capacity and warming accelerates. The more things change (loss of polar ice), the more they keep changing (polar ice melts more rapidly). This reinforcing loop is shown in Figure 9.2.

We will explore other examples of feedback loops shortly; however, that discussion will be helped along if we first examine two other basic tools of systems thinking: stock and flow diagrams and behavior over time graphs (BOTGs).

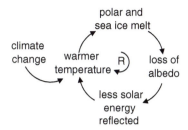

Figure 9.2 Reinforcing loop for loss of albedo due to polar ice melt

Stocks and Flows

Whereas causal loop diagrams illustrate the relationships within a system, **stock and flow diagrams** illustrate the structure of a system. The **stocks** are the variables in a system that can be observed, measured, or somehow experienced. Stocks can include tangible or measurable entities such as "water," "money," "carbon dioxide," "sea turtles," or "affordable housing" or less tangible entities such as "self-confidence," "neighborhood health," "fairness," "positive future orientation," or "happiness." Systems accumulate and store stocks over time, and stocks are affected by **flows**. Flows are the variables that affect the level of the stocks in a system. Flows can add to or decrease the level of stocks in a system in the same way that a stream flowing into a pond adds to the water level and a stream flowing out of the pond decreases the water level. In a stock and flow diagram, a flow that adds to the level of the stock is called an **inflow**, and a flow that decreases the level of the stock is called an **outflow**.

Figure 9.3 shows a typical stock and flow diagram. Stock and flow diagrams often use the standard plumbing schematic symbol for a valve to illustrate flows. In much the way that a valve controls the volume and rate of flow in a pipe, the flows in system can control the rate at which a stock is restored or drained. The cloud-shaped symbols indicate that the stock flows from somewhere (a **source**) and to somewhere (a **sink**). Often, it is useful to leave the sources and sinks unlabeled in order to isolate specific elements of the system for discussion.

For example, in the stock and flow diagram illustrated in Figure 9.4, the stock is the monthly balance in a bank account. Deposits (inflows) can come from a variety of undetermined sources, and money can be withdrawn from the account for a variety of expenditures.

Stock and flow processes are complementary with causal loops, and often systems are illustrated by graphs that include both. For example, suppose the bank

Figure 9.3 Typical stock and flow diagram

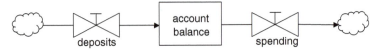

Figure 9.4 Stock and flow diagram for a bank account

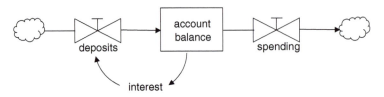

Figure 9.5 Interest on the account balance influences the inflow

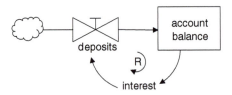

Figure 9.6 Reinforcing loop for interest-bearing account with no withdrawals

account in Figure 9.4 earns simple interest based on the account balance (stock) and that this interest is automatically added to the balance at the end of each month. This relationship is shown as a feedback loop in Figure 9.5. If no money is withdrawn from the account, a reinforcing loop is created, as illustrated in Figure 9.6.

In many situations, cause and effect relationships are subtle, and effects over time are not obvious. These situations are said to exhibit **dynamic complexity** (Senge, 1990). When we start examining dynamically complex situations using a combination of stock and flow and causal loop diagrams, it is possible to unpack quite complex interactions and relationships. For example, Figure 9.7 shows the complex array of feedback loops involved in the transmission of West Nile virus across species. Higher temperatures associated with climate change can increase the mutation rate of the virus and affect the life cycle of vector mosquitoes. There are permanent reservoirs of the virus in bird populations in temperate and tropical regions around the world, but host species such as birds and mosquitoes can be transported long distances by international air travel, introducing the virus to areas where it was not previously found. The virus can be transmitted from bird to bird, from bird to mosquito, or from mosquito to bird, creating multiple feedback loops for transmission. Transmission to humans and other species occurs primarily by mosquito, so measures to control mosquito populations can control the spread of the virus.

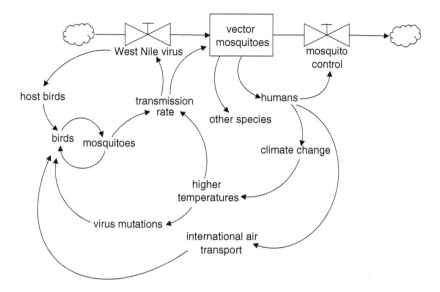

Figure 9.7 West nile virus transmission in multiple feedback loops

Behavior Over Time Graphs

So far, we have examined the manner in which interactions among system elements can be illustrated with causal loop diagrams, and we have examined the use of stock and flow diagrams to illustrate system structures. The third dimension of system thinking is analysis of how systems behave over time. Recall that one of the defining characteristics of a system is that it has a purpose or function. However, sometimes it is difficult to discern exactly what a system is supposed to accomplish, particularly when we deal with complex, nested, and overlapping systems. Unfortunately, most systems do not come with mission and vision statements and annual goals against which to measure their progress. Often, the best way to understand a system's purpose is to watch it behave over time and to graph its general patterns of change or behavior using **behavior over time graphs**.

Behavior over time graphs (or BOTGs) display time on the *x*-axis and the variable of interest on the *y*-axis. For example, if your students are comparing the number of pounds of compostable waste with pounds of waste sent to the landfill generated each day from the school cafeteria, they would show pounds of waste on the *y*-axis and days on the *x*-axis, as shown in Figure 9.8.

For ease of interpretation, behavior over time graphs sometimes show a **trend line** in addition to or instead of a graph of the raw data. A trend line (also called a **line of best fit**) shows the general direction or pattern in a set of data points. Trend lines are computed using regression analysis, and a technical discussion of that strategy is beyond the scope of this book; however, most popular spreadsheet programs, such as Microsoft Excel, allow you to add trend lines to simple line graphs. Trend lines for the compostable and landfill waste data are shown in Figure 9.9.

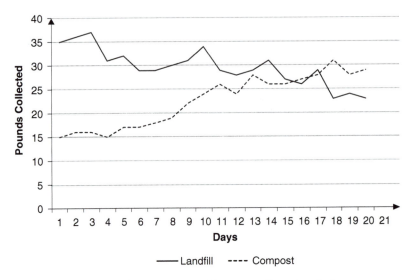

Figure 9.8 Pounds of landfill and compostable waste collected each day

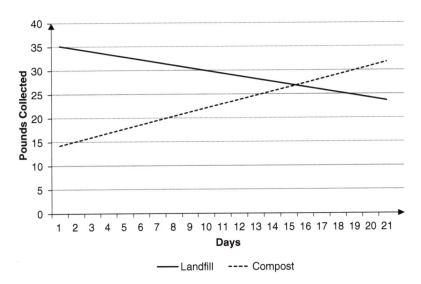

Figure 9.9 Trend lines showing pounds of landfill and compostable waste collected each day

Often systems exhibit recognizable patterns of behavior that facilitate prediction of future events as well as analysis of causal relationships and stock and flow processes. Figure 9.10 shows six common patterns of behavior over time that might be observed in systems. You should be aware that these graphs are only intended to illustrate various patterns of behavior and do not necessarily display real data. In the messy real world, graphs often intersect the y-axis at points other than the origin (as in Figures 9.8 and 9.9). Each pattern is described briefly below.

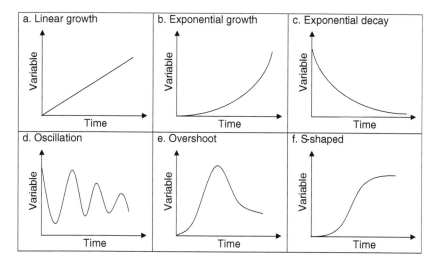

Figure 9.10 Common patterns in behavior over time graphs

Linear Change

Linear growth occurs when a variable increases at the same rate at each time interval. The rate of growth is constant across time, so the graph is a straight line, as shown in Figure 9.10a. For example, if you added exactly two dollars to your vacation fund every day, at the end of the year, you would have added $730 to the fund. The trend lines for the compostable waste and landfill data shown in Figure 9.9 also show linear change because they represent the average amount of change per day. The dashed compostable waste trend line shows linear growth. If you computed the slope of this line, you would find that, on average, the amount of compostable waste collected is increasing by about a pound per day. The solid line in Figure 9.9 showing the landfill waste trend line shows linear decay. On average, it is decreasing by about two thirds of a pound each day.

Linear change (growth or decay) is conceptually easy to understand because it is based on the basic operations of addition or subtraction. However, many systems display nonlinear patterns of behavior over time, and recognition of those nonlinear processes is an important systems thinking skill.

Exponential Growth

Exponential growth occurs when a variable increases at each time interval by a fixed percent of its current value. As the value of the variable grows, the proportion by which it increases also grows so the rate of growth accelerates. As shown in Figure 9.10b, exponential growth is displayed as a curved line that has an increasingly steep slope and approaches but never reaches the vertical. For example, bacterial growth occurs exponentially. Most bacteria reproduce by a process called binary fission, in which a bacteria cell divides into two new cells. If we start with a single cell of a bacterium that undergoes binary fission after an hour, and then each of the two new cells undergoes binary fission at the end of the second hour, and the process continues with each new cell, in 24 hours there would be 16 million bacteria cells. Eventually, the bacteria would run out of nutrients or room and growth would stop, but in the early stages, bacterial growth is exponential.

Exponential Decay

When a variable decreases by a proportion of its current value at each time interval, it is decaying exponentially. The rate of decrease becomes slower over time. This pattern is shown in Figure 9.10c. For example, **environmental persistence** refers to the amount of time a substance remains toxic in the environment and is sometimes expressed in terms of a substance's **half-life**. This is the amount of time required for a substance to reach half of its value at the beginning time interval. Thus, half-life refers to an exponential decay process. The longer a substance's half-life, the longer it poses a danger for organisms that become exposed to it. Because the rate of decay slows over time, a substance that decays exponentially may diminish rapidly at first but could persist at a toxic level for a very long time. For example, DDT has a half-life of up to 15 years in the environment. This means that it could take as long as 75 years for DDT to be fully dissipated once deposited.

Oscillation

Oscillation refers to a repeating pattern in which the value of a variable fluctuates around an average. This pattern is shown in Figure 9.10d. Oscillating processes are common. Think about the tides, predator-prey population cycles, economic boom and bust cycles, human sleep patterns, and student attentiveness throughout the school year. Often, oscillating system dynamics occur when there is a delay in a balancing loop that causes humans to overreact. You may have experienced oscillation if you have tried to adjust the heat in a room with a slow-to-respond heater. First, you feel cold, so you turn up the heat. The slow-to-respond heater takes a while to warm up, and you are still cold, so you turn the heat up higher. Then, when the heat finally reaches your room, you get too warm too quickly, so you turn the heat back down. However, that pokey heater is still blasting away, so you turn the dial back further. Pretty soon, the heater shuts off, and the room begins to cool until eventually you feel cold, and the cycle starts all over again. You may have noticed that the amplitude of the peaks and valleys in Figure 9.10d are decreasing over time. This is called **damped oscillation**, a pattern that occurs when a system gradually moves toward a desired goal and eventually reaches a state of stable equilibrium. When there is no change over time in the amplitude of oscillation, the system is said to be in **sustained oscillation**. A system in sustained oscillation is unlikely to reach a state of equilibrium without some form of outside influence.

Overshoot

The idea of overshoot was introduced in Chapter 2. As discussed in Chapter 2, currently a number of systems essential for the future survival of humans and many other species have crossed critical planetary boundaries and are in a state of overshoot. Overshoot is caused when there is a delay in a system that is experiencing very rapid or exponential growth. When a system has exceeded its limit and gone into overshoot, one of two outcomes can occur. The system could enter a period of oscillation around a goal that is below the limit and eventually reach a state of equilibrium. Alternatively, the system could go into overshoot and collapse. The graph in Figure 9.10e illustrates this overshoot and collapse scenario. Notice that after collapse, the system continues to decline until it eventually stops altogether. Overshoot occurs in nature when a population exceeds the **carrying capacity** of its environment. Carrying capacity is the optimal population size that can be supported by an ecosystem. For example, when the population of deer in an area becomes too large, there may not be enough food, water, or shelter to support the entire herd. When this occurs, deer, which would normally avoid built environments, may move into areas they would not previously have inhabited, such as suburban neighborhoods, areas along freeways, and city parks. This is a situation that is unhealthy for the deer and humans.

The concern has been expressed often that humans may have exceeded the carrying capacity of the planet and that systems collapse is imminent. This idea was first raised by Thomas Robert Malthus in 1798, who observed that exponential human population growth could eventually lead to poverty, disease, and starvation when the limits of the Earth's food systems were exceeded. Malthus advocated a number of political and economic measures aimed at slowing human population growth. This idea was revisited in 1972 in the first edition of *Limits to Growth* (Meadows, Meadows, Randers, & Behrens, 1972) and continues to generate interest and debate today.

S-Shaped

An S-shaped graph illustrates a system with balanced inflow and outflows. This pattern is shown in Figure 9.10f. After a period of rapid growth, the variable stabilizes below the limits of the system and enters a mode of long-term stability. An S-shaped curve indicates the system's behavior is not being affected by long delays and that the system is responding appropriately to feedback. An S-shaped curve can be an indication of the long-term health and sustainability of a system. For example, suppose a system has the goal of preserving biodiversity. When data show that a particular species is endangered by loss of habitat, effective policy and public education strategies are implemented, and the species population rebounds to a stable size below the carrying capacity of its environment.

Helping Learners Use Systems Thinking

The systems thinking tools described above can help learners understand a wide range of complex, dynamic problems and can be applied across disciplines. A minimal list of systems thinking tools would include the following four broad skill areas (Ben-Zvi Assaraf & Orion, 2010; Soderquist & Overlakker, 2010; Sweeny-Booth & Sterman, 2000; Waters Foundation, 2015):

1. *See whole systems and identify components within systems.* This skill can involve looking beyond isolated events and "snapshots" to see broader temporal and spatial boundaries of systems and looking for hidden dimensions of systems. This is the art of seeing the entire forest rather than focusing on specific trees.
2. *Analyze the relationships among systems components.* This skill entails seeing interconnectedness among overlapping and nested systems as well as recognizing how the components within a system affect and relate to one another.
3. *Recognize how elements within a system change over time and how systems can generate their own behavior.* This skill involves looking for patterns of behavior and analyzing cyclical cause-and-effect relationships. Attending to the temporal dimensions of systems can help students make predictions about future outcomes and better understand situations that display dynamic complexity. Looking for change over time also can help students see how information delays can affect system behaviors.
4. *Recognize and represent stock and flow and feedback processes.* This skill involves the ability to see the way systems behave and the ability to represent those processes graphically and in words. As students better understand the dynamics within systems, they can apply the skills of systems thinking to a broad range of problems in school as well as day-to-day life.

Although the knowledge domain associated with systems thinking can involve specialized knowledge and skills, you can help your students begin to apply systems thinking strategies before they have mastered the more technical aspects of systems dynamics. For example, the Waters Foundation (2015) has described a number of "habits of systems thinkers" that include the more technical skills listed above as well as these more general thinking habits that can be incorporated into a variety of classroom contexts beginning at early grade levels:

- Change perspectives to increase understanding. Looking at problems from differing points of view can help students see hidden dimensions and unexpected consequences.
- Identify and examine assumptions. Children can be taught from an early age to identify their own beliefs and assumptions and to test those assumptions against data.
- Examine issues fully and resist the urge to come to a quick conclusion. This habit involves taking time to fully understand all of the dimensions of a situation and avoiding quick fixes.

- Consider both short- and long-term consequences of actions, and look for unintended consequences.
- Check results and make changes if needed. This habit entails the use of successive approximations and ongoing assessment of solutions.

Finally, there are a number of skills and dispositions that are developed in traditional school subjects, particularly at the middle and high school level, that can be addressed through the lens of systems thinking. Those include:

- The ability to make generalizations;
- Creating, interpreting, and telling stories from graphs;
- Identifying units of measure;
- A basic understanding of probability, logic, and algebra; and
- Identifying nonlinearities and understanding their implications.

Indicators and Footprints

So far in this chapter, we have focused on the characteristics of systems and various tools that allow us to describe their behaviors. However, simply recognizing and describing systems is not the most powerful application of systems thinking. The real value of systems thinking is that it can help us make better decisions when those decisions involve complex and interconnected systems. This is where **indicators** can be helpful. Indicators are a type of data that provide information about how well the various elements of a system are working.

The terms **indicator** and **index** are closely related, both referring to the idea of "pointing out" or "showing" just as we use our index finger for pointing. Indicators point to the various components of a system so that we can monitor their status or condition in "real time," better understand how the components interrelate, or see how the various components or the overall system change over time. Indicators are particularly useful for monitoring large, complicated systems or complex sets of interconnected systems that are difficult to see holistically. Generally, multiple types of indicators are used to monitor a single system, with each indicator providing a specific single of information. Often, groups of related indicators are referred to as **indicator systems** because no single indicator is likely to provide enough information on its own, but when used together, groups of related indicators can greatly improve decision making effectiveness.

Indicators are most useful when they are easy to understand and interpret, provide relevant information about the health of the system, can be updated quickly and relatively easily, and are trustworthy (Tillman, 2007). Indicators can refer to a wide variety of types of data, including quantitative variables (e.g., time, quantity, rate, cost, etc.) or qualitative variables (e.g., "overall satisfaction," "ease of access," "type of communication," etc.). Therefore, the data that underlie an indicator can be collected through a wide variety of processes, including direct measurement, observation, or analysis of extant records, or interactively through strategies such as interviews and surveys. Similarly, indicators can be displayed in a variety of ways, including verbal descriptions, numbers, or graphic displays, depending the type of information involved.

Most of us interact with indicator systems on a regular basis, although we might not refer to them as such while we're using them. For example, the dials, gauges, and lights on the dashboard of an automobile provide the driver with information about engine temperature, oil pressure, electrical charge, fuel reserves, ground speed, and engine turnover rate measured in revolutions per minute (RPMs). When considered together, these various indicators provide a more complete picture of the overall performance and operation of the automobile than any single indictor would on its own.

Similarly, your annual health checkup probably involves a variety of indicators about the status of your body systems. Your health care provider may conduct a brief interview about your recent health status and history; measure your blood pressure, pulse rate, and temperature; and directly observe the quality and rate of your respiration and heart performance. Perhaps you also are asked to provide a blood sample so that levels of cholesterol, blood sugar, calcium, and electrolytes can be checked. None of these indicators would, on their own, be sufficient for making an informed judgment about your health, but when analyzed as a system of indicators, your health care provider is able to make educated inferences about your overall state of health and well-being.

Most of the time, we prefer not think of our bodies or mind as "systems," so our health care providers tend not to report the results of our personal annual check as a set of indicators. However, indicators are used frequently to report data about health and well-being at the community and planetary level. We will explore well-being in detail in the next chapter, with particular attention to strategies for helping learners improve their own personal well-being. In this chapter, we will focus on the use of indicator systems to monitor societal level measures of well-being, often are referred to as **quality of life** indicators.

Quality of life involves an assessment of the entirety of a society or community (Gaspers, 2010; Phillips, 2006). An assessment of quality of life can include environmental and health variables such as clean air and water and a safe climate; economic variables such as income equity and opportunities to earn a living wage or access to educational opportunities; and social system variables such good governance, gender equity, or access to adequate health care. Thus, quality of life describes the contexts that create the conditions for one's actual lived experiences—we can promote the well-being of individuals by improving societal variables related to quality of life.

However, quality of life and, as we will see in the next chapter, well-being are not just measures of "the good life." Assessment of quality of life involves a two-sided assessment that attends as much to avoidance of those things we find undesirable or harmful (i.e., ill-being variables) as to attainment of those things we find positive and desirable. These **ill-being** variables can include a wide range of social, economic, and environmental variables such as war or high rates of violence; poor governance; insufficient infrastructure to support community resilience; inadequate water or food systems; lack of basic freedoms, institutional inequalities based on variables such as race, gender, or religion; limited employment opportunities; or inadequate educational systems. Therefore, assessment of quality of life at a societal level must attend to the absence of factors that contribute to individual ill-being and the presence of factors that contribute to individual well-being.

Interest in societal level indicators of quality of life has grown in recent years as it has become clear that purely economic measures such as the gross national product (GNP) do not capture the variables that contribute to individual happiness or to sustainability and therefore do not accurately report the overall health and well-being of a society. For example, the Bhutan **Gross National Happiness** (GNH) index has received much attention in recent years because it was one of the first national efforts at characterizing the overall health of a country by including subjective measures of well-being in addition to traditional indicators of economic productivity.

The GNH index uses data collected from surveys of representative samples of Bhutan's citizens from all regions and social strata (Ura, Alkire, Zangmo, & Wangdi, 2012). The GNH uses a non-Western conception of happiness that moves beyond concern for one's self to embrace a concern for the health and happiness of the community. In this respect, the pursuit of happiness is collective as well as deeply personal. The GNH includes indicators from nine domains, as shown in Table 9.1:

TABLE 9.1 Domains and Indictors on the Bhutan Gross National Happiness Index

Domain	Indicators
Psychological well-being	Life satisfaction
	Positive emotions
	Negative emotions
	Spirituality
Health	Self-reported health
	Healthy days
	Disability
	Mental health
Education	Literacy
	Amount of formal schooling
	Cultural/traditional knowledge
	Community values
Cultural diversity and resilience	Zorig Chusum skills (traditional and ceremonial arts and crafts)
	Speak native language
	Driglam Namzha (etiquette)

(Continued)

Table 9.1 (continued)

Time use	Time spent working
	Time spent sleeping
Standard of living	Per capita income
	Housing
	Assets
Good governance	Politcal participation
	Services
	Government performance
	Fundamental rights
Community vitality	Connectedness with community
	Family
	Donation of time and money
	Sense of safety
Ecological diversity and resilience	Wildlife damage
	Urban issues
	Responsibility toward environment
	Ecological issues

The Bhutanese government uses the results of GNH surveys to improve conditions for the people it defines as "not-yet-happy." Data collected in recent years has tended to show that not-yet-happy people in rural Bhutan tend to be those who have attained less education, have lower living standards, or find that they are unable to balance their use of time between activities related to earning a living and leisure. Urban not-yet-happy people tend to be those who experience lower levels of psychological well-being and community vitality (Ura, Alkire, Zangmo, & Wangdi, 2012).

As you can see, the 33 indicators that underlie the GNH point to a number of complex and interconnected systems. While it would be theoretically possible to map out the stocks and flows and feedback loops associated with those systems, the GNH is a more streamlined and efficient strategy for monitoring those systems. When the results show an area where more attention is needed, it is still possible to do that more fine-grained systems analysis.

Perhaps one of the most well-known indicator systems in the context of sustainability is the **ecological footprint**. An ecological footprint is a metric for estimating the amount of pressure one's lifestyle and purchases place on natural planetary systems. In this respect, an ecological footprint is a measure of ill-being, not a measure of well-being. Ecological footprint analysis has grown in respectability and popularity in the last decade. There are a number of footprint calculators available on the Internet that allow users to enter information about consumption patterns, travel habits, and home energy efficiency. The calculators then create a report that tells approximately how much planetary surface area is required to support the respondent's lifestyle. Sometimes this is expressed as planet equivalents, with statements such as this: "If everyone on the planet had a lifestyle and consumption patterns similar to yours, we would need x number of planet Earths to support us all." Individual ecological footprint analysis can be helpful when used as a benchmark to establish goals, such as for an entire classroom or school. However, use of ill-being indicators such as ecological footprints must be tied to a constructive plan that will enable all members of the community to make meaningful contributions to reducing the group's aggregated footprint. If, as is often the case for children, an individual does not have direct access to the system variables that would need to be adjusted to reduce her or his individual footprint, the process can be frustrating and counterproductive.

Ecological footprint analysis at the societal level can be more useful, particularly when tied to measures of well-being. For example, the **Happy Planet Index** (HPI) (Abdallah, Michaelson, Shah, Stoll, & Marks, 2012) assesses the extent to which countries deliver long, happy, sustainable lives. The HPI is a ratio measure that reports the rate of production of long, happy lives per unit of environmental damage based on this formula:

$$Happy\ Planet\ Index \approx \frac{Subjective\ Well\text{-}being \times Life\ Expectancy}{Ecological\ Footprint}$$

In this respect, the HPI begins to factor in the true costs of ecological damage in assessing the overall health of a country or state. The HPI uses data from three well known and highly credible indicator systems:

1. Life expectancy information is obtained from the United Nations Development Programme (UNDP). The UNDP has, for over 20 years, issued annual topically focused Human Development Reports center around a definition of human development as

   a process of enlarging people's choices and enhancing human capabilities (the range of things people can be and do) and freedoms, enabling them to live a long and healthy life, have access to knowledge and a decent standard of living, and participate in the life of their community and decisions affecting their lives. (UNDP, 1990/2015)

2. Subjective ratings of well-being collected with an instrument designed by the Gallup organization that asks respondents to locate themselves on a scale in which zero represents the worst possible life for themselves and ten represents the best possible life for themselves (Cantril, 1965). This index (Gallup, 2014) defines well-being as a multidimensional construct that includes five elements that involve both individual and societal level dimensions:

   • Purpose: Liking what you do and being motivated to achieve your goals. Often purpose is associated with career or some form of professional identity.
   • Social: Having satisfying and supportive relationships in your life.

- Financial: Managing your economic resources so as to reduce stress and increase security.
- Community: Liking where you live, having a sense of safety, belonging, and pride in your community.
- Physical: Enjoying good health and having enough energy to accomplish your daily goals and activities.

3. Ecological footprint data for the HPI is collected using the Ecological Footprint calculator from the World Wildlife Fund for Nature (WWF, 2015). This is an online questionnaire that includes questions about consumption related to food, travel, home efficiency, and consumer items.

The most recent HPI report, published in 2012, ranked 151 countries. The top and bottom six countries on the HPI are shown in Table 9.2.

An outstanding resource for teachers interested in helping learners gain first-hand experience with the development and use of a sustainability indicator system is the *Healthy Neighborhoods, Healthy Kids Project Guide* (Tilman, 2007). This is a complete guidebook including lesson plans and activity suggestions for a middle level or early high school project-based unit focusing on the characteristics of a healthy neighborhood. Learners work in collaborative teams to identify the indicators most relevant for their particular community and then implement strategies to collect data pertaining to those indicators. Once a community profile has been developed, learners are encouraged to develop action research and service-learning projects to help improve the overall quality of life in their neighborhoods.

TABLE 9.2 Top and Bottom Six Countries on 2012 Happy Planet Index

Country	HPI	Well-being	Life expectancy	Ecological footprint
Top Six Countries				
Costa Rica	64.0	7.3	79.3	2.5
Vietnam	60.4	5.8	75.2	1.4
Colombia	59.8	6.4	73.7	1.8
Belize	59.3	6.5	76.1	2.1
El Salvador	58.9	6.7	72.2	2.0
Jamaica	58.5	6.2	73.1	1.7
Bottom Six Countries				
Bahrain	26.6	4.5	75.1	6.6
Mali	26.0	3.8	51.4	1.9
Central African Republic	25.3	3.6	48.4	1.4
Qatar	25.2	6.6	78.4	11.7
Chad	24.7	3.7	49.6	1.9
Botswana	22.6	3.6	53.2	2.8

Source: Happy Planet Index: 2012 Report.

EXTEND YOUR PROFESSIONAL KNOWLEDGE 9.1

1. Download the Healthy Neighborhoods Healthy Kids Guide at http://sustainableschoolsproject.org/tools-resources/hnhk
   a. Use the guide to explore your own neighborhood.
   b. Work with a group of youth to develop an indicator system for the area around their school.
   c. Develop a series of lessons or units that would extend the indicator project into a longer service-learning experience for the learners.

Notes

1 The terms "purpose" and "function" often are used interchangeably, but generally function refers to the behavior of nonhuman systems and purpose refers to human systems (Meadows, 2008).

2 There may be several feedback loops that operate *within* the tree to regulate metabolism and distribution of the products of photosynthesis such as CO_2 and sugar. Growth rate and rate of photosynthesis also may operate in a feedback loop, but this process is influenced by external factors over which the tree has no direct influence such as temperature and moisture (Sharkey, Weise, Standish, & Terashima, 2004). At the same time, trees are certainly components in very complex ecosystems that include numerous feedback loops.

References

Abdallah, A., Michaelson, J., Shah, S., Stoll, L., & Marks, N. (2012). *Happy Planet Index: 2012 Report*. London: New Economics Foundation.

Ben-Zvi Assaraf, O., & Orion, N. (2010). Four case studies, six years later: Developing system thinking skills in junior high school and sustaining them over time. *Journal of Research in Science Teaching, 47*, 1253–1280.

Cantril, H. (1965). *The Pattern of Human Concerns*. New Brunswick, NJ: Rutgers University Press.

Gallup, Inc. (2014). *State of Global Well-Being: Results of Gallup-Healthways Global Well-Being Index*. Princeton, NJ: Author.

Gaspers, D. (2010). Understanding the diversity of conceptions of well-being and quality of life. *Journal of Socio Economics, 39*, 351–360.

Kirkwood, C.W. (1998). *Integrated Business Process Analysis: A System Dynamics Sourcebook*. Tempe, AZ: Arizona State University.

Malthus, T. R. (1826). *An Essay on the Principle of Population*. London: John Murray. (Original work published 1798)

Meadows, D.H. (2008). *Thinking in Systems: A Primer*. White River Junction, VT: Chelsea Green.

Meadows, D.H., Meadows, D. L., Randers, J., & Behrens, W.W. (1972). *The Limits to Growth*. New York: Universe Books.

Meadows, D.H., Randers, J., & Meadows, D.L. (2004). *Limits to Growth: The 30-Year Update*. White River Junction, VT: Chelsea Green.

Phillips, D. (2006). *Quality of Life: Concepts, Policy, and Practice*. New York: Routledge.

Richardson, G.P., & Pugh, A. L. (1981). *Introduction to System Dynamics Modeling With DYNAMO*. Cambridge, MA: MIT Press.

Senge, P. (1990). *The Fifth Discipline: The Art and Practice of the Learning Organization*. New York: Doubleday Currency.

Senge, P. (2000). *Schools That Learn: A Fifth Discipline Resource*. Boston, MA: Nicholas Brealey.

Sharkey, T. D., Weise, S. E., Standish, A.J., & Terashima, I. (2004). Chloroplast to leaf. In W. K. Smith, T. C. Vogelmann, & C. Critchley (Eds.), *Photosynthetic Adaptation: Chloroplast to Landscape*. New York: Springer.

Soderquist, C., & Overlakker, S. (2010). Education for sustainable development: A systems thinking approach. *Global Environmental Research, 14*, 193–202.

Sweeny-Booth, L., & Sterman, J.D. (2000). Bathtub dynamics: Initial results of a systems thinking inventory. *System Dynamics Review, 16*, 249–286.

Tillman, T. (2007). *Healthy Neighborhoods / Healthy Kids Project Guide*. Shelburne, VT: Shelburne Farms.

United Nations Development Programme (UNDP). (1990/2015). United Nations Development Programme Human Development Reports. Retrieved from: http://hdr.undp.org/en

Ura, K., Alkire, S., Zangmo, T., & Wangdi, K. (2012). *A Short Guide to Gross National Happiness Index*. Thimphu, Bhutan: Center for Bhutan Studies.

Waters Foundation. (2015). Habits of a Systems Thinker. Retrieved from: http://waters foundation.org/systems-thinking/habits-of-a-systems-thinker/

World Wildlife Fund for Nature. (2015). WWF Footprint Calculator. Retrieved from: http://footprint.wwf.org.uk/

10

HAPPINESS AND WELL-BEING

If by renouncing a lesser happiness one may realize a greater happiness, the wise person would give up the lesser to behold the greater.

—Dhammapada, ch. 21, 290

All those who suffer in the world do so because of their desire for their own happiness.
All those happy in the world are so because of their desire for the happiness of others.

—Shantideva, *Bodhicary vat ra*, ch. 8, v.129

The human quest for happiness creates billions of dollars of commerce around the world. Every minute of every hour of every day, advertisers and marketers around the world work very hard to make us feel *un*happy in hopes that we will buy whatever it is they have to sell to make the unhappiness go away. . . .

Faster, tastier food.
More energetic energy drinks.
Up-to-the-minute fashions.
Alluring perfume.
A bigger, better, smarter mobile phone.
A sleeker, newer, more powerful automobile.
A perfect body and perfect hair!
A more prestigious job! Exotic vacations! A bigger house!
Bigger thrills! More! Bigger! Faster! Better! Newer! More!
More! Bigger! Better! Faster! Newer! More! Bigger! Better! Faster! Newer! More! More! More!

And yet. . . .
It seems like we are never satisfied for very long. As soon as we manage to acquire that bigger, better, faster, newer thing or that exciting experience, or that notable achievement

that we thought would bring lasting happiness, our expectations rise, and we soon find that we are no longer as happy as we thought we would be or as happy as we would like to be. So we start looking around for something else to make the unhappiness go away. And so the quest resumes and we search again for a bigger thrill, a better scent, a faster car, or that perfect job. Again and again and again . . . until. . . .

Until what?

Are we all just destined to suffer longing, disappointment, and unhappiness endlessly until we die? Can we ever get off of the treadmill of desire and dissatisfaction?

Is happiness, *true* happiness, even possible?

The answer to this question is unequivocally Yes! YES!

It is possible to experience a fulfilling and happy life that is not defined by endless consumption and suffering. There is no magic involved, no transformative religious conversion necessary, and no secret code to unlock. We can each learn strategies and ways of thinking that can help us live happier, more fulfilling, and healthier lives. In fact, this is one of the best benefits of a sustainability worldview.

BOX 10.1 THE HEDONIC TREADMILL

The phenomenon of repeatedly adjusting our expectations and desires as we accumulate more possessions, experiences, or accomplishments is called the **hedonic treadmill**. Each time we acquire the object of our desire, we rapidly adapt and take it for granted. Then we begin again to strive for that next possession, experience, or achievement that will make us feel happy. Ironically, and sadly, far from helping us achieve lasting happiness, life on the hedonic treadmill is often a source of great unhappiness.

Think of a time when you found yourself stuck on the hedonic treadmill.

What happened? Were you eventually able to break the cycle of desire and consumption?

What are some things each of us can do to get off the hedonic treadmill?

The sustainability worldview is hopeful, positive, and life affirming. Individuals who have developed a sustainability worldview understand the world holistically and see themselves as part of a vibrant, interconnected network of positive solutions. Indeed, working toward sustainability involves the opportunity to gain the one thing all humans want most: *a good life*.

This assertion is not idle rhetoric or empty hyperbole. While each of us has our own ideas of what constitutes a good life for ourselves, most people identify a similar set of variables that have come to be associated with the concept of **well-being**. For many of us, this list includes ideas such as health, financial security, positive relationships, and rewarding work—the things that make life worthwhile.

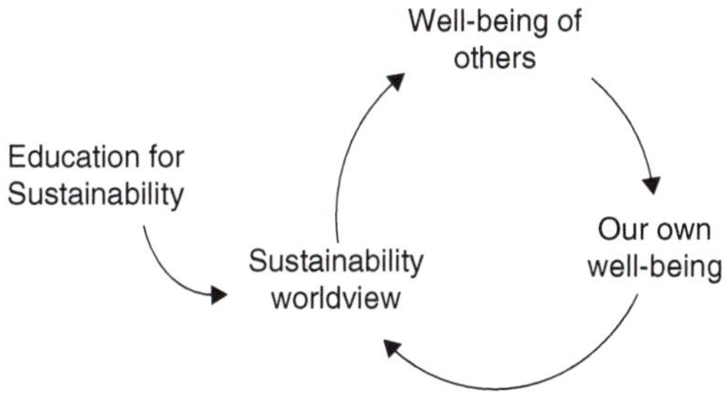

Figure 10.1 Well-being positive causal loop

Most assuredly, most people *do not* associate true happiness and well-being with life on the hedonic treadmill or the kind of rampant overconsumption that is responsible for so many of the sustainability challenges we face today. Moreover, a growing body of research is showing that when we act to promote the well-being of others and the various systems upon which humans and other species depend, we are also contributing directly to our own well-being (Dietz, Rosa, & York, 2009; O'Brien, 2010).

Here is how this works: Education for sustainability is aimed at helping learners develop a sustainability worldview that focuses on the well-being of all now and in the future. In turn, acting on behalf of the well-being of others has a positive impact on our own outlook and sense of well-being—we feel better about ourselves when we act on behalf of others. At the same time, the thinking skills and positive dispositions that help promote our own well-being are the same values, beliefs, and perspectives associated with a sustainability worldview. As we learned in Chapter 8, this positive relationship, illustrated in Figure 10.1, is called a causal loop or positive feedback loop.

CONSIDER THIS 10.1 DESCRIBE THE CAUSAL LOOP

- Think about how you would describe the relationship among the four variables in the causal loop shown in Figure 10.1 using words instead of a diagram. Write a short paragraph to describe the diagram.
- Perhaps you recognized that the hedonic treadmill is an example of a reinforcing loop—a vicious cycle. The more we consume, the more we feel dissatisfied, and then we consume more. Try sketching out the causal loop and behavior over time graph associated with the hedonic treadmill. Use a time when you found yourself on the hedonic treadmill as your example.

The well-being positive feedback loop is based on two findings that have emerged from the research on well-being that are particularly pertinent to education for sustainability. First, while pursuit of well-being for individuals is itself a worthy goal, societies also benefit from higher rates of well-being (Diener & Ryan, 2011). In general, people who are satisfied with their lives are more likely to be better citizens; better workers; and to live longer, healthier lives. Higher rates of subjective well-being in a society are associated with variety of desirable outcomes such as educational achievement (UNICEF, 2013), peace (Institute for Economics and Peace, 2013), health, (Lyubomirsky, King, & Diener, 2005), income (Graham, Eggers, & Sukhtankar, 2004), and participation in community (Oishi, Diener, & Lucas, 2007). The causal order here is important. It's not just that success causes well-being but rather that well-being helps people become better citizens and to become more successful. The message here is that if you want a better life, change your thinking first and success will follow.

The other important finding is that well-being is not something that just happens to us. We each have the ability to manage many of the variables in our own lives that affect our well-being, and it is possible to learn strategies that promote our own well-being. In this chapter, we will explore this well-being–sustainability connection and identify some strategies you can use to help yourself and your students experience greater well-being.

What Exactly Is Well-Being?

Well-being is a deceptively complex idea that defies easy definition. In contemporary usage, the term **well-being** often is used interchangeably or in tandem with other expressions such as "health," "happiness," "quality of life," "life satisfaction," "a good life," "welfare," or "sufficiency." This sense of the term has been in use in English since at least the early 17th century, generally referring to the state of being or doing well in life; a happy, prosperous condition; or the general property of good moral or physical welfare. However, the general ideas associated with well-being are nearly universal and can be found in indigenous cultures around the world; in Taoist, Confucian, Buddhist, and Hindu writings dating to the second century BCE (Ivanhoe, 2013; Ricard, 2013; Salagame, 2013); and in the writings of ancient Greek philosophers.

BOX 10.2 WELL BEING, WELL-BEING, OR WELLBEING?

In English, compound words often start out in the open form, are later joined in the hyphenated form, and then eventually metamorphose into the closed form. Today, the oldest, open compound form of *well being* is used infrequently, but the term is still in transition from the hyphenated to closed form. In most of the English speaking world outside of North America, the closed form *wellbeing* is the accepted spelling for the term. In the United States and Canada, both the hyphenated form *well-being* and the closed form *wellbeing* are used, and the hyphenated form is generally used in academic publications. All three forms are grammatically correct and refer to the same construct.

Today, well-being can mean many things, but in simple terms, it means feeling good—being healthy, happy, and judging life positively. However, well-being is more than just happiness. It involves an overall satisfaction with the way your life is going, a positive outlook on the future, and a general sense of fulfillment and positive functioning.

Interest in the science of well-being has grown significantly in the last two decades, and today the scholarly literature on well-being is large, diverse, and vibrant. In recent years, well-being has been studied through the lenses of economics, sociology, psychology, public policy, health sciences, education, environmental sciences, philosophy, and religion (Gasper, 2004). In addition, a growing body of research is investigating the cross-cultural dimensions of well-being and the ways in which notions of well-being vary around the world (Knoop & Delle Fave, 2013).

Two areas of inquiry related to well-being have particular relevance in the context of education for sustainability: research focusing on societal level indicators of well-being or **quality of life** to inform public policy (LaPlaca, McNaught, & Knight, 2013) discussed in the last chapter, and investigation of the nature of well-being at the individual level, frequently called **subjective well-being.**

Subjective Well-Being

Generally, well-being refers to a longer-term aggregate of all life circumstances rather than to the short-term ups and downs that everyone experiences, although our overall sense of well-being often is colored by our immediate circumstances (Diener, Lucas, Schimmack, & Helliwell, 2009). We each assess own individual well-being according to a variety of evaluations we make of the various aspects of our lives (physical, emotional, psychological, etc.). These evaluations are based on a comparison of our personal goals, hopes, and desires with our lived circumstances and experiences. We judge our level of well-being according to how satisfied we are with this comparison. Naturally, each of us has a unique set of life experiences and a uniquely personal set of desires, goals, and aspirations, so we also each have a highly individualized definition of well-being that cannot be directly verified by others. This is why well-being at the individual level is often referred to as subjective well-being. At the same time, one's subjective assessment of well-being is directly influenced by the larger, societal milieu that surrounds those individual perceptual and thinking processes, particularly quality of life variables such as those discussed in the last chapter.

As was discussed in the last chapter, quality of life involves a two-sided assessment that attends as much to avoidance of those things we find undesirable or harmful as to attainment of those things we find positive and desirable. Similarly, well-being is not only an evaluation of the good and desirable aspects of life. It also involves the absence of variables associated with ill-being—those aspects of life that most people would classify as bad and undesirable.

At the individual level, these ill-being variables include factors that could limit one's overall satisfaction with life, such as poor physical or psychological health, insufficient financial resources, unhealthy or unsatisfying relationships, insufficient education, or underemployment. Indeed, millions of people around the world experience very difficult lives due to circumstances such as extreme poverty, brutal oppression, inequality, or inadequate health care. For people living under these circumstances, well-being might involve meeting their basic needs for things like food, clean water, or shelter; survival in an occupied territory or under an oppressive government; avoiding diseases; or coping with the catastrophic effects of climate change.

There are two important points that must be considered here. First, well-being does not only involve the positive emotions commonly associated with happiness. It has been theorized (Lyubomirsky, King, & Diener, 2005) that there are three major factors that affect a person's happiness: a genetically determined "set-point" around which our level of happiness generally hovers; (b) circumstantial factors such as health, income, and education; and (c) activities and practices known to promote happiness. This third factor is of particular interest for educators, and we will return to it shortly. Well-being can promote positive emotions; however, happiness is a more episodic and situationally dependent. Well-being is a longer-term and more holistic state.

Second, well-being cannot be equated with wealth. Well-being and happiness have much more to do how you interact with the world and the people around you than it does with what you own or can buy. One need only look at the high rates of obesity, violence, addiction, and domestic violence in the United States to see this. While financial security certainly makes it easier to care for one's health, to obtain healthy food and adequate shelter, and to afford an education, even very poor people can experience the positive emotions, healthy relationships, and a sense of accomplishment that are associated with well-being (White, 2013).

The process that underlies subjective well-being is called **self-determination**. Self-determination theory assumes that people are intrinsically active, vital, self-motivated, curious, and eager to succeed because success is itself satisfying and rewarding (Deci & Ryan, 2008). These basic traits result in three psychological needs that are experienced by all humans across cultures (Deci & Ryan, 2000).

The need for **competence** involves the feelings of effectiveness; efficacy; and mastery of challenging, nontrivial behaviors. The need for **relatedness** involves feelings of close connection with important others in one's life, and the need for **autonomy** involves feelings of ownership of one's own behavior, freedom to follow one's interests, and to consider for one's self the relevance of various social norms and values. It is thought that these are evolved and therefore "hard-wired" needs—humans who were more competent at skills important for survival, who were better able make autonomous decisions, and who were better able to negotiate social relationships were more likely to survive and reproduce.

When these needs are satisfied, we experience higher levels of self-motivation and mental health, but when they are thwarted, we experience diminished motivation and lower levels of subjective well-being (Deci & Ryan, 2000). However, because these are intrinsic needs, they often operate at a subconscious level, and we may not always recognize when they are influencing our behavior. When we lack effective ways to get these basic self-determination needs met, we may behave in ways that are not only unhealthy for ourselves but for others. Advertisers know this and are very skilled at appealing to our needs for competence, for relationships, and for autonomy. Think about the feelings that arise when you watch an automobile commercial showing a beautiful couple driving off into the wilderness in their sport utility vehicle. Perhaps you feel a twinge of envy or a desire to "be like" like the people in the commercial because they appear to be happy and having fun (experiencing positive emotions), enjoying one another's company (experiencing a satisfying relationship), and about to engage in a challenging if not dangerous activity (experiencing feelings of competence) in a vehicle that provides freedom and autonomy (cha-ching!).

CONSIDER THIS 10.2 UNMET SELF-DETERMINATION NEEDS

How could real or perceived unmet self-determination needs drive these unsustainable practices?

* Overconsumption
* Direct or indirect acts of violence toward others
* Waste of nonrenewable resources
* A focus on one's current needs without consideration of the needs of future generations.

Much of the research on subjective well-being has been conducted in a relatively new field called **positive psychology** that is rooted in self-determination theory (Donaldson, 2011; Seligman & Csikszentmihalyi, 2000). The primary aim of positive psychology is to identify psychological and educational interventions that facilitate the positive feelings, behaviors, and cognitions that enhance well-being

(Sin & Lyubomirsky, 2009). This approach represents a significant departure from the 20th-century psychological theories that were concerned primarily with processes associated with decreasing suffering. Instead, positive psychology "emphasizes building individual and societal well-being by identifying and fostering strengths of character" (Peterson & Park, 2011, p. 49). One of the pioneers of this new approach, Martin Seligman (2011), asserts that well-being is not something that can exist solely in one's head but involves a combination of positive emotion (often associated with happiness), finding meaning in one's life, having satisfying, healthy relationships, and having a sense of accomplishment. Seligman (2011) has coined the acronym PERMA to refer to these five elements. Each of the letters in PERMA represents one of the elements that contributes to subjective well-being:

P stands for **positive emotions**, particularly happiness but also including emotions such as, gratitude, pleasure, peace, hope, inspiration, satisfaction, curiosity, and love.

E refers to a high level of psychological **engagement**, sometimes referred to as "flow" (Csikszentmihalyi, 1990). This occurs when we are so deeply engaged in a task that time seems to stop as we concentrate intensely on what is happening in the current moment.

R stands for positive and satisfying **relationships**. In general, people who have meaningful, positive relationships with others are happier than those who do not.

M refers to **meaning**, which entails belonging to or pursuing something bigger than oneself. For some people, this involves involvement with a religion or belief system. Others may find meaning by working for humanitarian or social justice causes that helps humanity in some way.

A stands for **accomplishment** or mastery in some area. For some people, this may entail mastering a particular skill, such as playing a musical instrument. For others, it might involve winning a competitive event or achieving a particular goal in one's profession.

CONSIDER THIS 10.3 PERMA IN YOUR LIFE

What contributes to your own well-being?

Think about the five elements in PERMA. Which of these elements is most important in your life right now?

- Positive Emotions
- Psychological Engagement

- Satisfying Relationships
- Meaning
- Accomplishment

What are the sources of PERMA in your life?

Much of the emphasis in positive psychology is on helping individuals identify and use their **character strengths** to improve daily functioning, resilience, health, and overall success. Character strengths are thinking habits that are reflected in thoughts, feelings, and behaviors (Park, 2004). They are relatively stable over time and across situations, but they are not fixed traits or entities. We can each learn to recognize and refine our use of character strengths and, in so doing, improve our own subjective well-being and the well-being of others with whom we interact (Peterson & Park, 2011).

One of the early initiatives of the positive psychology movement was to develop a classification scheme for **character strengths** and **virtues**. This work was led by Chris Peterson and Martin Seligman (2004). According to Peterson and Seligman (2004), virtues are characteristics that are universally valued by philosophers and religious thinkers as the overarching categories of good character. Character strengths are the psychological processes and mechanisms that define the virtues. Character strengths involve the acquisition and use of knowledge in the service of enacting the various virtues.

Peterson and Seligman reviewed hundreds of works dating from ancient Buddhist and Daoist texts to modern psychological research literature to identify core virtues and corresponding character strengths that are universally valued across cultures and history. The resulting framework, the *VIA Classification of Character Strengths and Virtues*, comprises six virtues and 24 corresponding character strengths. The six overarching virtues (Wisdom and Knowledge, Courage, Humanity, Justice, Temperance, and Transcendence) and corresponding character strengths identified by Peterson and Seligman (2004) are shown in Figure 10.2.

Character is a multifaceted construct that is manifested uniquely in each individual. Therefore, we each have our own unique profile of character strengths. Any two individuals could have very different profiles but both be considered as being of "good character." In fact, the word "VIA" in the character strengths framework title is not an acronym but actually is the noun *via*, which refers to the idea of "the path" or "the way" (R.M. Niemiec, pers. comm., October 6, 2014). This name captures the notion implicit in the framework that each of us is on our own journey toward being the best person we can be. According to Peterson and Seligman (2004, p. 13), it would be rare for an individual to show all of the 24 character strengths, but a person of good character would likely display one or two character strengths from each of the categories of virtues.

1. **Wisdom and Knowledge**—*Cognitive strengths that entail the acquisition and use of knowledge*
• **Creativity** [Originality, Ingenuity]: Thinking of novel and productive ways to conceptualize and do things; includes artistic achievement but is not limited to it • **Curiosity** [Interest, Novelty Seeking, Openness to Experience]: Taking an interest in ongoing experience for its own sake; finding subjects and topics fascinating; exploring and discovering • **Judgment** [Open-Mindedness, Critical Thinking]: Thinking things through and examining them from all sides; not jumping to conclusions; being able to change one's mind in light of evidence; weighing all evidence fairly • **Love of Learning**: Mastering new skills, topics, and bodies of knowledge, whether on one's own or formally; obviously related to the strength of curiosity but goes beyond it to describe the tendency to add systematically to what one knows • **Perspective** [wisdom]: Being able to provide wise counsel to others; having ways of looking at the world that make sense to oneself and to other people
2. **Courage**—*Emotional strengths that involve the exercise of will to accomplish goals in the face of opposition, external or internal*
• **Bravery** [Valor]: Not shrinking from threat, challenge, difficulty, or pain; speaking up for what is right even if there is opposition; acting on convictions even if unpopular; includes physical bravery but is not limited to it • **Perseverance** [Persistence, Industriousness]: Finishing what one starts; persisting in a course of action in spite of obstacles; "getting it out the door"; taking pleasure in completing tasks • **Honesty** [Authenticity, Integrity]: Speaking the truth but more broadly presenting oneself in a genuine way and acting in a sincere way; being without pretense; taking responsibility for one's feelings and actions • **Zest** [Vitality, Enthusiasm, Vigor, Energy]: Approaching life with excitement and energy; not doing things halfway or halfheartedly; living life as an adventure; feeling alive and activated
3. **Humanity**—*Interpersonal strengths that involve tending and befriending others*
• **Love**: Valuing close relations with others, in particular those in which sharing and caring are reciprocated; being close to people • **Kindness** [Generosity, Nurturance, Care, Compassion, Altruistic Love, "Niceness"]: Doing favors and good deeds for others; helping them; taking care of them • **Social Intelligence** [Emotional Intelligence, Personal Intelligence]: Being aware of the motives and feelings of other people and oneself; knowing what to do to fit into different social situations; knowing what makes other people tick
4. **Justice**—*Civic strengths that underlie healthy community life*
• **Teamwork** [Citizenship, Social Responsibility, Loyalty]: Working well as a member of a group or team; being loyal to the group; doing one's share • **Fairness**: Treating all people the same according to notions of fairness and justice; not letting personal feelings bias decisions about others; giving everyone a fair chance • **Leadership**: Encouraging a group of which one is a member to get things done and at the time maintain time good relations within the group; organizing group activities and seeing that they happen

(continued)

5. *Temperance*—*Strengths that protect against excess*	

- **Forgiveness**: Forgiving those who have done wrong; accepting the shortcomings of others; giving people a second chance; not being vengeful
- **Humility**: Letting one's accomplishments speak for themselves; not regarding oneself as more special than one is
- **Prudence**: Being careful about one's choices; not taking undue risks; not saying or doing things that might later be regretted
- **Self-Regulation** [Self-Control]: Regulating what one feels and does; being disciplined; controlling one's appetites and emotions

6. *Transcendence*—*Strengths that forge connections to the larger universe and provide meaning*	

- **Appreciation of Beauty and Excellence** [Awe, Wonder, Elevation]: Noticing and appreciating beauty, excellence, and/or skilled performance in various domains of life, from nature to art to mathematics to science to everyday experience
- **Gratitude**: Being aware of and thankful for the good things that happen; taking time to express thanks
- **Hope** [Optimism, Future-Mindedness, Future Orientation]: Expecting the best in the future and working to achieve it; believing that a good future is something that can be brought about
- **Humor** [Playfulness]: Liking to laugh and tease; bringing smiles to other people; seeing the light side; making (not necessarily telling) jokes
- **Spirituality** [Faith, Purpose]: Having coherent beliefs about the higher purpose and meaning of the universe; knowing where one fits within the larger scheme; having beliefs about the meaning of life that shape conduct and provide comfort.

Figure 10.2. The VIA classification of character strengths

For a complete description of each of the character strengths in the *VIA-IS*, readers are encouraged to refer to *Character Strengths and Virtues Handbook and Classification* (Peterson & Seligman, 2004) and to visit the *VIA Institute on Character* website.

The Well-Being–Sustainability Connection

Positive education is the application of positive psychology in elementary, secondary, and higher education settings (Green, Oades, & Robinson, 2011; Seligman, Ernst, Gillham, Reivich, & Linkins, 2009). Research in positive education has shown the efficacy of programs that help learners identify their most dominant (or "signature") character strengths and then use those strengths to handle day to day stressors, overcome depression and anxiety, and become more successful in school (Duckworth, Peterson, Mathews, & Kelly, 2007).

In many respects, education for sustainability is positive education writ large. Education for sustainability aims to help people manage their own well-being by adopting new ways of thinking and behaving and by working to promote the well-being of others around the world and in the future. It is concerned with helping the planet and all of the species it supports to flourish and thrive. In this respect, education focused on helping learners develop a sustainability worldview extends positive education with three assertions:

- The well-being of everyone on the planet is of equal importance. No one should expect to promote her or his own well-being in ways that diminish opportunities for others around the planet to promote their own well-being.
- The well-being of future generations is of equal importance to that of people alive today. No one should expect to promote her or his own well-being in ways that diminish opportunities for future generations to promote their own well-being.
- Individual well-being is dependent on the well-being of interconnected environmental, social, and economic systems. Education efforts aimed at promoting the well-being of individuals also should attend to helping learners actively participate in the well-being of these larger systems.

It is easy to see that helping learners identify and use character strengths also better enables them to enact the principles and values associated with a sustainability worldview. For example, many of the virtues and character strengths that form the basis for positive education map directly onto the principles articulated in the Earth Charter. This mapping is illustrated in Figure 10.3.

CONSIDER THIS 10.4 THE EARTH CHARTER AND CHARACTER STRENGTHS

- As you examine Figure 10.3, think about how the virtues and character strengths associated with each Earth Charter principle can support the development of a sustainability worldview.
- What changes might you make to Figure 10.3?
- Would you add any character strengths not listed?
- Would you remove any of the strengths that are listed?

Positive Education Practices That Support the Development of a Sustainability Worldview

In the past decade, Peterson and Seligman's (2004) handbook of character strengths and virtues and the development of the *VIA Inventory of Strengths* have been the basis for a robust program of research, resulting in hundreds of articles and reports addressing psychological and educational strategies to help people use their character strengths to improve their satisfaction with life and overall well-being. As a

Earth Charter principles	Associated virtues and character strengths
Protect and care for the community of life 1. Respect life in all its diversity. 2. Care for the community of life with understanding, compassion, and love. 3. Build democratic societies that are just, participatory, sustainable, and peaceful. 4. Secure Earth's bounty and beauty for present and future generations.	**Humanity** • Love • Kindness • Social intelligence **Justice** • Citizenship • Fairness **Temperance** • Prudence • Self-control • Transcendence
Ecological integrity 5. Protect and restore the integrity of Earth's ecological systems and the natural processes that sustain life. 6. Prevent harm as the best method of environmental protection, and when knowledge is limited, apply a precautionary approach. 7. Adopt patterns of production, consumption, and reproduction that safeguard Earth's regenerative capacities, human rights, and community well-being. 8. Advance the study of ecological sustainability, and promote the open exchange and wide application of the knowledge acquired.	**Wisdom and knowledge** • Open-mindedness • Perspective **Humanity** • Kindness • Social intelligence **Justice** • Citizenship • Fairness **Temperance** • Prudence • Self-control
Social and economic justice 9. Eradicate poverty as an ethical, social, and environmental imperative. 10. Ensure that economic activities and institutions at all levels promote human development in an equitable and sustainable manner. 11. Affirm gender equality and equity as prerequisites to sustainable development, and ensure universal access to education, health care, and economic opportunity. 12. Uphold the right of all, without discrimination, to a natural and social environment supportive of human dignity, bodily health, and spiritual well-being, with special attention to the rights of indigenous peoples and minorities.	**Courage** • Persistence • Integrity **Humanity** • Kindness • Social intelligence **Justice** • Citizenship • Fairness **Temperance** • Humility and modesty • Self-regulation **Transcendence** • Hope • Spirituality
Democracy, nonviolence, and peace 13. Strengthen democratic institutions at all levels, and provide transparency and accountability in governance, inclusive participation in decision making, and access to justice. 14. Integrate into formal education and lifelong learning the knowledge, values, and skills needed for a sustainable way of life. 15. Treat all living beings with respect and consideration. 16. Promote a culture of tolerance, nonviolence, and peace.	**Wisdom and knowledge** • Open-mindedness • Love of learning • Perspective **Justice** • Citizenship • Fairness **Transcendence** • Hope

Figure 10.3 Virtues and character strengths associated with earth charter principles

result, there are now a number of research-validated instructional practices that are highly compatible with the professional practice of teaching for sustainability. We will explore three approaches that connect well-being and sustainability in the remainder of this chapter: strengths-based approaches, sustainable happiness, and mindfulness.

Strengths-Based Approaches

Strengths-based education focuses on helping learners become more aware of character strengths and then become more deliberate about using them daily. According to Linkins, Niemiec, Gillham, and Mayerson (2014), these approaches fall in to three broad categories:

- Helping learners develop the language and perspectives associated with a strengths approach;
- Helping learners recognize and deploy their own strengths or support the strengths of others; and
- Recognizing and supporting the strengths of groups.

In programs based on signature character strengths, learners typically obtain a personalized character profile using the *VIA-IS* and then learn how to use their top character strengths on a daily basis. Exercises to promote this process involve activities intended to help learners better understand their signature character strengths, recognize when they are overusing the strengths with which they feel most comfortable, or find novel ways to use those that may be lower on their strengths profile.

Programs that aim to cultivate specific character strengths seek to help learners improve their use of character strengths that correlate highly with key outcomes such as life satisfaction, positive emotions, or success in school. In these approaches, learners are taught specific exercises designed to heighten their awareness of these character strengths and to prompt them to activate that strength when engaging in daily activities. For example, Park (2004) reported that the strengths of curiosity, gratitude, hope, love, and zest are strongly correlated with subjective well-being, and optimism in particular is consistently associated with better adjustment among children and youth. Exercises to strengthen gratitude might entail recounting three good things that happened to you that day each evening before you go to bed or counting the number of times each day you say "thank you" and noting whether you really mean it (Rashid & Anjum, 2005). An exercise to help improve hope and optimism might encourage a learner to envision themselves at some point in the future when they are being their "best possible self" and to think about what strengths would enable that best self to become realized.

Probably the most well-known example of an approach aimed at strengthening specific character strengths is Angela Duckworths's program of research focusing on **GRIT**. GRIT involves a combination of character strength perseverance plus a commitment to complete long-term goals. In a series of studies, Duckworth (Duckworth & Quinn, 2009) validated a brief assessment to assess GRIT and then showed that individuals who score high on this GRIT Scale consistently show improved outcomes on difficult long-term tasks such as national spelling bee competitions, success at a military academy, and school completion. This work has been described extensively in the literature and does not need to be explored in detail here.

A large variety of exercises aimed at helping learners identify and use character strengths have been described by Rashid and Anjum (2005) and Seligman (2011), as well as in numerous publications of studies conducted by the *VIA Institute on Character* and *Penn Resiliency Program* (e.g., Linkins, Niemiec, Gillham, & Mayerson, 2014; Seligman, Ernst, Gillham, Reivich, & Linkins, 2009).

Sustainable Happiness

While positive education and the research on character strengths conducted through the *VIA Institute* has a great deal to offer in the context of helping learners develop a sustainability worldview, this work is not directly focused on educating for sustainability and makes no claims to that effect. To date, the most explicit connection between positive education and education for sustainability is the *Sustainable Happiness Course* (O'Brien, Murray, Foster, & Hicks, 2014; O'Brien, 2011, 2013). Sustainable happiness is "happiness that contributes to individual, community, and/or global well-being and does not exploit other people, the environment, or future generations" (2014). The *Sustainable Happiness Course* is an online course that is intended to help individuals improve their level of subjective well-being generally and happiness specifically while at the same time contributing to the development of a sustainability worldview. The course includes videos, downloadable study aids, resource materials, and descriptions of a variety of activities focused on eight "happiness domains" (Foster & Hicks, 1999) that are described in Box 10.4.

BOX 10.4 EIGHT HAPPINESS DOMAINS IN THE SUSTAINABLE HAPPINESS COURSE

Intention: The active desire and commitment to consciously choose attitudes and behaviors that lead to happiness for you, for others, and for the planet.

Accountability: The choice to create the life you want without harming anyone else or the Earth by assuming personal accountability for your actions, thoughts, and feelings and the refusal to blame others or see yourself as a victim.

(continued)

Box 10.4 (continued)

Identification & Centrality:	The ongoing process of looking inside yourself to assess your talents and what makes you uniquely happy, and the insistence on making these things central to your life.
Recasting:	The three-step process that transforms problems and trauma into learning, opportunity, and forward action for you and your community.
Options:	The decision to approach life by creating multiple scenarios, to be open to new possibilities, and to be flexible in the way you live your life.
Appreciation:	The choice to appreciate your life and the environment, to express appreciation to others, and to stay present by turning each experience into a treasured event.
Giving:	The choice to share the best of yourself with friends and community and to give to the world at large without the expectation of a return.
Truth:	The choice to be honest with yourself and others and not allow societal, workplace, or family demands to violate your internal contract.

The *Sustainable Happiness* course is intended as an adult, self-study guide, but O'Brien (2011) also has developed a variety of strategies for applying the activities and happiness domains to work with children and youth.

Mindfulness

Mindfulness is the awareness that emerges through paying attention on purpose, in the present moment, and nonjudgmentally to the unfolding of experience moment by moment (Kabat-Zinn, 2003). Mindfulness derives from Buddhist meditation practices that promote undistracted awareness of what is taking place in the here and now. It involves the ability to notice and observe one's own thoughts, feelings, sensations, motivations, and behaviors without attempting to change or evaluate them. Mindfulness might be thought of as the opposite of processes such as daydreaming and automaticity, the process in which a person executes a complex, well-learned activity without thinking about it.

In recent years, a variety of mindfulness-based programs have been applied in counseling and mental health contexts, in business and industry, in the military, and in work with children and adolescents. School-based programs that help students develop mindfulness often involve simple meditation practices such as attending to one's breathing, metacognitive strategies such as simple reminders to prompt mindfulness, and movement strategies such as basic yoga practices (Napoli, Krech, & Holley, 2005). Mindfulness practices have been found to be effective for helping reduce stress and improve feelings of well-being among elementary and high school-aged students (Kuyken et al., 2013) and to help learners develop more thoughtful and deliberative decision making strategies by encouraging them to notice the emotional and cognitive messages that lead to hasty or risky behaviors. When learners are encouraged to engage in simple practices, such as pausing before responding rather than reacting automatically and to notice their affective state during a decision process, they are more likely to engage in analytic thinking and metacognitive strategies (Hollis-Walker & Colosimo, 2011).

Mindfulness is extremely well aligned with a strengths approach to promoting subjective well-being and with the development of a sustainability worldview. Indeed, in his groundbreaking book *Mindfulness & Character Strengths: A Practical Guide to Flourishing*, Niemiec (2014) integrates mindfulness practices with character strengths practices in an approach he refers to as *Mindfulness-Based Strengths Practice (MBSP)*. The book is intended for a wide variety of practitioners, including counselors and educators, and includes an extensive array of activities and exercises that can be used in a variety of classroom and nonclassroom settings.

Mindfulness practice is highly compatible with the core concepts and principles that underlie a sustainability worldview. For example, Niemiec (2012) showed the direct alignment of the Buddhist monk Thich Nhat Hanh's (1998) five mindfulness trainings with character strengths-based interventions. At the same time, the central principles of Buddhist practice, or **Noble Eightfold Path**, are directly synergistic with a sustainability worldview. The Noble Eightfold Path involves a reverence for life in all of its forms; a commitment not to bring harm others as result of our verbal, mental, or physical actions; a commitment to refrain from taking what is not freely given; a commitment to engage in work that is peaceful, honest, and not harmful of others; and the practice of disciplined thought, typically through meditation (Bodhi, 1994). It is easy to see that these ideas align with a sustainability worldview. For example, taking only what is freely given would include not depriving future generations from meeting their needs, and a respect for life in all of its forms is directly aligned with the first Earth Charter principles "respect life in all of its diversity."

EXTEND YOUR PROFESSIONAL KNOWLEDGE 10.1.

Visit *VIA Institute on Character* website atwww.viacharacter.org/www.

1. Take the VIA survey.
    a. What are your character strengths?
    b. Were you surprised when you discovered your strengths?

(continued)

Box (continued)

> c. How do you think you could use this information to improve your own well-being?
> d. How could you use your signature character strengths in your professional practice of teaching for sustainability?
> 2. *Visit the Sustainable Happiness Course* at http://sustainablehappiness.ca/.
>   a. Register for the course and begin working through the modules.
>   b. Monitor your own sense of well-being and happiness as you take the course.

References

Bodhi, B. (1994). *The Nobel Eightfold Path: The Way to the End of Suffering*. Onalaska, WA: BPS Pariyatti Editions.

Csikszentmihalyi, M. (1990). *Flow: The Psychology of Optimal Experience*. New York: HarperCollins.

Deci R.M., & Ryan, E.L. (2000). Self-determination theory and the facilitation of intrinsic motivation, social development, and well-being. *American Psychologist, 55*, 69–78.

Deci R.M., & Ryan, E.L. (2008). Facilitating optimal motivation and psychological well-being across life's domains. *Canadian Psychology, 49*, 14–23.

Dhammapada. (2013). Pakinnakavagga: Miscellaneous. *The Dhammapada: The Buddha's Path of Wisdom*, ch. 21, 290. Translated from the Pali by Acharya Buddharakkhita, with an introduction by Bhikkhu Bodhi. Access to Insight (Legacy Edition). Retrieved from: www.accesstoinsight.org/tipitaka/kn/dhp/dhp.intro.budd.html

Diener, E., Lucas, L., Schimmack, U., & Helliwell, J. (2009). Defining well-being. In *Well-Being for Public Policy* (pp. 8–23). Oxford: Oxford University Press.

Diener, E., & Ryan, K. (2011). National accounts of well-being for public policy. In S. Donaldson, M. M. Csikszentmihalyi, & J. Nakamura (Eds.), *Applied Positive Psychology: Improving Everyday Life, Health, Schools, Work, and Society* (pp. 15–34). New York: Routledge.

Dietz, T., Rosa, E.A., & York, R. (2009). Environmentally efficient well-being: Rethinking sustainability as the relationship between human well-being and environmental impacts. *Human Ecology Review, 16*, 114–123.

Donaldson, S. I. (2011). Determining what works, if anything, in positive psychology. In S. Donaldson, M. M. Csikszentmihalyi, & J. Nakamura (Eds.), *Applied Positive Psychology: Improving Everyday Life, Health, Schools, Work, and Society* (pp. 3–13). New York: Routledge.

Duckworth, A.L., Peterson, C., Matthews, M.D., & Kelly, D.R. (2007). Grit: Perseverance and passion for long-term goals. *Journal of Personality and Social Psychology, 92*, 1087–1101.

Duckworth, A. L., & Quinn, P. D. (2009). Development and validation of the short grit scale (Grit–S). *Journal of Personality Assessment, 91*, 166–174.

Foster, R., & Hicks, G. (1999). *How We Choose to Be Happy*. New York: Perigee.

Foster, R., Hicks, G., & O'Brien, C. (2014). Introduction to the Sustainable Happiness Course. Retrieved from: www.sustainablehappinesscourse.com/introduction/

Gasper, D. (2004). *Human well-being: Concepts and conceptualizations*. Discussion Paper No. 2004/06. The Hague: United Nations University-Wider.

Graham, C., Eggers, A., & Sukhtankar, S. (2004). Does happiness pay? An exploration based on panel data from Russia. *Journal of Economic Behavior and Organization, 55*, 319–342.

Green, S., Oades, L., & Robinson, P. (2011, April). Positive education: Creating flourishing students, staff and schools. *InPsych.* Retrieved from: http://www.psychology.org.au/publications/inpsych/2011/april/green/

Hollis-Walker, L,. & Colosimo, K. (2011). Mindfulness, self-compassion, and happiness in non-meditators: A theoretical and empirical examination. *Personality and Individual Differences, 50*, 222–227.

Institute for Economics and Peace. (2013). *Pillars of Peace: Understanding the Key Attitudes and Institutions That Underpin Peaceful Societies.* Sydney: Author.

Ivanhoe, P.J. (2013). Happiness in early Chinese thought. In S. A. David, I. Bonniwell, & A. Conley Ayers (Eds.), *The Oxford Handbook of Happiness* (pp. 263–278). Oxford: Oxford University Press.

Kabat-Zinn, J. (2003). Mindfulness-based interventions in context: Past, present, and future. *Clinical Psychology Science and Practice 10*, 144–156.

Knoop, H.H., & Delle Fave, A. (2013). Positive psychology and cross-cultural research. In H. H. Knoop & A. Delle Fave (Eds.), *Well-being and Cultures.* Heidelberg: Springer.

Kuyken, W., Weare, K., Ukoumunne, O. C., Vicary, R., Motton, N., Burnett, R., . . . Huppert, F. (2013). Effectiveness of the Mindfulness in Schools Programme: Non-randomised controlled feasibility study. *British Journal of Psychiatry, 203*, 126–131.

LaPlaca, V., McNaught, A., & Knight, A. (2013). Discourse on wellbeing in research and practice. *International Journal of Wellbeing, 3*, 116–125.

Linkins, M., Niemiec, M., Gillham, J., & Mayerson, D. (2014). Through the lens of strength: A framework for educating the heart. *Journal of Positive Psychology, 10*(1), 1–5.

Lyubomirsky, S., King, L., & Diener, E. (2005). The benefits of frequent positive affect: Does happiness lead to success? *Psychological Bulletin, 131*, 803–855.

Napoli, M., Krech, P., & Holley, L. (2005). Mindfulness Training for Elementary School Students: The Attention Academy. *Journal of Applied School Psychology, 2005, 21*(1), 99–125.

Niemiec, R. (2012). Mindful living: Character strengths interventions as pathways for the five mindfulness trainings. *International Journal of Wellbeing, 2*, 22–33.

Niemiec, R.M. (2014). *Mindfulness & Character Strengths: A Practical Guide to Flourishing.* Boston, MA: Hogrefe.

O'Brien, C. (2010). Sustainability, happiness and education. *Journal of Sustainability Education, 1.* http://www.jsedimensions.org/wordpress/content/2010/04/

O'Brien, C. (2011). Sustainable happiness for teachers and students. *Canadian Teacher Magazine*, 18–19.

O'Brien, C. (2013). Who is teaching us about sustainable happiness and well-being? *Health Culture and Society, 5*, 294–307.

O'Brien, C., Murray, I., Foster, R., & Hicks, G. (2014). Sustainable Happiness Course. Retrieved from: http://sustainablehappiness.ca/

Oishi, S., Diener, E., & Lucas, R.E. (2007). Optimal level of well-being: Can people be too happy? *Perspectives on Psychological Science, 2*, 356–360.

Park, N. (2004). Character strengths and positive youth development. *Annals of the American Academy, 591*, 40–54.

Peterson, C., & Park, N. (2011) Character strengths and virtues: Their role in well-being. In S. Donaldson, M. Csikszentmihalyi, & J. Nakamura (Eds.), *Applied Positive Psychology: Improving Everyday Life, Health, Schools, Work, and Society.* New York: Routledge.

Peterson, C., & Seligman, M. (2004). *Character Strengths and Virtues: A Handbook and Classification.* Oxford: Oxford University Press.

Rashid, T., & Anjum, A. (2005). *340 Ways to Use VIA Character Strengths*. Cincinnati, OH: VIA Character Institute. Retrieved from: www.viastrengths.org/Applications/Exercises/tabid/132/Default.aspx

Ricard, M. (2013). A Buddhist view of happiness. In S.A. David, I. Bonniwell, & A. Conley Ayers (Eds.), *The Oxford Handbook of Happiness* (pp. 344–356). Oxford: Oxford University Press.

Salagame, K.K. (2013). Well-being from the Hindu/San tana Dharma Perspective. In S.A. David, I. Bonniwell, & A. Conley Ayers (Eds.), *The Oxford Handbook of Happiness* (pp. 371–383). Oxford: Oxford University Press.

Seligman, M.E.P. (2011). *Flourish: A Visionary New Understanding of Happiness and Well-Being*. New York: Atria Paperback.

Seligman, M.E.P., & Csikszentmihalyi, M. (2000). Positive psychology: An introduction. *American Psychologist, 55*, 5–14.

Seligman, M.E.P., Ernst, R.M., Gillham, J., Reivich, K., & Linkins, M. (2009). Positive psychology and classroom interventions. *Oxford Review of Education, 35*, 293–311.

Shantideva. (1997). *A Guide to the Bodhisattva Way of Life: Bodhicaryavatara* (V.A. Wallace & B.A. Wallace, Trans.). Ithaca, NY: Snow Lion.

Sin, N.L., and Lyubomirsky, S. (2009). Enhancing well-being and alleviating depressive symptoms with positive psychology interventions: A practice-friendly meta-analysis. *Journal of Clinical Psychology, 65*, 467–487.

Nhat Hanh, T. (1998). *The Heart of the Buddha's Teaching: Transforming Suffering Into Peace, Joy, & Liberation*. Berkeley, CA: Parallax Press.

UNICEF Office of Research. (2013). Child well-being in rich countries: A comparative overview. *Innocenti Report Card 11*. Florence: Author.

White, S. (2013). *Beyond the grumpy rich man and happy peasant: Subjective perspectives on well-being and food security in India*. Bath Papers in International Development and Wellbeing No. 25. Bath: The Centre for Development Studies, University of Bath.

INDEX